Bristol
Polytechnic

Author: LLOYD

Title: Rolls-Royce· the years of endeavor

ROLLS-ROYCE
THE YEARS OF ENDEAVOUR

Sir Henry Royce

ROLLS-ROYCE

THE YEARS OF ENDEAVOUR

IAN LLOYD

First published 1978 by
THE MACMILLAN PRESS LTD
London and Basingstoke
Associated companies in Delhi
Dublin Hong Kong Johannesburg Lagos
Melbourne New York Singapore Tokyo

Printed in Great Britain at The Pitman Press, Bath

British Library Cataloguing in Publication Data

Lloyd, Ian
  Rolls-Royce, the years of endeavour
  1. Automobile industry and trade – Great
  Britain – History
  I. Title
  338.7′62′922220941   HD9710.G74R5

  ISBN 0-333-24018-9

To Frances

Contents

List of Appendixes

List of Illustrations

Preface

The concluding chapter of *Rolls-Royce: the Growth of a Firm* describes the unprecedented expansion of the company's aero-engine production, during the First World War, the novel experience of its management in high-level negotiations with Air Ministry, Admiralty and War Office ministers and officials within the United Kingdom, and the British Purchasing Mission and various sub-contractors within the United States. The procedures involved in the disengagement from war were themselves complex and demanding. It was the company's first extensive experience of what was to become, after little more than a decade of apparent pre-war normality, the complex environment of State monopsony in the field of aircraft engines, to which the motor-car business eventually became almost a secondary interest.

In 1919 and 1920 there was evidently a strong belief that much of the pre-1914 environment could be restored and the reflex actions of the company generally suggest a concerted effort to return to the familiar. But great wars shatter the moulds in which they originate. Things are never quite the same. Markets change, the old security is challenged by new products and opportunities. Imagination and enterprise are at a premium and firms which give full scope to both survive at the expense of those which do not.

Two of Rolls-Royce's three founding patrons, Royce and Johnson, were still alive, although Royce was an invalid whose energies had to be most carefully sustained and husbanded in an environment specially arranged for this purpose. Johnson maintained a vigorous and forceful presence in the company's affairs, though he continued to be as self-effacing as ever, declining the knighthood which he was offered at the end of the war. Both these men nevertheless realised that adaptation was the key to survival in an era which was to prove as testing as any which the company had lived through. It could accurately be described as 'The Years of Supremacy', for in both the chosen fields of technology – aero-engine and automobile – the company was to entrench the world-wide reputation which its products had acquired. But this required prodigious efforts and many mistakes were made – and, within the family at Derby, admitted. The qualities which predominate are those of endurance, the ability to anticipate and survive great technical challenges, strong commercial competition, the appalling near-disaster of the Great Depression, and the immense problems which rearmament presented both to designers and administrators.

At the end of the period covered in this volume (1939) a new generation was at the helm. The personalities who gave their names to the institution had disappeared, leaving a reputation to be sustained which was as challenging as any that has ever been inherited by the management of a British institution. There are a few – the Brigade of Guards, the Royal Society, All Souls, the Royal College of Surgeons, the Cavendish Laboratory – in which a tradition of excellence and achievement is regarded as fundamental to the survival of each in its own sphere. In this great and continuing national tapestry Rolls-Royce represented a similar ambition in a field which has increased steadily in importance as the nation's survival has come to depend less on the traditional factors which dominated the nineteenth century and much more on industrial performance. New men were required in new institutions. New traditions of excellence had to be established in an unfamiliar environment. The arduous nature of that continuing challenge is described in the chapters which follow.

I.S.L.

September 1977

Sources and Acknowledgements

The list of sources and acknowledgements in the first volume of this series, *The Growth of a Firm*, applies to that book, this volume and its successor, *The Merlin at War*. Comparatively little new and relevant material appears to have been published in the intervening years (1946–49) since the original work on these books was undertaken, but I would like to mention four books, each of which is based on enquiry into original sources, some of which were not available to me at that time. Anthony Bird and Ian Hallowes' *The Rolls-Royce Motor Car* (Batsford, 1964) contains some particularly interesting analyses of Rolls-Royce automobile technology, especially within the 'Silver Ghost' and 'Phantom' periods, and I have decided that it would be helpful to the reader to give references to this at the appropriate places.

Wilton Oldham's life of Claude Johnson, *The Hyphen in Rolls-Royce* (G. T. Foulis, 1967), is based on Johnson's papers and personal diaries and greatly enlarges one's view of this interesting and modest man. The correspondence between Johnson and Lord Northcliffe, a powerful and influential figure in his day, is of considerable historical interest.

Arthur W. Soutter's *The American Rolls-Royce* (Mowbray Co., 1976) has contributed a most comprehensive view of the Rolls-Royce Springfield venture, based on the author's intimate personal experiences in the management of that concern. It contains, in particular, one of the most detailed analyses of the technical procedures of Rolls-Royce car manufacture within the 'Silver Ghost' and 'Phantom' eras which has ever been published and throws considerable light on the Springfield venture, as seen by a particularly well-informed participant. References to this work have been added, where appropriate, to my own text. I would like to acknowledge warmly the considerable contribution which those four authors have made to our understanding of Rolls-Royce history.

Finally, it would be churlish not to mention Lord Montagu's interesting biography of C. S. Rolls, *Rolls of Rolls-Royce*, (Cassell, 1966).

Though I have not made any reference to this, either in my earlier volume, *The Growth of a Firm*, or in this book, it is the most authoritative biography of Rolls which has yet appeared and throws a great deal of light on the complex and unusual personality of this pioneer of the British motor-car and aviation industries.

As before, I would like to acknowledge the very generous assistance I have received from both Rolls-Royce Motors and Rolls-Royce Ltd with photographs. Their comprehensive libraries of pictures have again been placed freely at my disposal and I can only express my regret that the cost of printing prevents my making an even wider selection available to the reader.

1 A Flirtation with Monopoly

After the first somewhat premature attempts to lay in stocks of material for the resumption of car manufacture nothing further was done until after the Armistice. The surviving founder of the company, Royce himself had never altogether ceased to give some thought to the problems of car design and it was on 7 July 1917 that he announced in a West Wittering memo[1] that all post-war chassis would have electric self-starters and that he had been studying the Lanchester gearbox.

The problems of what car to make, how many, and at what price, became once again the main concern of management. Within a few days of the Armistice the process of retooling and reorganising the factory for car production had started, and the first post-war car was sent to test early in 1919. The senior executives were generally optimistic and considered that the market would absorb all the cars that Derby could produce. The backlog of pre-war orders was quite considerable and a large number of new orders had been taken. On 21 January 1919 a meeting was held at West Wittering at which it was decided to increase the chassis programme beyond the previous limit of 500 per annum. The standard Silver Ghost 40/50 h.p. chassis, suitably modernised in the accurate sense that Royce defined the term, was to remain the company's principal product, but despite this decision the ever-recurring suggestion of a small car soon led to a specification being drawn up. Some years later, a 20/25 h.p. chassis was to be designed and produced.

Long before the war had ended, the management had been obliged by developments of a different character to give serious thought to the higher policy of the company. On 4 April 1917 an invitation was received from Sir William Peat, the head of a distinguished firm of accountants, to attend a meeting which was being held to discuss a project for 'some form of amalgamation or union of interests between the leading British motor car manufacturers in order more effectively to combat the American and foreign competition which is likely to obtain after the war'.[2] The first meeting, at which Sir William presided, was held on 17 April and was attended by Sir Victor Caillard, a director of Vickers, Ernest Hopwood, the managing director of Wolseleys (a Vickers subsidiary), Edward Manville, the chairman of Daimlers, and Claude Johnson, managing director of Rolls-Royce. The managing director of Sunbeams had been invited but did not attend. Sir William started the proceedings by announcing that he had good reason to believe that the combination which they had met to discuss would be welcomed in 'other quarters' without specifying what these mysterious quarters were. 'There was,' he said, 'unnecessary competition and waste of money' among British motor-car manufacturers, and the proposed scheme was designed to avoid this. Three reasons were put forward to support a merger. Some British manufacturers tried to make several types, the war had enlarged the car capacity of all factories and the capacity of the market was unlikely to remain 'the same . . . or considerably smaller.'

The result, Sir William inferred, would be that the 'weaker companies, who are now temporarily financially and physically fat, will go out of business' and a scheme of co-operation was thus necessary to ensure 'economy and strength'. Sir William detailed the many advantages which such a scheme as he envisaged possessed, and described its structure. A merger company would be formed which would issue preference shares in exchange for a proportion of the physical assets, valued on a common basis, of each participating company. The average annual profits of the past five years would be ascertained, and ordinary shares issued for a one or two years' purchase of this average, plus the remainder of the physical assets. Special war capital expenditure was to be valued on a post-war basis by a committee of valuers. The merger company would pay a fixed dividend on the preference shares, and a variable dividend on the ordinary shares. As far as possible the merger company would 'allot to each company a type of car on which it would concentrate', and though control would be exercised by the central board, each company would remain under the control of its own board. The following advantages were enumerated:

(1) The economies resulting from the allocation of one model to one works;
(2) Economies and advantages obtained from the bulk purchase of materials and parts would be very great;

(3) Substantial economies in selling and advertising at home and abroad;

(4) A 'reduction of competition';

(5) A reduction in 'general establishment charges resulting from the possibility of uniformity of design, the centralisation of drawing offices, the centralisation of experimental departments, etc.';

(6) Concentration of personnel;

(7) The avoidance of overlapping 'both in design and types of motor cars which are offered to the public';

(8) 'It was pointed out that by such a combination pressure would be more effectively brought to bear upon the legislature in all matters affecting the interests of the trade';

(9) The strength of the merger company would enable it to resist foreign imports and the 'undue demands of labour'.

Sir William also pointed out that such a company would be able to provide 'working capital for the support of companies which are in need of it'.

It was suggested to Johnson that Rolls-Royce would be required to contribute only a small proportion of the profits, and that the Singer Company, which was one of the suggested participants, might do very well under such a scheme, the shareholders of both Rolls-Royce and Singers 'participating equally in the profits of the combination'. Sir William quoted as an example the case of a successful merger which had just been achieved in the explosives trade.

Johnson was justifiably suspicious and in a report which he sent to all the directors, made several pertinent observations:

> It appeared to me peculiar that Vickers were represented by three people at the conference, and that one of them, Sir Victor Caillard, should produce from his pocket a typewritten statement of the statistics which each company should supply. I came to the conclusion that Vickers arranged the meeting and that it was to the interest of Vickers (and probably not of Rolls-Royce) that the combination should be formed.

Rolls-Royce, he argued, had now produced a chassis of great repute. Both cars and aero-engines were famous and the value of the works had increased by £360,000 (£225,000 at pre-war prices). These, he thought, were the reasons why Vickers were displaying a sudden interest in Rolls-Royce which they had elaborately disguised as an interest in the entire motor industry. 'Under the circumstances', he continued, 'Vickers would probably desire to swallow up Rolls-Royce as part of a combination which they would control rather than face Rolls-Royce in open markets. Personally, I would sooner risk Rolls-Royce going out of business than be a part of a combination in which there would be unholy and dirty elements. This', he concluded, 'may be short-sighted prejudice.'

Here, indeed, is the surprising spectacle of the traditional entrepreneur refusing to increase corporate profits, quite possibly to his great personal disadvantage, by joining a monopoly which would undoubtedly have reduced competition and might have reduced waste, and doing so largely on moral grounds. The word moral may do more than justice to his reasons, but pride in the organisation created by the diligent co-operation and effective leadership of a small team of men devoted to ideals greater than mere financial profit and the valuation of the independence and good name of their firm far above financial reward cannot be described as 'economic' reasons. Though Johnson was now in a position to act independently, his attitude towards these proposals reflected a far-sighted faith in the advantages of independence. This is one of the not infrequent occasions in his life in which Johnson exemplified the spirit of private enterprise at its best.

Johnson evidently suspected the motives of those promoting the merger and was determined that Rolls-Royce would retain its complete competitive independence. The mere fact of the offer probably confirmed his belief in its ability to do so. On 15 May the board decided to continue negotiations, but neither Johnson nor the other members thought that they would lead to anything. Though Royce rarely took an active interest in such matters (the board having done everything possible to ensure that he should be able to devote his energies unreservedly to the problems of design), he was invariably consulted on major questions of policy, and his opinion was always valued. In a letter to the chairman, Ernest Claremont, Royce reveals an ability to uncover the essentials of any problem which was by no means confined to engineering design.

This is a very difficult subject. When I mentioned it to Mr. Johnson some time ago, if I remember rightly, my ideas were that if we wanted to stay in government work and be in a strong aero position we ought to be associated with one of the bigger armament companies, preferably Armstrong Whitworths. Vickers have their motor car and aero engine departments. The only other combination of this type that I can call to mind with which we could associate ourselves would be John Brown's of Clydebank and Sheffield, which I believe includes Coventry Ordnance. The Daimler Company are associated with or owned by B.S.A. This is one form of combination. Another form of combination would be to be associated with and control the manufacture of a comprehensive list of vehicles, such as our own luxury car, a small horse power utility chassis like a taxi and a motor lorry, which two latter would be made in separate factories and have a separate name, but would have the guarantee of being good because of being associated with Rolls-Royce. Such an amalgamation would have for its object economy of selling, manufacture and technical management.

It is difficult to see the position of the luxury car after the war. One has the impression that there will be somewhat limited use for such a car, probably much more limited than before the war. It is from this point of view perhaps that the advantages of amalgamation should have full consideration. We have always felt some effects of our isolation, and the effects of jealousy through success and I think that after the war it will be difficult to stand against it.

The amalgamation proposed by Sir William Peat appears, however to be of a different character to what I had thought of, in which companies doing much the same work are to be amalgamated and specialised, and a point appears to be that if such an amalgamation were brought about, and we were the isolated successful Company, competition would be brought around us that would make it difficult to live.

From a personal point of view, I prefer to be absolute boss over my own department (even if it was extremely small) rather than to be associated with a much larger technical department over which I had only joint control. This ought *not* to be considered. We would endeavour to work together.

An amalgamation of the kind mentioned has, of course, enormous economical possibilities, both commercial and manufacturing and could be represented in every civilised land, and would have a chance of competition with strong companies, or combinations of companies that will exist in America and Germany. I do not see any objection to giving the necessary figures for the proposed combination, so that we can go in or stay out, according to the character the amalgamation acquires.

I do not think the present way, that is the multitude of small companies doing a great variety of work, can possibly stand the competition after the war, and I am anxious that our own position shall not be equally weak. I feel that something must be done, otherwise the trade of motor manufacturing will leave England.

This letter reveals a curious blend of attitudes. There is the ever-present fear that one day there will no longer be a market for the Rolls-Royce car through the development of economic circumstances beyond the control of the company. It shows that Royce did not underestimate the importance of the personal element in industry – 'jealousy of our success' – or the danger of advances in production methods abroad. It suggests that he was not unaware of the 'effects of our isolation', and that Rolls-Royce had been subject to pressures of one sort or another and the strong influence towards amalgamation which such pressures can exert on the independent firm, particularly if coupled with offers of generous compensation for the executives responsible for the final decision.

What is much more remarkable, however, is the striking applicability not only of Royce's analysis, but also of the original proposals of the amalgamation scheme (which might easily have been suggested by a government department in 1947) to the British motor industry thirty years later. But while this analysis was also applicable at the time, the inherent conservatism and apparent financial strength, both of the individual companies and of the country, enabled those responsible to postpone the awkward implications for many years. Royce's self-confessed preference for a small concern in which he himself could be head was symptomatic of a general preference for economic and technical independence in the industry. The technical and productive reorganisation which the impending change in the national fortunes was to demand, not only of the motor industry, was at this stage unacceptable for the important reason that the basic foundation of any industry, its human organisation, was not prepared to evolve in parallel. The decision was not of the same far-reaching importance for Rolls-Royce as for other firms in the industry, for obvious reasons.

The Cassandras of 1917, with whom their counterparts in 1947 would no doubt have found much in common, were confounded by two favourable developments whose strength they had underestimated. These developments had the unfortunate effect of convincing the industry's leaders that the course they had neglected to pursue was unnecessary. The first was the buoyant demand for motor vehicles, the second the extent to which the expansion of this demand enabled the weak and the strong alike to prosper. In the sunny warmth of economic prosperity the thinly clad were not aware of their rags, nor were the strong able or willing to foresee the threat which the future posed to their security. The liquidation of foreign investments and the depreciation of capital equipment, though serious, were not as great as in the Second World War. Nor had the economy yet experienced the internal restrictionism and apathy which was to characterise the inter-war years. The British motor industry was not, in the twenties, unsuited technically or temperamentally to the somewhat conservative home market which was still its main support. The influence of internal competition among manufacturers, all of whom were hampered to some extent by production techniques which were rapidly becoming obsolete as Detroit began to develop mass production, was not strong enough to induce the integration which was forced on the industry after the Second World War by a crisis which was general in its impact and origins. Whether or not this integration could have been brought about by the methods contemplated by Sir William is not altogether certain. But the individuality and the powers of technical innovation shown by Rolls-Royce, always an exceptional unit within the industry, would have suffered substantial impairment had the firm been forced to adopt methods and a scale of output which were considered undesirable and unsuitable. The negotiations nevertheless continued through several further conferences before the project was finally shelved.

The next meeting, held on 9 May, was attended in addition by Mr Siddeley of the Siddeley-Deasy Motor Car Company, and the figures which had been supplied by all except Sunbeams were discussed. Siddeley, who had apparently been acting on behalf of Sir William, had approached thirteen companies,[3] and of these Napiers alone had shown no interest. He also proposed to approach four other companies[4] manufacturing cars and five principal lorry manufacturers, and expressed the opinion that it would be wise to associate Messrs White and Poppe and E. G. Wrigley & Co. in the scheme. The delegates did not approve the much more grandiose scheme which was now being put forward. It was emphasised, in Johnson's words, that 'the main purpose of the amalgamation would be that the energy which was not spent in fighting to kill one another in this country should be directed to killing foreign competitors, especially American'. The metaphors were somewhat virile, but it must be remembered that the United States had only just entered a war from which its industries had been making substantial profits. The suggestion of a tariff against American imports was turned down by the meeting as being 'politically impossible'. It can be assumed from the fact that the total contemplated output of the group was £5 million per annum that no real mass-production scheme was planned. The economies to be achieved were not primarily those obtained from an increase in output, but from reducing waste by rationalisation within the existing organisation of the industry.

When Sir William finally proposed that the meeting should adopt the existing scheme and that those present should form the nucleus of the new organisation, Johnson realised that he could go no further and said flatly 'that we would not adopt any scheme until, firstly, we had seen it in concrete form and had examined it and considered it carefully and, secondly, until we were assured that a sufficient number of important motor companies would join'. Rolls-Royce was not, he said, prepared to join a group of four. 'It occurred to me that the Wolseley Company were not anxious about a large combination, but showed great anxiety that Rolls-Royce should put their neck in a noose at which Vickers and Daimler would pull with a view to strangulation.' His language grew more intemperate as his suspicions increased.

On 10 May, however, Mr Siddeley, somewhat alarmed by Johnson's intransigence, called on him and disclosed that he was the originator of the scheme. He argued that no threat was intended to Rolls-Royce and that the position of executive directors would be safeguarded, but Johnson was not reassured.

At the next meeting, held on 16 May at Vickers House, the figures of net assets and average profits in pre-war years were produced and discussed at some length. There is little point in speculating on the possible influence of such an amalgamation on the future of the firm. The participants would not long have retained their separate identities, still less their actual independence of policy. Many of the very real advantages enumerated in the original proposals would undoubtedly have accrued both to the firms and to the motor industry as a whole, but it is unlikely that the character and independence of judgement, which the Rolls-Royce management had developed so conspicuously, would have long survived. The interests of the firm were now deeply embedded in the aero-engine industry, an industry of even more unusual and novel features than the motor industry, in which success is dependent on precisely those qualities of vigorous initiative and the power of rapid and thorough product development which large-scale and over-centralised undertakings tend to inhibit. While the complex character of the relationship between vitality and size in economic institutions particularly in the same institution at different stages of its life, has never been fully explored, there is certainly no simple correlation between them. But the developments which the firm was shortly to experience in the United States throw further light on the elusive nature of the qualities and characteristics which seem to be responsible for success or failure, both of the unit within the economy, and, by a process of simple addition, of the economy of which it forms a part.

2 Return to the *Status Quo*

The management faced many new problems in resuming chassis manufacture in 1919. A large volume of unfulfilled orders received just before and during the war had been placed in chronological order and the customers informed that their orders would be executed as soon as possible. Many had signed contracts for chassis at pre-war prices or provisional prices which bore little relation to post-war costs, and this error of judgement required tedious negotiation with each individual customer. To preserve goodwill Johnson decided that the order had to be fulfilled at the agreed price if the customer would not voluntarily agree to an increase. Apart from these orders demand was a completely unknown quantity. The important export trade had been completely disrupted and had to be re-established under very different conditions, often in the face of heavy tariffs (the French tariff was 70 per cent) imposed for balance of payments reasons or to protect the recovery of local vehicle manufacture. The damage which war causes to the commercial structure of the economic system is usually far more serious than the destruction of physical assets. Its repair depends upon the re-creation of mutual trust and confidence and economic stability. Both are invariably absent in the immediate aftermath of a war.

Manufacturers in England were, moreover, apprehensive of the power of labour. Johnson had come to the conclusion quite early in the war that England would not provide a suitable market for the Rolls-Royce car. Many suggestions that the firm should manufacture abroad were carefully considered. The car's pre-war reputation had been enlarged by the outstanding achievements of the armoured car and the aero-engine,[1] and proposals were made by Messrs Handley-Page that Hispano-Suiza should manufacture the aero-engine under licence in Spain, and by Vickers that a Vickers-Rolls-Royce factory should be built in Australia. A request for a licence to manufacture the Eagle received from the Imperial Japanese Navy was politely declined. The Handley-Page offer was also turned down, mainly on the quite accurate grounds that Rolls-Royce was not able to provide the necessary staff. The Vickers proposals to form a joint company to be known as

10

Vickers-Rolls-Royce Aviation reached a fairly advanced stage, but the project did not materialise, probably for reasons which may be judged from the earlier negotiations on a different subject. More serious consideration was given to the offer of a section of the British Government aero-engine factory at Clichy, in France. Johnson inspected this, but rejected the offer on the grounds that Hispano-Suiza intended to lease adjoining shops for the manufacture of their chassis. He also visited a works at St Denis which he thought might be purchased for £180,000, but though he thought this a more serious possibility the board did not approve.

Attractive though many of these schemes appeared at first sight, management's main concern was to assure a market for the output of the Derby works, which had been greatly enlarged by the war. The fees received from licences for foreign manufacture would hardly be sufficient to compensate for a severe reduction of Derby output. Though the company's experience in the United States was of a somewhat different character, this confirmed the wisdom of the decision to concentrate output at Derby.

The Silver Ghost chassis produced in 1919 was not substantially different from that produced in 1914. Royce had not much opportunity during the war to consider the problems of car design, still less to design a new chassis. The idea of designing a completely new chassis just for the sake of doing so would in any case have struck him as very foolish. Royce had never submitted to the tyranny of an annual model produced to give an impression of progress which has not taken place.

Soon after the war Royce set to work on the design of a 20 h.p. car known as the Goshawk which was eventually to appear in 1922. The management was afraid that the market would not support the sales of the 40/50 h.p. at a level of output which they considered economic, and that the constant increase in its cost of manufacture would price it right out of the market. The pre-war works cost of the 40/50 h.p. chassis was £506 (made up of wages £124, materials £196 and overheads of 150 per cent on wages) and it was estimated that the war had increased this figure to £1083. To this figure had to be added the agent's fee of 20 per cent on the selling price of £1145, which increased the cost to £1373, the final profit thus being £77 per chassis on those sold through the trade, and £387 on those sold direct by the firm. In a footnote to this particular estimate appears the comment that 'both labour and material costs at the moment are purely a matter of guesswork'. Royce thought that the price should be fixed between sixteen and eighteen hundred

1.   The 20 h.p. Goshawk

pounds and remarked: 'You will notice I am against making the Company suffer from the unreasonable demands of labour, which I think is the present attitude of labour, in demanding shorter hours and not permitting maximum output for even these short hours.' This price-fixing decision was certainly influenced by the price increases on other cars and it is significant that the management did not only regard those cars in the same horsepower or price range as competitive.[2]

In January 1919 the price was fixed at £1350, which Claremont thought far too low, and in March it was raised to £1450 for six months. In December it was raised to £1850, in the following April to £2000 and finally in June to £2250. The last of these increases, following upon heavy wage increases and rising material costs, was watched very closely, and did in fact result in 26 cancellations from a total of 110 current orders. By November no less than 48 per cent had cancelled, a trend which strongly confirmed the opinion of those who thought that the car was pricing itself out of the market. In consequence the board asked Royce to press ahead with his design of a 20 h.p. car which would sell for approximately £1500, and he agreed to do so 'on the understanding that the quality would be equal to that of the large car'. Although the Goshawk project caused a great deal of controversy and aroused little enthusiasm, on 7 January 1921 the board authorised an expenditure of £25,000 on jigs and tools for its manufacture.

This expenditure was approved despite the fact that only two months previously Johnson had written to Royce asking him to economise wherever possible on development work, and to suspend all work on the Buzzard and Vulture designs. Johnson believed that the firm's economic survival depended on its ability to produce economically in the automobile industry, and the car thus received a much higher priority than the aero-engine. This continued for some years as the R.A.F. possessed considerable stocks of aero-engines suitable for military aircraft and the general state of international security was such that European governments did not feel it necessary to foster either development or production on a scale which would have made it possible for a firm such as Rolls-Royce to rely on State patronage for the bulk of its orders. As Schlaifer has pointed out in his comprehensive study of aero-engine development, the major engine firms, both in Britain and the United States, have never found development contracts, however liberal their terms, a sufficient incentive in themselves for a firm to do intensive development on an engine. The prospect of profits on quantity production has always been required.[3] For some years yet financial solvency had to be bought by strenuous efforts in the open market of a highly competitive industry.

The composition of the firm's output was continuously studied by the Works Committee, a policy-advisory body consisting of various departmental heads or their assistants. At this time its membership included Platford, Hives, Haldenby, Wormald and Bailey. This Committee estimated that works costs had increased by 130 per cent and that a 20 h.p. car engine would cost 85 per cent of the 40/50 h.p. on the basis that the Falcon had cost 85 per cent of the Eagle. A reduction of the production target of 1000 chassis per annum was discussed and the committee considered that this would involve the cessation of the night-shift (with the dismissal of 1300 men) as well as the dismissal of 200 day-shift employees, causing no less than 250 machines to remain idle. The members of this Committee seemed keenly conscious of the social responsibilities which such a decision involved. Several months earlier they had minuted a resolution that 'it is necessary of course to have a sufficient turnover to meet all our responsibilities' and they now added, in a rather plaintive parenthesis, that 'the problem is very complex and to our minds not in any way satisfactory to the Company'. They considered that output should be maintained by the discovery of new markets.

The situation was again discussed in December. It was pointed out that 750 chassis had been sold at an average price of £1500 in 1914, and that of this total 150 had gone to France and the United States, both of which were now closed markets. This left a market of 600 'if the buying capacity of the world remained the same' and on the assumption that the 40/50 chassis would now cost £3000 the Committee concluded that a figure of 500 would be an optimistic estimate. The balance of the turnover would comprise 700 'Kites' – the experimental name for the Goshawk at this time – which it was then thought would cost £1800. This volume of production would only half fill the works, which the Committee estimated to have a capacity for 2000 40/50 h.p. chassis. The options were to close half the works, to manufacture a third car, a four-cylinder selling at £500–£600, or to manufacture other goods. If the company were to survive, its capital would have to be turned over four times, giving an annual turnover of £5 million. This was £800,000 greater than the turnover in 1918, and nearly £4 million greater than the turnover actually achieved in 1922. All these estimates excluded any prospect of aero-engine revenue.

Johnson immediately attacked these conclusions. 'Why is it necessary', he asked, 'in order that the Company may live for it to have a turnover of £5 million?' 'Would this', he asked, 'be the case if a portion of the works were closed?' The Committee replied with some diffidence that they realised they were not financiers but suggested that their conclusions appeared to be 'common sense'. They did not think that closing part of the works would be sufficient. Johnson had earlier requested an estimate for a 10/15 h.p. chassis similar to a Humber model of this size. With an obstinacy born almost entirely of technical pride the Committee had answered that it could not give a valid estimate. In his reply Johnson asked them outright to estimate what a 10/15 h.p. Humber improved to Rolls-Royce standards would cost. The Committee replied that it could be produced for a selling price of £850 provided not less than 1000 were produced.

The tenor of these discussions and interchanges, which did not lead to any decisive action, indicates that the Works Committee regarded the closing of part of the works as insufficient mainly on the grounds that it was undesirable. It would involve a reduction in employment, an unpopular policy which they themselves, as departmental heads, would have to administer. Johnson, being somewhat more remote from the social impact of such a policy, could be more ruthless in following through the logic of his thinking and he refused to accept the argument that the company would not survive simply because the Works Committee would rather not face up to the consequences of essential change. His question, in turn, implied the conclusion that he preferred, as an executive responsible for the survival of an institution which must vary the volume of its activities at a greater speed than might be desirable on social grounds, to pursue a policy which would achieve this objective on the basis of a small turnover rather than one which would threaten bankruptcy on a large turnover for which there was no market.

The problems of a progressive industrial society are not generally produced by institutions, by malice or by carelessness, though these all make their contribution. They are produced by change, by insufficient information, poor judgement and by the fact that the allocation of function, responsibility and power between the state and its subsidiary economic institutions, is always to some extent obsolete, particularly in the aftermath of war.

As the year 1921 progressed the problems increased in number and difficulty. The overdraft was £400,000, and the bank was not prepared to allow it to increase. Taxation was heavy, and permission had to be obtained to pay this in instalments. In May the price of the 40/50 was reduced to £1850 in an attempt to prevent the accumulation of unsold chassis. This price reduction followed on a general reduction of wages made by the Engineering Employers Federation. In July a further reduction to £1600 was considered by the board, but it was decided to wait. In August the number of unsold chassis amounted to 84, and an additional 23 cancellations had been received.

At a board meeting on 17 August Johnson maintained that 'the number of people with £1000 or more to spend on a chassis was too small to support the Company's business' and recommended that 'as an insurance against closing the Company's business Mr. Royce be asked to devote his energy exclusively to the completion of the Goshawk II and to design for a chassis of 12 h.p. at a works cost not exceeding £500–£575'. The board decided that the Silver Ghost price should remain at £1850 on the grounds that 'a further reduction would lead to the impression that the present chassis was not up to the past Rolls-Royce standard'.

Energetic steps were taken to deal with a situation largely beyond the control of the management. Arrangements were made for customers to purchase cars on an instalment basis if they wished to do so, and a proposal to supply the trade with accessories was discussed, but not approved. Direct negotiations took place with suppliers of raw materials and components (drop forgings, alloy steels and castings) in an endeavour to obtain reduced prices. Proposals for a joint concern run by Rolls-Royce and Thos. Firth & Sons for the manufacture of springs reached a fairly advanced stage but were finally shelved, though a supplies agreement was concluded.[4] Two firms which had made castings for Rolls-Royce had been threatened with purchase by a combine and had approached their principal customers in the motor industry in the hope of persuading them to forestall this move, which would have reacted unfavourably on the price of castings. But in both cases Rolls-Royce decided not to purchase the shares offered and if necessary to manufacture their own castings.

In December a very thorough analysis of establishment charges was made and the staff were invited to make suggestions. Some interesting figures have survived in consequence. It was estimated that in 1914 36.5 'unproductive' hours were worked for every 100 productive hours, and that the former figure had risen to 54.7 in 1920. In May 1920 the ratio of 'productive' to 'unproductive' employees was 3.301–2.243. By January 1921 these figures had become 3.774–1.458 and the 30 per cent reduction in unproductive employees was hailed as an achievement.[5]

The establishment charges as a percentage of productive wages had increased from 122 per cent in 1913 to 129.3 per cent in 1920, in which year the total establishment charges amounted to £991,700. In discussing an analysis of this figure the board decided in February 1921 to reduce the output of chassis to 25 per week, to stop night shift and to reduce the total establishment charges, if possible, to £680,000. But despite this the situation deteriorated steadily in 1921, and Claude Johnson's absence in the United States and his preoccupation with the problems of the American company[6] did not help matters in England.

In an editorial written in June 1925 the editor of the *Automobile Engineer* summed up the immediate post-war period as 'a series of frustrated attempts to re-establish the pre-war status-quo'. As the failure of the Vickers negotiations clearly reveals, this criticism is substantially valid as regards the general structure of the industry – the number of units in the industry, their size, volume of production and share of the market. But the industrialists upon whom fell the immediate impact of the post-war years did not appreciate the significance of what was happening, either to the nature of their markets, the potentialities of their industry as revealed first by quantity and then by mass production proper in the United States, or to the evolution of automobile design which in certain major essentials had become relatively stable.

In some ways, the industry was relatively quick to respond to one important misjudgement of the market. In the 1919 Paris Show there was a preponderance of large and costly cars most of which showed very little change from pre-war practice, though cantilever springing, battery ignition and overhead valves were making their appearance. By the 1921 Olympia Show this preponderance had vanished completely. At this Show there was a large number of very small cars. This was no doubt due both to the depressed economic climate and the extensive imports of low-priced, quantity-produced vehicles from the United States in 1920 after import restrictions imposed during the war had been raised. Vehicle production in Europe in 1919 was negligible and the very heavy demand could be met in no other way. Since British industry could also sell all the cars it could produce there were few objections at the time, and despite the tariff and the unfavourable exchange rate, the value of vehicles imported from the United States in 1920 reached £16½ million. This was an exceptional year, however, and it is unlikely that this figure would have been maintained in the following year even had the 1915 McKenna tariff of 33⅓ per cent not been reinforced in 1921 by a variety of duties imposed by the Safeguarding of Industry Act. The fact that this tariff was raised in 1924, albeit for a short period, without any serious effects indicates that its importance for the motor industry was not very great, and that the division of the market between imported and home-manufactured vehicles must be explained by factors other than cost preference. It was prejudice against imported vehicles which, more than any other factor, made it possible for the British motor industry to complete its laborious and painful readjustment without resort to major structural change. As *The Economist* pointed out in 1923, the total British output of 37,753 vehicles, valued at £20½ million, was produced by no less than 90 separate undertakings with an aggregate capital of £32 million. This production represented just over half the capacity of the home market, then estimated at 72,000 cars.

Nevertheless the Rolls-Royce car was by no means the only high-priced car at this time. The Napier 40/50 h.p., the greatest pre-war rival, sold for £1750, Daimlers had three types ranging from £1000 to £1900,

Crossley four types ranging from £1200 to £1450, and Sunbeam had no less than seven types ranging from £1125 to £1650. The Sizaire-Berwick, a much advertised post-war car which greatly resembled the Rolls-Royce, was produced in four models ranging from £1400 to £1500. The imported continental cars also offered Rolls-Royce very little price competition. The Delaunay Belleville 40/50 h.p. sold for £2280, and the Hispano-Suiza for £1400. Lanchester produced two models, one at £1500 and the other at £1850. Until the appearance of the Goshawk late in 1922 Rolls-Royce and Rovers both pursued the intelligent policy of producing only one car, a policy which enabled both firms to survive the difficult post-war period without any grave financial embarrassment, a fact which caused *The Economist* to comment in its review of the industry in 1923 that these two firms 'stand out prominently as our best managed motor concerns'. But the fact that Royce was urged to expedite the design of the Goshawk indicates that the management was not complacent.

The market for the aero-engine was even less predictable and offered no financial security. Until the thirties sales of new engines were to average about £200,000 per annum, though the turnover of spares and repairs almost doubled this figure. Royce was joined shortly after the war by Lt.-Col. T. B. Barrington and A. R. Rowledge, who had resigned from Napiers and was working on the Condor III, which was a complete

2.   The Rolls-Royce Condor I aero-engine

re-design of the original Condor, and on new marks of the Eagle and Falcon. As always, he favoured a policy of obtaining improved performance from existing basic types, and if possible from existing marks of engine, but in the early twenties lack of development finance ruled out any alternative policy. A request for £10,000 for the development of an experimental aero-engine made to the board in February 1922 was turned down. Shortly after this the position became so acute – due primarily to the small turnover (lower in 1922 than in any other post-war year) and the heavy cash outlays which the reconversion of plant had demanded – that the possibility of a £250,000 debenture loan was discussed with Arthur Gibbs and the Midland Bank. The latter agreed to an overdraft of this amount provided it was secured by debentures, but their issue was fortunately avoided by the timely arrival of a substantial income tax rebate.

In June of the same year, however, the Board decided that 25 per cent of whatever sum was voted for development would be allocated to aero work. In view of the minor importance of aero-engine turnover this was a courageous decision. Nevertheless trading conditions improved considerably towards the end of the year and in September 1922 a decision was taken to produce an entirely new 40/50 h.p. chassis, a car which was eventually named the Phantom I. The need for a new model was never doubted, especially as the company had spent heavily after the war modifying all the chassis of those owners who asked for front-wheel brakes and an improved type of springing. The front-wheel brake modification to some six hundred vehicles cost the company nearly fourteen thousand pounds. This was a particularly heavy expense to be written off against goodwill at such a difficult time. The decision to fit four-wheel brakes as a permanent feature of the car, forced on the company by American and Continental practice, was responsible for a fairly substantial increase in cost of production, amounting in 1924, when it was fully applied for the first time, to £77,000. There was, of course, no possibility of raising the price to cover this outlay since it had become almost standard practice on mass-produced American chassis selling at a quarter of this price.

Operations may be said to have returned to something approximating 'normal' by the end of the year 1922 when the Goshawk 20 h.p. was introduced to the public for the first time, but the period between the abnormality of the First World War and its aftermath, and the abnormality of the Second World War and its preceding period of rearmament – a period of at most eleven years – merits separate consideration.

The vast majority of the policy documents, reports, and correspondence relating to this period were unfortunately destroyed as salvage during the early part of the Second World War. This is to some extent compensated by the rather surprising completeness of the records relating to the affairs of Rolls-Royce of America, though even these were preserved, and discovered, more by accident than by design.

Before the scene shifts once more to the United States, mention must be made of an important domestic development which took place despite the adverse economic conditions. This was the introduction by the management of a comprehensive welfare scheme and the issue of workers' shares.

The original suggestion, which was made, as might be expected, by Claude Johnson, caused a considerable stir on the board. His first proposal, to issue 200,000 ordinary shares to employees, was made at a board meeting on 17 December 1918, and aroused Claremont's instinctive opposition. Though the dogs which he preferred to let lie were far from sleeping, Claremont thought that this was asking for trouble. He described, in the words of the board minute, 'A great divergence between capital and labour, and suggested that until the Government had determined the fundamental basis upon which they could be reconciled, such measures on the part of individuals might be very embarrassing to all concerned'. For a businessman Claremont displayed a surprising faith in the ability of the Government to solve a problem over which it had little or no control. He clearly did not consider that management should be prepared to carry the responsibility for good industrial relations.

But Johnson was not deterred. Nor was he content to wait for government initiative on such questions. He finally persuaded the board that the responsiblity of the management for their employees extended beyond the payment of a satisfactory wage and a reasonable continuity of employment. The board consented to issue a statement which he supported, although he did not entirely approve its contents:

> The Directors desire to secure the closer co-operation of the workpeople, and with a view to preparing a suitable scheme for submission to the shareholders, invite such of the workpeople as would be prepared to take up shares in the Company on advantageous terms to notify the Secretary.

The company's solicitors were asked to investigate and report on various profit-sharing schemes then in existence and at a board meeting on 3 March Johnson suggested that the workpeople should elect two of their representatives to serve on the board. The minutes of this meeting reflect the consternation with which the board heard this proposal. It was rejected outright. That Johnson should have made such a suggestion was interesting. It was certainly ahead of its time, and he must have been well aware of the antagonism which it would arouse. He was no doubt equally aware of the 'growing divergence between capital and labour' which Claremont had described, since he had

3. The Short Singapore I flying boat, powered by Rolls-Royce Condor engines

probably observed at closer quarters some of the irrational and undesirable developments in British industry which this divergence was already causing. He appreciated more fully than most the extent to which restrictionism on the part of labour is a reaction against the factory system, and that dissatisfaction with the actual distribution of income between capital and labour is a symptom rather than a cause of a revolt which neither party understood then, or for that matter fully understands today.

The board nevertheless authorised Johnson to approach the employees and ask them which of three possibilities – workers' shares, profit-sharing, or welfare schemes they preferred. Johnson cannot have relished approaching the employees in this 'cake or biscuits' spirit.

On 20 June 1919 the board met in London in an expansive mood to congratulate Royce on the success of his engines in the first non-stop transatlantic flight which Alcock and Brown had just completed in a Vickers Vimy powered with Eagles. The flotation of the American company was under way on very favourable terms to Rolls-Royce and the board was in a generous frame of mind. The conversation turned to the subject of welfare, and it was resolved to ask the shareholders to contribute to a welfare fund 50 per cent of each year's profits after a 10 per cent dividend had been paid on paid-up capital, and not more than 20 per cent transferred to reserve after providing for taxation and other contingencies.

Numerous suggestions had been received covering a very wide field and the board decided that it would consider ten of these.[7] The employees were invited to form a committee to ascertain the cost and to choose which they preferred. Some of the suggestions – the terms of apprentice indenture, the encouragement of inventions, and complaints about supervision – the board would not consider under this heading since they were management problems. Others, such as holidays with pay and refreshment during working hours, the board considered to be industrial problems which would have to be settled on an industry-wide basis by the Engineering Employers Federation. A few, such as the suggestion that employees should be conveyed to the works in company vehicles, were ruled out as quite impracticable.

An employees' committee was set up in due course, and in December this committee and the trade unions agreed unanimously to recommend the workers' share scheme to the employees. This at first aroused great suspicion and hostility, and the scheme was very largely still-born. Some years passed before the obvious advantage of high dividends on shares bought at par were appreciated. A Welfare Fund was, however, established and this was expanded in scope and importance as the company grew and the fund's income expanded.

The immediate post-war period was thus one of considerable change and experiment in all fields. The pre-war mould was too decisively shattered to permit it to be entirely rebuilt, and the management had to improvise constantly and to adapt old administrative, technical and social methods to new conditions and new possibilities. The most interesting experiment of all was to take place in the New World.

3 Rolls-Royce of America Incorporated: a Venture into the Unknown

A combination of circumstances, some of them normal and some exceptional, had often directed the attention of the management towards the North American continent. A small number of cars had been sold there before and during the war and a considerable number had been bought by Americans visiting England and Europe. Rolls himself was the first to appreciate the possibilities of the American market when he went out there to race the 20 h.p. Rolls-Royce in 1906, and it is possible that even if the war had not occurred, Johnson would have followed his inclinations and made a serious attempt to expand the 'natural' market which he had long believed existed in America.

It seemed at first that the war had put paid to most of these ideas. The manufacture neither of aero-engines nor cars was seriously considered until the crisis of 1917 which took Johnson to America to organise the Eagle programme. The wealth of the country, the size of the upper income groups, the efficiency of American production methods and the relative freedom from restrictions of all kinds which American manufacturers enjoyed all combined to persuade him to maintain and expand the organisation which Rolls-Royce had established during the war, and to undertake production of the Rolls-Royce chassis in America as a form of major insurance against the economic and political disasters which he feared would prejudice the future of the company at Derby.

The company's representatives in America at the end of the war included Bagnall, Olley and Kenneth Mackenzie. Soon after the war had ended Johnson instructed Mackenzie to explore the possibilities of obtaining a suitable plant and financial backing. Mackenzie's first interview of any importance was with Duke, the tobacco magnate, who was believed to hold a substantial block of Rolls-Royce shares and who had earlier advised the company on aero-engine production. Duke had novel, but by no means exceptional, views on the post-war situation, which he outlined to Mackenzie. He thought that the times were quite out of joint for new undertakings. Taxation in the United States, he believed, was 'crippling to initiative' and the taxation of profits on the realisation of capital assets he found especially distressing. In order to live he found it necessary to invest in tax-free municipal bonds, and these circumstances made him pessimistic about the industrial and commercial future both of the United States and the United Kingdom. He believed that Britain would have to raise $7000 million annually to discharge her debts and this, being 9 per cent of her gross capital of $80 billion, would inevitably cause a slump. The United States he thought to be in an equally precarious position because the Government was 'pandering to labour'. Duke's reasoning on these subjects, of which the following paragraph is a good example, is of more than passing interest in that the most naive and amusing rationalisations did not prevent him from reaching pertinent and accurate conclusions.

> The United States has raised loans of $25 billion, interest on which at four per cent is $1 billion a year. Adding to this the expenses of the Government which are expected to have increased from one to two billion dollars a year in the last few years, and the financial loss on the railroads as at present operated, the total bill against the United States is about $5 billion a year, which is 2% per annum on her rated capital at the least estimate, under a Republican Government, and perhaps 4% on her present capital, which is estimated as having decreased nearly 50%, under the present administration.

Duke certainly was no fool. He pointed out, in Mackenzie's words that 'a consideration which is contrary to our manufacturing in the United States is the fact that in the eyes of at least some of our customers, the Rolls-Royce car has an inflated value simply because it is made in England'. Duke estimated that this was from 3 to 10 per cent of the value of the car, and thought that if the value of the imported cars, after paying the 30 per cent *ad valorem* import duty, was only 5 per cent greater than the selling price of the same car manufactured in the United States, it should be manufactured only in England. He was doubtful as to the best policy if this figure was 10 per cent, and only if it was as high as 15–20 per cent did he consider that manufacture in the United States would be justified.

Duke did not underestimate the advantages to be gained from manufacture in the United States rather than in England, and cited the example of similar factory buildings erected simultaneously in Liverpool and Petersburg, North Carolina. The Liverpool buildings had cost 18 per cent more than those in Petersburg although the wage rates in the latter case were twice as high.

From the outset Rolls-Royce intended to form a company under the direct control of Derby. The idea was that it should be virtually financially self-sufficient, full control being given to Derby in return for access to all designs, chassis and aero-engine development information, as well as technical assistance on production.

Duke immediately saw the danger inherent in this arrangement which he thought was bound to lead to difficulties. He advised Rolls-Royce to raise all the capital itself and exercise full control over its subsidiary quite independently of outside financial interests. He suggested finally that Rolls-Royce should wait two or three years before launching this project, but Mackenzie pointed out that this would mean wasting the organisation which had been built up in America during the war. There is little doubt that Johnson thought this a great advantage, but he did not weigh it in the scales of comparative advantage, and neglected the disadvantages of starting production during the reconversion period. Had he accepted Duke's advice to wait two or three years, Rolls-Royce of America might well have had a more auspicious start.

Though Duke was very sceptical about the possibility of Rolls-Royce making a success of this scheme, an acquaintance of his in the American Tobacco Company by the name of Patterson (who had a plant by that name at Newark, New Jersey) was very interested, and put up an alternative scheme to Mackenzie. Mackenzie's original scheme was for the new company to issue 400,000 preferred and 400,000 ordinary shares of a value of £1 each, the subscriber of £400,000 in cash receiving the preferred and 100,000 of the ordinary shares, the remaining ordinary shares being held by Rolls-Royce. Patterson's scheme was similar in form, but of a total of 500,000 preference and 500,000 ordinary shares, Rolls-Royce would receive 250,000 ordinary shares for the manufacturing rights. Mackenzie believed that Patterson was in fact backed by Duke, and that this was therefore Duke's own scheme.

At this stage of the negotiations J. E. Aldred and Co.[1] appeared on the scene. Aldred, an entrepreneur financier of the old school, was a personal acquaintance of Arthur Gibbs, who had in all probability told him of Rolls-Royce's intention in America.

On 4 June Mackenzie cabled London as follows:

Aldred close business associate of Holt of Montreal wished us locate Baltimore where they have power interest and to assist in financing our new Company. Cannot now tell whether business with him advisable. In view of our other channels for financing will depend on developments. Are Holt or Beaverbrook substantial shareholders with us? Patterson pressing early decision. Think we should deal with him on supposition he acting for Duke and the latter interested in Newark plant.

At a board meeting on 20 June 1919 in London the problem was discussed. The proportion of preference to ordinary shares and conversion rights was considered, Claremont maintaining that 'from his experience it had in the past been possible to obtain in America startling sums for goodwill and patents'. He suggested that Rolls-Royce should not part with these rights for under £500,000, but Johnson thought that this was too small for an outright sale, a scheme which he did not, in any event, approve.[2]

At a subsequent board meeting on 27 June it was decided that Johnson should go to America and that he should invite Arthur Gibbs to accompany him. The latter accepted with some reluctance as he did not look with any great favour on the new scheme. They left almost immediately on the *Mauretania* and arrived in America early in July.

On his arrival, Johnson found four schemes awaiting his examination.[3] Three of these were relatively firm offers. He decided that the Aldred offer was the best and cabled the Board to this effect. The fact of Aldred's past successes, combined with the reputation the firm had acquired of never financing a company in which they did not retain a permanent interest, with the power to appoint some members of the board, strongly recommended them to Johnson. Aldreds were also agreeable to Rolls-Royce retaining technical and commercial control of the American company.

Aldreds offered to issue $3,500,000 in 7 per cent ordinary preference shares of a nominal value of $100 at $90 per share. This they were prepared to underwrite entirely for $10 per share. These shares were to carry a further dividend not exceeding 3 per cent, ranking equally with the dividend on ordinary shares. A further $3,500,000 of ordinary shares was to be issued, a quarter of which would be allotted to Aldreds or their nominees, and the remainder to Rolls-Royce. This scheme differed radically from that put forward by the English board as a basis for discussion. This contemplated a total capital of $8,000,000 comprising $3,000,000 in the 7 per cent convertible preference shares and $5,000,000 ordinary shares. It was intended that the ordinary shares would be issued for the purpose of acquiring the 'American business and prospects of Rolls-Royce' and that $750,000 should be issued to pay for the underwriting of the preference issue.

It is not surprising that this offer made no appeal to the American financiers with whom Johnson and Mackenzie were negotiating. They wanted the preferred shares to have conversion rights (from preferred to ordinary) and suggested that the preference shares should not carry a vote unless no dividend were paid within a specified period. The figure of 10 per cent discount on the preference issue was the minimum acceptable to any of the finance houses, and Patterson was not prepared to underwrite the issue for less than this plus an additional consideration of $875,000 in ordinary shares and $80,000 in cash.

None of these schemes was acceptable in their turn to the English board, who cabled Johnson on 22 July that they considered that the terms were excessive, 10 per cent being an 'outside price' for underwriting in England. Johnson was advised to continue the negotiations in an endeavour to obtain better terms. This he attempted to do, but Aldreds would not budge and pointedly asked the Rolls-Royce board to inform them which English underwriters were prepared to provide $3,500,000 for 10 per cent of the ordinary stock, considering that there were many more attractive 7 per cent offerings in New York than Rolls-Royce, that there was no guarantee that the American buyer would pay $11,000 for a chassis made in the United States, that there was no guarantee that the American chassis could be made as good as the British and that under their proposals Rolls-Royce would have three-quarters of the eventual earnings although they were putting no cash into the venture, taking no financial risks and giving no guarantee of the company's earning capacity.

Aldred considered that he was already carrying a considerable risk only because of the good name of the English company. He described the terms of another $5,700,000 issue which he was underwriting at a discount of $12\frac{1}{2}$ per cent. For the underwriting Aldreds were also to receive 49 per cent of the common stock. He said that a large New York banking firm had refused business when told that the maximum fee would be 25 per cent of the value of the issue. This threw very cold water on any hopes that the English board may still have held of their terms being met.

Before proceeding further Johnson made discreet enquiries in New York to disprove or substantiate Aldred's claims. He consulted J. P. Morgan who approved of Aldred on the grounds that he had successfully financed several large and successful companies such as the Montreal Heat, Light and Power Company and the Gillette Safety Razor Company. 'We do not', they said, 'consider him in the first rank, but nevertheless think well of him and upon the basis of his past performance would be inclined to think that he was capable of handling the matter you mention.'

Johnson also approached Lee Higgison & Co., one of the oldest financial houses in the United States, and obtained from them the opinion that the Aldred offer was most generous and that the proposal was one which they themselves 'could not begin to consider'.

Thus reassured, Johnson rapidly concluded an agreement with Aldred. The creation of a voting trust disposed of the main item of disagreement – the question of whether or not Rolls-Royce was to retain majority control of the new company. This trust was created for five years, and the first members were Johnson, Aldred and Claremont. All the ordinary shares were deposited with the trustees, who were thus in a position to control the board and the company. In October 1919 Aldred issued a prospectus, inviting subscription to the preference stock, which was oversubscribed. This prospectus gave the authorised capital as $15,000,000 equally divided between preference and ordinary. Of this sum, $3,500,000 of the preference shares were issued to the public out of a total issue of $7,000,000, the remaining shares being stock of no declared value. C. E. F. Clarke, a school-friend of Aldred, and a man with little knowledge of the industry, was made President. Johnson, Claremont, Royce and Mackenzie represented the English company, and Clarke, L. J. Belnap,[4] Aldred and H. J. Fuller represented the American financial interests on the board. The division of interest was thus built into the foundation of the enterprise.

The prospectus declared that the products of the two companies would be identical and indistinguishable and contained a letter from Johnson referring to the strong financial position of the English company. The English board would act in an advisory capacity and the English company would supply certain 'prominent technical officials'. The production target was stated to be 380 chassis per annum, though the factory was to be designed in anticipation of demand 'speedily justifying a substantial increase in capacity of plant'. The new company was to take over the Long Island Service Station previously operated by Rolls-Royce, and to pay Robert Schuette, the former Rolls-Royce agent in New York, a sum of $100,000 as compensation for loss of profit on his agency agreement. It was hoped that this substantial sum (which was far less than the final figure actually paid to this individual) would be partially redeemed by the profit accruing from the sale of chassis imported from England which the new company would handle before output from its own works commenced. The prospectus also stated that the parent company was precluded by war legislation from raising capital in England for investment abroad.

An interesting comment on the announcement that Rolls-Royce intended to manufacture in America appeared a few months later in the London *Times*, which interviewed the managing director of a large American motor firm then visiting England.

> If the American Rolls-Royce [he said] is to be made of English material, by English workmen, with English workmanship in the real Rolls-Royce way (as if each car were a special order); if, in short, the Derby works are going to be reduplicated exactly over here, then I consider the venture to be a serious menace to the American high-class car. If, however, the car is going to be turned out on real American lines, frankly it does not give me the smallest uneasiness. It won't be a real Rolls-Royce.

This was undoubtedly the attitude of the English board, and from his own point of view the American manufacturer could not have done better than to encourage them in their belief, though no doubt the comment was made in all sincerity.

An agreement was now included between the two companies (Rolls-Royce of America and Rolls-Royce) whereby Rolls-Royce agreed to supply all design, patent and manufacturing information requested by the American company, and one set of drawings of 'everything now or hereafter manufactured' and to withdraw completely from the American market except on agreed terms. The American company agreed not to compete in any way with the English company in England or the rest of the world outside the North American continent.

The prospectus made no mention of any specific plant which the promoters had in mind and merely stated that the intention was to acquire a plant in New England 'which after careful investigation will be deemed most advantageous for the Company'. The choice of plant was being actively considered in November, and four works had been seriously investigated, rough estimates being made of the capital

4.   Maurice Olley

outlay per chassis required at each. These varied from $39,446 at Willimanset to $54,782 at the King Works, the planned output being seven chassis per week.

Belnap, Johnson, Nadin and Olley were all in favour of the Wire Wheel Works at Springfield, since its choice would avoid the risks of delay which the erection of new buildings would involve and offer the possibility of getting into production quickly. Great difficulty was experienced in persuading any builder to give a firm estimate for the erection of new works, due mainly to the severe fluctuations then taking place in the prices of building materials. They also stressed the 'beneficial impression on the public which must result from the immediate acquisition of land and buildings'.

Belnap, Johnson and Nadin favoured the Sumner property (also at Springfield) as second choice, because of its 'altitude, dryness, healthiness, accessibility to Springfield, isolation from other automobile concerns and ample supplies of labour'. Mackenzie and Olley favoured the Willimanset property as second choice on the grounds that the district was likely to become a neighbourhood of great industrial importance, the land which could not be acquired cheaply would increase in value and that the neighbouring town of Holyoke provided 'ample attractions to satisfy workers'. There was also a good supply of labour and cheap power and low rates.

For these reasons and because it was thought a good thing *not* to locate the production of the Rolls-Royce in the centre of an automobile manufacturing district such as Detroit, the Wire Wheel Plant at Springfield was finally chosen, and part production began on 12 July 1920. It was thought that this geographical isolation would accentuate, in the eyes of both customer and manufacturer, the difference between the Rolls-Royce and an ordinary car. Springfield had long established a tradition for craftmanship labour in other industries.[5]

In view of later developments, some of the forecasts and estimates of costs and financial requirements made at this stage are of some importance. At Johnson's request De Looze analysed the 1911 Derby figures as a basis for calculation. This gave a figure of £176,689 for the fixed and floating assets at Derby at this time, excluding goodwill and deducting debtors, but De Looze preferred to include them and bring the figure up to £260,849, 'since we are always working on credit for at least two months and the bank balance either for or against us depends entirely on our turnover and the speed with which we get our bills paid'. On the basis of this figure and an annual output of 356 chassis in

5.   The Springfield-built Rolls-Royce Phantom I

the financial year of 1911, a figure of £531 working capital per chassis was obtained. Total costs came to £506 per chassis (wages £124, material £196 and establishment charges £186) or £189,236 per annum. It was thought that costs in America would be 120 per cent to 150 per cent higher than at Derby, and this gave figures of £986 and £1067 per chassis (£351,000 and £379,000) for the production of a similar quantity at Springfield. To these figures would have to be added £70,000 for jigs and tools and installation costs. On this basis it was finally calculated that £400,000 would be required for working capital at Springfield.

A more detailed estimate of working capital requirements made by Nadin in July seems to have been used during the following six months. This estimate predicted that expenditure would not be covered by receipts until May 1921, twenty months after the commencement of operations. He estimated that there would be a quarterly deficit, starting at $616,000 and averaging $209,000 a month for the first year. This was calculated on the assumption that the first cars would not be delivered into the hands of customers until September 1920. The total anticipated deficit in this period was $3,218,000, $160,900 a month over the period of twenty months. This total was increased to $3,714,000 by preference dividends at the rate of $64,000 a quarter and the purchase price of the Long Island Service Station. Against the absorption of $256,700 per annum by the preference dividend it was estimated that there would be a profit of $576,000 on the year's output of 384 chassis ($1500 per chassis). The total cost of the chassis was estimated to be $9805,[6] including the item of profit. The proposed selling price was fixed provisionally at $11,750, a figure which would yield approximately $2000 profit per retail sale. A trade discount of 10 per cent reduced the figure for total profit to $535,000, and if this was raised to 15 per cent the profit would still further be reduced to $436,000. Nadin's estimates of cost were considered to be excessive by several other members of the management.

After satisfying himself that the organisation had been successfully launched, Johnson returned to England and made a very favourable report to the board. Shortly after this Belnap succeeded Clarke as President, a position which he held for several years thereafter. This change was generally approved both in America and in England, but Mackenzie (the Rolls-Royce solicitor in the United States) was given very careful instructions to report quite independently to the English board on all developments at Springfield. This was bad psychology on Johnson's part since Mackenzie's position obviously implied a lack of trust in the integrity of the Springfield board.

The first sign that all was not well appeared in a letter from Mackenzie to Johnson in which he remarked that 'there has been some difficulty in getting the necessary information to keep track of what is going on at Springfield, but I think that this has been largely overcome'. He told Johnson that Belnap had planned for the first chassis to be ready in October and that he was doubtful if the target would be reached.

On 15 March 1920 Belnap wrote to Johnson suggesting that a more extensive publicity campaign would be needed. He believed that it should be widely made known that 'the American Company is the American factory of Rolls-Royce Ltd. and that the product we produce in the American factory is to be identical with that produced in the British factory . . . my reason for making this point is that we are constantly confronted, directly or indirectly, with the fact that we will probably do the same as others who have attempted to manufacture a foreign car in the U.S. and failed. Of course we all know why they have failed.'

These remarks suggest that there was more going on than met the eye, and it would seem legitimate to conclude from the above that the American company was experiencing unforeseen difficulties, even at this early stage in its career, and that the President himself was not altogether confident of success. One of the rocks on which the American company ultimately foundered was undoubtedly a complex psychological prejudice, deliberately aggravated wherever possible by the company's competitors, that the Springfield product was an inferior imitation of the real thing. Moreover, those Americans who already owned Derby Rolls-Royces were quite prepared, without any malice aforethought, to fan these flames to maintain the prestige and distinction of their own vehicles. Such idiosyncrasies are undoubtedly

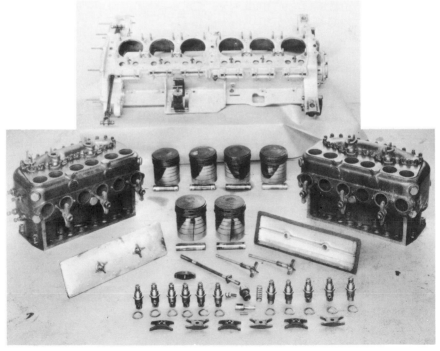

6.   The Rolls-Royce Springfield Silver Ghost engine components

of great importance. Manufacturers in such fields who ignore these idiosyncrasies do so at their peril. Thus it would appear that as far as the Springfield Rolls-Royce was concerned product defamation had started even before the first car had been sold.

Belnap's letter also informed Johnson that the prices for many materials had been lower than expected, though he expressed some concern over the tool position. 'We have now', he said, 'about 300 toolmakers in 38 jig, tool and fixture specialty shops working for us in cities adjacent to Springfield. We have been rather anxious about the price of this work for we found that the toolmakers were expending entirely too much time on high price and finish.'

This was one of the unforeseen consequences of the Rolls-Royce reputation. Belnap went on to discuss price policy and said that he considered he would be able to sell a sufficiently large number of chassis at $11,750. The first final selling price which had been suggested by Springfield was $9300, but the increased cost of materials had soon forced this up.

Johnson's reply did not reveal any undue concern. 'I am very glad', he said, 'that you think you can sell chassis in sufficient numbers for $11,750. By all means keep the price up.' Many of these problems were discussed with Aldred and his partner, H. J. Fuller, when they visited England in April 1920, and in June Johnson went over to Springfield again and on this visit found everything to his satisfaction. Shortly after his return in July he wrote: 'I was much pleased with the spirit of the men and their determination to excel the English quality and not merely to equal it. Surely that is the spirit of Rolls-Royce.'

In August serious difficulties arose over the problem of the accessories which were to be fitted to the American chassis, and to the interim chassis being supplied from Derby. These accessories were far more widely standardised in America than they were in England, and the American board considered that the market might be seriously jeopardised if spares were not readily available. In particular, the American board wished to fit Bijur starters and Bosch magnetos on the Springfield chassis. The Springfield engineers complained that the Watford magnetos and Lucas dynamos were giving more trouble than any other parts of the car and, to substantiate this claim, pointed out that several owners had fitted the Bosch magneto at their own expense.

E. W. Hives, who had been working under Royce for some considerable time as chief of the Experimental Department, was sent out to America to report on the situation and to discuss the prospective changes with the Springfield engineers. His competent and thorough report was wholly characteristic of the man who was subsequently to become the Company's chairman, but unfortunately little attention was paid to its direct suggestions and even less to its indirect implications. Hives also took out a new experimental Derby chassis to test under local American conditions, and obtained some valuable information from this car.

Hives went to America fully imbued with the Derby prejudice against the local accessories, very largely as a result of a series of exacting tests carried out by the Experimental Department on a Bosch magneto. He later discovered that this particular magneto was an admittedly inferior model produced for what the American Bosch Company's representatives described as 'the competitive market'.

Hives visited both the Bosch[7] and Bijur works and the American manufacturers were quite prepared to put their products through any test which he requested and to compare them with any other productions. The Bosch Company offered to make special magnetos to the Springfield specification, to allow Springfield inspectors to supervise their production, and to test – and if necessary reject – any magneto. The price they asked was $35, for which they were prepared to guarantee their product in the same general terms as the guarantee given to the whole car. The company also offered to design and produce a special starter for the Springfield chassis.

Hives also visited the Westinghouse factory, which was only half a mile from the Springfield works, and again the management offered to design special equipment for the Springfield Rolls-Royce if their existing products were not up to standard.

On 12 January 1921 a conference was held on the subject of Springfield, which was attended by Bagnell,[8] Beaver, Belnap, Hives, Kein, Nadin and Olley. At this conference, Hives declared his readiness to recommend the Bosch magneto on both technical and financial

English make	Cost when manufactured at Springfield	Cost of U.S.A. Equivalent
Starter	$216.68	$40
Lucas generator	$116.31	$40
Watford magneto	$ 92.74	$35

grounds. In his report to England he remarked that 'the inspection for workmanship and efficiency and the guarantee which the American manufacturers are prepared to give are much better than we obtain from any English suppliers'.

From the point of view of cost alone, as the figures reveal, the argument was overwhelmingly against importing the accessories from England.

In a report on American-made parts, in particular the Bijur motor, written in July 1920 before he went out to America, Hives had made the following comment:

> As regards other parts such as magnetos, generators, switch-boards, etc., we agree that if the parts which America have submitted and are going to submit are as good as they believe them to be, then we ought undoubtedly to adopt them on all Rolls-Royce cars, those made in England as well as those made in America . . . We do not see how we can justify our position of making the best car if we have two standards.

The ability to change one's mind decisively is often the indication of a vigorous and progressive intellect. In his report to Royce on the running of the experimental Derby chassis in America, Hives shows very clearly that he had come to understand the precise nature of the problem of producing a Rolls-Royce in America. It is unfortunate that his main conclusion was totally neglected, because if such a policy had been followed consistently from the start at Springfield, the enterprise might well have been successful. It is as much the fault of Derby as of Springfield that it was not followed until it was too late.

> In considering [he said] the policy of making the Rolls-Royce car in America identical with the Derby car I consider that we should always have in mind that it is *the results of the car in the customers' hands which we want to be identical*. It is futile to have the cars look the same if, owing to variations in conditions, they give different results.

The behaviour of the experimental Derby chassis had proved this conclusively. The car did not perform as it did in England for several reasons, principal among which were the lower-quality petrol and the wider range of atmospheric temperatures. The carburation was inadequate and the car was very difficult to start. As a result, some American customers were returning their new cars (the imported chassis)[9] and the proportion of dissatisfied customers was much higher than in England. After recommending a series of important modifications to remedy these defects, Hives turned his attention to the general comparison between costs of manufacture in England and the United States. This is of considerable interest. It establishes the fact that the 'identical product' policy involved an immediate sacrifice of very great advantages.[10]

Springfield was unable to take advantage of the low costs achieved by mass production of accessories or of the servicing facilities which local accessory manufacturers had developed. The inevitable consequence was that the overheads of the Springfield organisation soon began to spiral almost completely out of control.[11]

Hives pointed out that the Springfield forgings were not only cheaper than in England but were also nearer to size. American frames were also cheaper than their English counterparts, although they were heat-treated. On the subject of costs Hives concluded with the following recommendation:

> There ought to be some scheme developed whereby the costs of Derby and Springfield are constantly compared, not only raw material costs, but machining costs, fitting costs, testing costs and office costs. I saw enough in the U.S.A. to realise that in all departments there is something to be learned from American methods.

But the validity of these remarks did not increase the cost-consciousness of the Derby works, and no attempt at a running comparison was ever made in the thorough manner which would have been of such great value.[12] Sixteen years were to elapse before Hives was able to put some of his ideas into practice and in doing so come to appreciate very fully the natural conservatism of industrial organisations.

The report concluded with a reference to coachwork in the United States, something about which London had previously had no doubts whatever. 'One of the surprises,' he said, 'was the excellence of their custom-built bodies ... The best American bodies were better made and better finished than the English. They were made to more practical designs and had better fittings.' The Smith Body corporation at Springfield he considered to be 'far and away more up to date than Barkers'.

This report must have been very strong medicine for the English management, but in presenting it Hives was no more than continuing the tradition, which Royce himself had established, of bringing the strongest criticism to bear on the Rolls-Royce chassis itself. In a memorandum referring to the cost of handwork and of the special electrical department at Derby, Royce made known his point of view without committing himself to any specific recommendations.

> We must thank Mr. Hives for pointing out the entire dissimilarity of our procedure with reference to this work on this side of the Atlantic compared with the practice adopted in the States. I am sure that the points mentioned above, the careful avoidance of handwork and the realisation that the cost of handwork is at the rate of 1d. per minute, will enable us to do much towards getting on a better foundation.

Royce finally approved of the American Bosch magneto, and by April 1921 the policy of complete identity of product had been abandoned for the simple reason that it was totally impracticable. Though abandoned in practice it was never fully abandoned in spirit, and production at Springfield continued under a two-fold handicap. It was not until 1930 that Royce was to find himself in emphatic agreement with Hives' recommendations.

4 A Cascade of Problems

Though the technical problems at Springfield were of great importance the attention of the management was very soon absorbed almost wholly by the threat of a financial avalanche, the first rumblings of whose approach were heard in September 1920.

Calculations made on 1 October 1920 had revealed a very serious position. Several important items of expenditure had been grossly underestimated, and the existing cash resources of the American company were not nearly capable of meeting the requirements for working capital. The expenditure on jigs, tools and dies in particular greatly exceeded the original estimate. This was $300,000; and $848,000 had been spent. The payments to Schuette, which were originally estimated to require $100,000, amounted finally to $239,000. There was also an unexplained increase of $228,000 on the chassis and body trading account. The figures in Appendix II reveal, however, that although there had been a serious miscalculation of expenditure, the real cause of the trouble lay elsewhere. Nadin's original calculation of the disbursements required in the first fourteen months' operations had produced a figure of $3,218,000 for the total working capital required. The amount of cash actually provided by the underwriters, after they had deducted their heavy fees and discounts from the proceeds of the issue, was $2,721,250. The net cost of the issue was thus $778,750, 28.5 per cent of the money actually raised for the company's use and 22.2 per cent of the value of the shares issued to the public. This meant that the rate of interest which the American company had to pay on its capital was a good deal higher than 7 per cent.

In November 1920 Aldred again visited England and the English board discussed the financial problem with him in London. He intimated that the American company would require £400,000 to enable it to pull through the crisis, and said that this amount could not be raised unless the English company was prepared to offer some sort of guarantee. This guarantee the English directors declared themselves neither able nor willing to give. The overdraft was limited to £200,000 until the issue of the next balance sheet, and the board was seriously contemplating an issue of £600,000 worth of debentures to finance its own operations. The bank had moreover warned De Looze that if a guarantee were given to America the overdraft would be correspondingly curtailed.

The board finally agreed, with considerable reluctance, to guarantee a maximum figure of £125,000, and Johnson was authorised to guarantee this sum on condition that the interest did not exceed 10 per cent and on the further condition that Rolls-Royce would not be called upon to repay the capital sum in under ten years. A further proviso was that the American company was not to create any new loans without Derby's consent. Johnson consulted Arthur Gibbs on the subject, but the latter thought that the risk was negligible to the shareholders and he raised no new objections.

Aldred returned to America in December 1920 and a further series of discussions took place with Johnson and Belnap. Aldred thought that the English bankers were 'disregarding the substantial security to be had' and to this Johnson replied that he was of the opinion that 'the English bankers were influenced in their view by the fact that the American financiers who were connected with the administration of the American Company, and who had found the original $2,800,000, did not show sufficient confidence in the future of the American Company to find the further $1,880,000 now required.' Johnson maintained that when, on 30 September, he had made Aldred aware of the large sum of money required to get Springfield into full production, the latter had assured him that there would be no difficulty in raising it.

At a Springfield board meeting on 16 October 1920 no mention had been made of there being any necessity for Derby to participate in the raising of the required sum, then estimated at $1.5 million. Aldred was not prepared to accept this and indignantly repudiated the suggestion that he had undertaken to provide the additional finance. He maintained that he could never have agreed to provide Springfield with the considerable additional funds which it required, and declared that it was up to the English company as holders of all the common stock to provide these funds. It is difficult not to sympathise with Aldred's point of view since, despite the onerous terms on which he had raised the capital, he had borne the entire financial risk, and the underwriting charges would hardly have compensated him for the loss of the considerable sum which he had personally invested in the company.

On 23 December Johnson cabled two alternative proposals to Derby. The first of these was for Derby to guarantee an issue of bonds or debentures for $2,000,000, of which half would be reguaranteed by the American bankers or an American syndicate. Derby would still retain full control of the American board but would have to pay the American bankers $50,000 as a consideration for their re-guarantee. The second proposal was that Derby should transfer 33⅓ per cent of its common stock holding to the American syndicate as a payment for their placing $2,000,000 of bonds of debentures. Under the second proposal Derby would incur no new liability or responsibility and would retain the same voting power.

The English board considered these proposals on 1 January 1921 and favoured the second on the condition that the payment for underwriting was made out of the unissued common stock of the American company, or alternatively borne proportionately by the American syndicate and the English company. The first proposal they were prepared to accept only on the following conditions:

(1) That $2,000,000 was the upper limit of the issue;
(2) That the rate of interest should not exceed 10 per cent;
(3) That there should be a ten-year period within which Derby could not be called upon to pay in full;
(4) That the issue was secured by first mortgage debentures, a general charge on the floating assets, and a specific charge on the real estate;
(5) That the American syndicate should guarantee to pay half of any capital sums which Derby was called upon to pay;
(6) That the American company should create a ten-year 5 per cent sinking fund;
(7) That premises and machinery appeared in the balance sheet at cost value less depreciation;
(8) That Derby would have the right to require immediate realisation if any of the above conditions were broken.

It was noted at this meeting that Springfield already owed Derby £77,697 on general account, but despite this the board decided to support Johnson and cabled their acceptance of the proposals, subject to the above conditions. On 4 January, Johnson replied that this was not good enough. 'The bankers', he said, 'who usually follow Aldred have refused Ordinary Share bonus set out in mine of 23.12.20 . . . but there are faint hopes of very fine bankers accepting half and Aldreds will accept other half on same terms. But the bankers will not agree that we should retain votes on Ordinary Shares sacrificed as bonus.' The language of this cable had an air of plaintive desperation about it. 'Have English Directors forgotten,' he continued, 'that Ordinary Shares are owned by men who found original money, that the Preferred Shares are not now worth 50 cents and that we have to ask them to sacrifice their preference position in favour of our notes?' He asked the board to agree to his suggestion that the voting powers on this stock should be relinquished.

They were not in the least ready to approve any development of this nature, and had all along been in favour of a scheme suggested by Messrs Claremont Haynes, whereby all the common stock holders, including Aldred, should sacrifice an equal proportion of their hold-ings. They were also in favour of an issue of new common stock, and examined a great variety of ingenious schemes designed to satisfy the bankers' demand for 8750 shares and yet retain the voting control in Derby.

The Atlantic cables were kept very busy. One of the schemes which Johnson suggested was that Derby should purchase $190,000 worth of notes with the money already owed by Springfield for chassis. The board replied acidly that it would 'find no cash' and that it was 'determined not to lose control, but to support you and Mackenzie will forego another 1,000 shares'. This they would only do on the condition that Johnson 'repudiated Aldred's suggestion of their responsibility for the embarrassing situation'.

Johnson was obviously unable to appreciate the attitude of the English board. He agreed that it was not desirable that England should lose control but if he could not persuade Aldred to surrender the 1188 shares asked of him on the proportionate scheme was he then to close the works?

Throughout these negotiations the English board maintained very close contact with the company's solicitors in London, Messrs Clare-mont Haynes. The latter were asked to advise and report on both proposals and they pointed out that the result of the first scheme (whereby England guaranteed capital and interest, and the American syndicate half the capital but not the interest) depended on the profits which the American company made. For it to be able to meet all obligations a net surplus of $615,000 was required, $200,000 for the debenture loan instalment repayment, $160,000 for interest, and $245,000 for a 7 per cent dividend on the preference shares. If the profit was sufficient to cover the first two payments, Derby would not be called upon to provide funds but would lose voting control through the preference shareholders acquiring votes. If the profit was insufficient to meet all three payments, then Derby might have been called upon to pay half the capital sum ($100,000) and the whole of the interest ($100,000).

In regard to the second proposal they pointed out that England would lose control immediately the transfer of ordinary shares was made, and suggested that all common stock-holders should give up an equal proportion. Claremont condemned the first proposal on the grounds the Derby would never wish to dispose of its shareholding if the American company were successful.

Ordinary business prudence and good sense naturally suggest that the management of any concern should be well advised legally in its relations with other corporations, but the extreme care taken (where the American company was concerned) to obtain legal advice in every move, even when it was wholly controlled from Derby, reveal a curious psychological approach towards the whole affair. The Derby management seemed anxious to retain voting control purely for the purpose of retaining control and without the apparent ability or intention of merging the interests of Derby and Springfield into a joint interest composed of two distinct, but inseparable, part-interests. This attitude was sensed, and resented, at Springfield, and it is hardly surprising that it led to an equal and opposite polarisation of the financial interests in the United States.

Whenever any development at Springfield was considered in London (where the board usually met) it was always related primarily to the effect this would have on the English company. Aldreds consequently came to consider such developments purely in relation to their financial interest in Springfield. These attitudes were mutually antagonistic, and the one aggravated the other. The first development in this direction was undoubtedly the high charge which Aldred made for raising capital; the second was the English company's refusal to even *appear* anxious to come to its assistance in the period at present under discussion in the text. In the end, neither party would accept full responsibility for the Springfield company which, already facing great natural difficulties, was unable to develop the vigorous and sustained policy required to establish itself on a sound economic basis.

The situation now began to deteriorate very rapidly. Though the first car had just been produced early in January 1921, it looked very much as though a complete fiasco was imminent and that the Springfield Rolls-Royce would never reach the market either to confound or confirm the gloomy forebodings of the critics. While the negotiations with Aldred continued on the basis of a new suggestion that Derby should receive half of a new bonus issue, Johnson had to cable England for immediate financial support. To this request the Board replied as follows:

> Most sympathetic America but duty to shareholders here paramount. Must have regard industrial and financial outlook. Cannot accept underwriting liability, would restrict our bank credit.

This reply exasperated Johnson, who was unable to bring his great personal powers of persuasion to bear on the English directors. His view of the English company's responsibility was wider than theirs and he realised that the failure of the Springfield company before the first car was produced and sold would have very serious repercussions not only on the name and goodwill of the company in America and on the American market for either English or American chassis, but also on the standing of the English company itself. He replied immediately in the following terms:

> Previous Board's verdict of death by starvation of undertaking having limitless possibilities for English shareholders can only result from definite statement from McKenna that underwriting would seriously restrict bank credit and that McKenna realises that Aldred cannot extricate himself from liability attached to underwriting without also extracting England.

The board accepted the logic of the situation and agreed to provide $100,000 in 'stop-gap' aid. Almost immediately after this Aldred came forward with an entirely new scheme. He undertook to provide $1,500,000 and underwrite all the notes in return for 8750 of the common stock plus an undertaking by the English company to guarantee the repayment to the New York banks of $1,600,000 at the end of six months. The common stock was to be provided by all the holders putting up 28.7 per cent of their holding.

This proposal was received in England on 19 January and considered by the board on the following day. It was pointed out that the maximum liability which Derby might have to meet was $750,000, an amount which would not be recoverable except by selling the bonds (if a purchaser could be found), or from the American company at the end of ten years. The financial situation of the English company was carefully reviewed before reaching a decision. There was no cash immediately available at Derby, although the bank had intimated that it was prepared to allow an overdraft of £300,000. A sum of £220,000 was required in the immediate future for dividends and bonuses, and an equal sum was due to the Government for arrears of taxation. A changeover of production (to the Goshawk) 'with its attendant risks' was impending, and on top of all this the board felt that it could not neglect what it termed 'the prevailing industrial and financial depression'. It was not an easy decision to have to make.

After weighing these adverse factors, not so much against the favourable factors (which are not mentioned and appear either to have been taken for granted or not considered at all), as against the risks attendant upon not coming to some agreement with Aldred to assist Springfield, the board decided to offer the required guarantee. Before doing so, however, it took the precaution of making some discreet enquiries about Aldred's standing and reputation. They were advised that Aldred was quite capable of meeting his obligations as he had just spent $1,500,000 on his private home. The Midland Bank also promised that it would see the firm through if it was called upon to meet this guarantee, without its existing overdraft being affected.

An agreement was finally signed for a debenture issue of $2,000,000 (not $1,500,000 as originally contemplated), and in February 1921 Johnson returned to England, exhausted by worry and responsibility, and suffering badly from insomnia. For the time being the cash problem was solved. Of the authorised issue $1,700,000 was actually issued at 90 per cent, to yield just over $1,500,000 to the company. The board instructed Johnson to sign the agreement providing the guarantee on condition that Aldred agreed to purchase the ten-year loan notes within six months at a minimum price of $90 per 100. This obligation he fulfilled in due course.

No sooner had the problem of finance been solved than others materialised with indecent haste. On 31 March Belnap wrote to England saying that production had by this time reached a figure of five cars a week, the planned output then being twelve per week, or six hundred per annum. He added, ominously, that 'sales are not anything like we would wish. Our sales average just now about three a week, but judging from the last two or three weeks' reports prospects are brighter than they have been at any time.' In another letter to England Mackenzie pointed out that a rigid adherence to English designs and standards would do more harm than good. 'The American Company must', he said, 'attempt to meet American demands even if it does mean a slightly different car. Petrol gauges for example are not fitted, but are universal in the United States.'

The sales problem now began rapidly to overshadow all the others. It was plainly of little use pouring resources into the production of a vehicle which, whatever its price, the American public would not buy. At a meeting of the American board on 14 February a senior member of the sales staff reported on a market survey which he had just undertaken. Both the evidence from this survey and from the Chicago Show proved conclusively that 'purchasers in the West showed a disposition to favour the American made chassis[1] and in almost every instance preferred to purchase a complete car including the body'.

The thorny question of retailers' discount was a further problem. Springfield originally offered a discount of 10 per cent on sales provided that the dealer purchased a demonstration model. Those dealers, usually the best-known in the town or area, who had been approached had turned this offer down almost unanimously. They made a counter-offer of 15 per cent and pointed out that some American manufacturers were offering discounts of up to 40 per cent. The American board decided that it would negotiate these discounts individually, but insisted that 15 per cent should be considered as an outside maximum.

During 1921 the sale of imported chassis and bodies through the Long Island and Boston Sales Depots was the only profitable section of the company's activities. During the first six months of the year the gross turnover of the Long Island Service Station and the New York, Chicago and Boston Sales Depots was $876,300 (54 chassis and 23 bodies valued at $748,831) on which the net profit was $120,800 (13 per cent). This figure is significant since it is some indication of the business which Derby had to forgo in the American market during the period when Springfield was producing cars. This might conceivably have yielded the English company a net profit of $300,000 annually had a really aggressive attempt been made to build up the sales of the English Rolls-Royce in America.

Detailed records of operations between October 1922 and 1927 have unfortunately not survived,[2] but production was more or less stabilised during 1922, the sales varying from $107,000 in January to $335,000 in May, the average for the first six months of the year being $233,000 per month as compared with $145,561 during the same period in 1921. It is interesting to note that in Nadin's original estimate the sales from Springfield production alone during the first six months of 1921 were

expected to average $223,320 per month. During this period the total
sales of Springfield-made cars in fact amounted to only $124,000.

The situation at Springfield in July 1922 was not encouraging.
During that month the sales of new cars amounted to 24 chassis and 20
bodies. This was an annual rate of 288 chassis, a figure well below the
planned output. Yet the superficial signs were encouraging. A loss of
$32,000 in the first quarter had been converted into a profit of $96,000
in the second quarter, an annual rate of $387,000. But for a new and
unestablished company without any reserves the burden of capitalisation was far too heavy. The total operating deficit had amounted by this
time to $958,300 and unliquidated formation expenses appeared in the
balance sheet as an asset valued at $529,000. The capital now consisted
of $3,500,000 in 7 per cent preferred stock, 36,000 ordinary shares of no
par value, the majority of which were held by Derby, and $1,700,000
ten-year 8 per cent gold notes, as the debentures were called. Trade
names, designs and patents were valued on the asset side of the balance
sheet at $4,316,000, a very high proportion of the total assets. The
company had to make a profit of $605,000 per annum in order to meet
the debenture charges and interest, the preference dividends, and the
debenture sinking fund payments. On the basis of a turnover of 350
chassis, the figure originally contemplated, a profit in excess of $1700
per chassis would have had to be realised solely in order to fulfil these
obligations.[3]

A circular written to the preference shareholders on 28 August
shows that the Aldred organisation still had every confidence in the
future of the American company, although it is of interest that as early
as December 1920 one of the senior partners, H. Murray, had predicted
disaster. But Murray was by nature a pessimist and his views were
disregarded. The circular letter reveals clearly that the Springfield
organisation was still dominated by the 'identity of product' principle:

. . . Having in mind the abnormal business and industrial conditions
through which the Company has passed in the initial stages of its
development we feel that its progress has been remarkable and that it
is today upon a thoroughly sound basis, having reached a period in
its development where it is in a position to reap the fullest advantage
from the bettering of business conditions.

The real problem in the development of Rolls-Royce of America,
Inc., has been the building of a chassis equal in mechanical perfec-
tion and workmanship to the famous car produced by the Rolls-
Royce Company in England. We are completely satisfied that this

problem has been solved and that the product of the plant at Springfield is in every respect the equal of the English chassis. . . .

A careful study and analysis of every phase of the Company's business justifies the following conclusion: that the Company with its present equipment can manufacture 10 cars a week; but that in view of the fact that the Rolls-Royce car has no competition in its field there will be no difficulty in selling the entire output of the plant; that with a comparatively insignificant capital expenditure for equipment the output can be raised to 750 cars per year, and a survey of market possibilities indicates that this number of cars can be readily disposed of under ordinary business conditions . . . The Company's cash position is good, and there *seems little question of its ability to show substantial earnings from now on* . . . In our judgment the future of the enterprise now seems assured.

Aldreds were, nevertheless, fully aware of the excessive financial burden which the company had to carry, and in August 1922 suggested that the ten-year notes should be converted into 15-year notes in order to throw some of the burden on to the later years of operation when it was hoped that the company would be in a stronger financial position. The original proposal was that the company should issue $1,835,000 $7\frac{1}{2}$ per cent notes in exchange for the $1.7 million 8 per cent notes which were very largely held by Aldred and had proved completely unmarketable. This suggestion was made by Henry J. Fuller, one of the most able and energetic executives in the Aldred organisation, who joined the Rolls-Royce (Inc.) board at the start and became its chairman in November 1921. He had been asked by Aldred to devote his entire energies to straightening out the affairs of the Springfield company, and made strenuous and far-reaching efforts to bring this about. In a letter to Johnson in which he claimed that the Rolls-Royce representatives on the American board were opposing this scheme on the grounds that the requirements for a successful note issue would interfere with the voting control exercised by Derby, Fuller pointed out that 'we on our side have put up not only the money, but our reputation, and must see this enterprise through. But to do so we must have the co-operation of Rolls-Royce, and I believe that on reconsideration you will not stand in the way of the necessary thing being done to take care of the financial situation.' This particular requirement, to which Mackenzie objected, was that the notes should be convertible on certain terms to preference stock.

Aldred and Fuller considered that this was essential to the success of the issue, and in a letter to Mackenzie Aldred pointed out that 'to market this issue successfully will be of great value to the Company because it will establish its credit and make open certain bank lines which are now closed to it by reason of the carrying of these notes.

The motives which seem to have actuated the English board's desire to retain control at all costs present a rather interesting study. From the earliest days of the American company two possibilities were uppermost in the minds of the English directors. The first was that the American company, though nominally controlled from England, would succumb to the dangerous temptation to mass-produce the Rolls-Royce on American lines. The mere thought of this horrified Royce, to whom the very phrase was objectionable.[4] The second was that Derby might lose control of a company which had the full legal right to use the name Rolls-Royce, the right of access to the Derby factory, and to the designs and manufacturing technique of the English company. The English board went to considerable expense to ascertain its position throughout, and sought the advice of eminent British and American counsel. Far too much attention was paid to the problem of ensuring that the legal and financial position of the English company was in no way prejudiced. Little constructive effort was directed towards the much more important problem of ensuring that the American company was a success and that the car it produced was, as Hives suggested, one which produced the same results in the hands of the American customer as did its counterpart in England. Only in this way could the English board have obtained some return by way of the capital appreciation of the ordinary shares which they held, and which were never reflected at any value in the balance sheet of the English company. Johnson alone seems to have appreciated the full magnitude and the nature of the opportunity which presented itself on the American continent, but he was unable to induce the remaining Derby executives and directors to widen their vision and perspective sufficiently and to give Springfield the enthusiastic and wholehearted support which alone could have ensured its success.

Aldred cannot be blamed for regarding his interest in the company as being purely financial. He was, after all, a financier and entitled to consider only this side of the firm's activities. This much he had stated quite openly, having several times expressed to Fuller a desire to 'get out while the going was good'. Unfortunately, the going never became good enough for him to do so. He was not really interested in establishing a reputation for the name and products of the Springfield company comparable with that which the courageous, patient and persistent endeavour that characterised the activities of the English management and employees had established for the English company. Their interest in Derby sprung from faith in an ideal, and respect for a tradition. Aldred could not be expected to look upon the concern in this way, but the fact that he provided the capital which he did suggests that if he had been approached differently he might well have developed a similar regard for the best interests of both concerns.

The American management, though undoubtedly able,[5] found itself enveloped by the conflict of self-interest between the financiers who had no intention of becoming motor-car manufacturers, and the motor-car manufacturers who had no intention of becoming financiers. Between the Scylla and Charybdis of disinterest and distrust the company ultimately foundered. To some extent the Springfield management might be blamed for not resolving this conflict more successfully, since it cannot be said that it was the responsibility of the other parties (Rolls-Royce and Aldred) to do so. It was, however, obviously in the best interests of all three that a solution should be found. But of all three parties the greatest share of the responsiblity must be laid at the feet of the English management of this period, whose inflexibility denied them the opportunity of establishing a firm manufacturing base in the United States.

On 5 September 1922 Johnson developed his views on this subject very fully in a letter to Mackenzie:

> Having in view the future welfare of the American Company, we are entirely opposed to any action which might deprive the American Company of the benefit of control by Directors holding our views – to wit, that quality must be maintained at the expense of quantity and output. The danger which we foresaw before the formation of the American Company, and against which we endeavoured to protect the American Company by maintaining English control, may, at any time, become rampant by reason of the administration of the American Company believing that sales in certain quantities are necessary in order to maintain the life of the American Company.

Johnson's statement begged the question on two counts. The first was whether the strict dialectic of quantity verus quality applied with such uncompromising intransigence to the American conditions, or even for that matter to the British; and the second was whether a control which was very largely of a negative character was in fact beneficial to the American company. Johnson was occasionally obstinate and dogmatic, and he concludes his letter by pointing out to Mackenzie that the same 'battle', as he termed it, of quantity *versus* quality, had to be fought out in the early days of the English company. The correspondence between the two organisations at this period reveals a strong divergence of views on numerous topics and the acrimony is barely disguised by the conventional politeness of business language.

On 26 September 1922 Fuller cabled a new proposal to Derby. He suggested that the new issue, instead of being convertible, could be made at a lower rate and a better price if, in order to secure continued voting control for another five years, Derby would guarantee the notes. He also suggested that Aldreds might surrender 3000 of their holding of ordinary stock to Derby as a consideration for this guarantee. Johnson's reply to this suggestion was quite unequivocal:

> When I was in New York in connection with first issue I stated repeatedly and emphatically that the English Company would *not* guarantee an issue of notes under any circumstances or consideration whatever. This attitude in maintained.

Johnson paid another visit to Springfield in November 1922 to discuss these matters, the final outcome of this controversy being that Aldred adhered to the original scheme and converted the ten-year 8 per cent bonds to fifteen-year 7 per cent bonds. These were also to be redeemed by a sinking fund towards which the main contributions would be made in the later and more prosperous years. On 15 December Aldreds advanced the company a line of credit of $200,000, and the Derby proposals were finally accepted on 18 December.

Early in 1923 Fuller informed the board in England that production at Springfield was proceeding fairly smoothly and that the capacity of the works was 400 chassis per annum. The floor space had recently been doubled by the rental of additional premises from the Knox Company[6] to allow the incorporation of a complete body-building division, employing a substantial number of the specialist coachbuilders previously employed by the Knox Automobile Co. The sales staff had found that the average American customer, even in this price range, could not be bothered with the complications of buying a chassis and having to wait several weeks while a custom-built body was fitted. Sales during 1922 had averaged six a week (312 per annum) and to achieve this figure the company had to maintain three main branches with elaborate showrooms and to retain the services of fifteen dealers outside the large centres. Despite these sales, a net loss of $294,000 in 1922 increased the total deficit to $1,486,000, a figure which represented 65 per cent of the tangible assets at balance sheet valuation. This deficit was however a good deal lower than that incurred in 1920 and 1921.

On the basis of these figures a calculation was made that even if sales increased to 650 per annum no dividend could be paid on the ordinary stock under five years. The year 1923 saw some improvement. The gross profit was $660,000, and the net profit after paying bond interest and depreciation charges $336,000. This was set off against the accumulated losses. Johnson was dissatisfied with these figures, which he considered to have been achieved in some measure by inadequate depreciation of jigs and tools. The unliquidated flotation expenses had also been merged into the goodwill and patents figure in the balance sheet and he strongly disapproved of the misleading impression which this created. The argument again resulted in a compromise, since Aldred considered that it was essential from the point of view of maintaining public confidence in the company to show a profit in excess of $300,000, even if this had to be achieved by deferring certain charges and expenses.

In September and October 1923 the question of four-wheel brakes was causing considerable agitation at Springfield. These were by now almost standard in the United States, but Derby would not permit the modification to be introduced independently at Springfield. This was a very serious matter for Springfield, and on 18 October Fuller cabled Claude Johnson that he was prepared to come to Europe to discuss the problem. Four days later Johnson cabled that they had decided to adopt four-wheel brakes. This is a typical example of the cumbersome working relationships between the parent company and its subsidiary. As a result the first 600 left-hand-drive Silver Ghosts produced at Springfield had two-wheel brakes, as did the first 65 Phantoms, marking the beginning of an increasingly serious divergence between the rate of chassis development in Springfield and Derby.

5 The Beginning of the End

A knight-errant of much more formidable appearance now entered the lists of controversy. The American company was bound by the terms of the agreement with Derby to produce a car identical to that produced in England. The introduction of the 20 h.p. Goshawk at Derby raised the problem of whether or not the Springfield factory was obliged to produce this model as well. It was finally decided that the car was unsuited to American conditions, and that its sales would be severely limited by the competition of several American vehicles which offered a similar performance and capacity at a lower price. It was estimated[1] that the tooling costs alone for this model would have been in the region of $750,000 and the financial position did not permit an expenditure of this order to be considered. The constant modification and improvement of the Silver Ghost, which culminated in the introduction of the Phantom I series in 1926, presented an even more serious threat to the future of the Springfield company which would have had to close down if unable to finance retooling costs for the new chassis, estimated to have amounted to some $450,000, or $366 for each of the 1225 Phantom I chassis eventually built at Springfield.

Quite apart from the financial and legal complications presented by this change, the mere rumour that the Springfield Rolls-Royce was 'out-of-date' would have been sufficient to close the factory in a country where being 'out-of-date' is one of the most heinous errors which any manufacturer can commit. The changeover to the production of the Phantom I was both legally and commercially obligatory, and absorbed a very large amount of working capital. The Springfield management had no alternative but to introduce this change.

Yet another source of controversy between the English and American boards was the practice of 'trading-in' second-hand cars, which the American branches and dealers found to be absolutely unavoidable. The Derby management did not think it good policy to display new and second-hand Rolls-Royces in the same showroom, but under the long established trade-in system in the U.S.A. this was inevitable. A dealer would frequently lose the order if he was not prepared to accept the customer's old car in part-exchange. In England the position of the Rolls-Royce car was so strongly established that the company could virtually sell the car on its own terms. But the English directors seemed unable to appreciate the fact that conditions were entirely different in America and that Springfield was not exactly in a position to change them. In England the company could, if it wished, act in the spirit of the phrase 'the public be damned', but the policy of accepting 'trade-ins' had inevitably to be continued by the Springfield organisation.

These developments in the relationship between the two companies in 1923 had unfortunate repercussions. Johnson finally lost confidence in Belnap as President, and attributed a good deal of the trouble to him. This was unfair and unwarranted, except in so far as Belnap himself had by this time become convinced that the existing policy was simply not realistic. Fuller was about to visit Europe on a general survey of Aldred interests, and arranged to meet Johnson at Gibraltar where the whole problem was discussed. Fuller defended Belnap's administration and persuaded Johnson that he should continue as President. This he did, but it is not surprising that, in view of his own conviction about the company's future, and the critical attitude which he must have sensed, Belnap resigned in April 1925 and was succeeded as President by H. C. Beaver, whom he himself had brought into the Company, and ultimately by Fuller.

The year 1924 saw little real improvement. Up to the end of July a loss of $79,000 was sustained, but in the following three months a profit of $97,000 was made, though full allowance for depreciation was made in neither case. The net loss incurred in the first ten months of the year, if full allowance for depreciation and losses on second-hand cars ($108,000) was made, was $90,300. The cash position had been improved and the debtor–creditor ratio improved by a reduction in stock amounting to $403,500. The ratio of the cost of goods invoiced to the selling price had also improved from 72.9 per cent in the first three months of 1924 to 63.4 per cent in the corresponding period of 1925, transforming a net loss of $39,000 on a turnover of $1,121,000 to a net profit of $52,000 on a turnover of $1,152,000.

In 1925 prospects at Springfield seemed to improve, following on the changeover from right to left-hand drive. In a letter to Lord Wargrave, then chairman of the English Board, Fuller was sufficiently optimistic to declare that he thought the factory would have difficulty in meeting the demand, both for chassis and bodies. In the third week of July, twenty cars were sold, and he concluded that 'any doubt in my mind as to the future of the enterprise has passed'.

In the same year, a new development in the body-building division of the company occurred which was to have interesting consequences. A large number of bodies for the Springfield chassis had been built by the independent coachbuilding firm of Brewsters, whose work had a very high reputation in the United States and elsewhere. The Brewster

7.   Miss Mary Pickford's Brewster-bodied Phantom I

Company was a long-established firm of custom coachbuilders founded in 1810 by James Brewster, a lineal descendent of William Brewster, one of the Pilgrim Fathers.[2] Heartened by the apparent improvement in its position in the early part of 1925 the American board discussed the possibility of purchasing the Brewster Company outright. Two further reasons prompted this interest. The first was the body shortage referred to previously, the second was a rumour that Henry Ford intended to acquire this company. Fuller considered that the name Lincoln–Brewster would be a very serious threat to Spring-field. The Springfield board therefore decided to purchase the company and Aldreds negotiated the transaction on their behalf. Rolls-Royce of America received the controlling interest (5100 shares) in return for guaranteeing the interest and sinking fund on the first and second mortgages on the Brewster property, amounting to $184,000 per annum. The Springfield board considered this a bargain in that the property was worth $1,650,000 and they considered that the profit of Brewsters' own business would easily equal this figure. Unfortunately, the profit did not materialise and the debt remained.

Towards the end of the year Johnson crossed the Atlantic once more on what was to be his last visit to the United States. On his return, he reported at length on the position at Springfield. He appreciated that some of the difficulties were far beyond the control of the American management and, in effect, declared that it was difficult for a company to change the economic environment within which it has to operate:

> The difficulties are enormous. One can buy three or four fine American cars for the price of a Rolls-Royce car. The American citizen cannot believe that the Rolls-Royce can possibly be superior to his own cars to this extent and turns his back on the Rolls-Royce. Further, the American citizen has a great fear of being laughed at locally by his neighbours as being a pretentious ass. Our big competitors in America have been most industrious and inventive in rubbing in these views. Consequently the difficulties of making the American citizen believe that in buying a Rolls-Royce he is making a sound investment and that he can afford to laugh at those who buy a new car every year instead of buying the best, have been, and still are prodigious.

Belnap himself entertained Johnson on this visit, and retained the impression of an effective and calculating individual who in his opinion came nearer than anyone else to appreciating the problems of the American management. Johnson remarked to him on one occasion that 'to know a business one has to live it, and I have the business in England to live'. This remark sums up a great deal. Belnap was convinced that, although Johnson did not admit it, he realised at this time that the American company had little chance of being successful. No one, with the possible exception of Fuller, who had considerable interests outside the company, had either the opportunity or inclination to 'live' the business. Johnson had thought Belnap a pessimist when the latter had visited England in 1924, and it could not have been easy for him to admit that he was wrong. He would only do so indirectly, by implication.

Belnap had, in the meantime, become more and more uncertain of the future of the company and dissatisfied with his own position. He finally resigned, much to the relief of some members of the management who had found him an exacting executive. Before resigning, however, he had brought in several new men in an endeavour to infuse new life into the business. A college friend of his by the name of H. C. Beaver, with whom he had worked at Allis-Chalmers as an engineering pupil, and who had joined the company at its first Treasurer now succeeded Belnap as President for a short while until Fuller himself took over this task. He had also been impressed by W. E. Hosac whom he had met in the course of dealing with the company's advertising programme, and the latter accepted the offer of a position as sales manager for Rolls-Royce. R. E. Fulton, a friend of Fuller's and managing director of the Mack Truck Company, was also induced to join the Springfield Board. Johnson heartily approved of all these changes.

But it was ultimately Henry Fuller who took full control himself and made a most enterprising effort to restore the company's fortunes. He made an extensive tour of the central and Western States and, in Johnson's own words, 'preached the Rolls-Royce gospel to his many influential friends in the big cities, and generally did magnificent missionary work, the effects of which are only beginning to be felt'. His active intervention had a marked effect on the short-run fortunes of the company, but he was in the end able to do little more than stave off the ultimate collapse.

The attempt by competitors to secure 'control or co-operation' is taken by most businessmen as a sure sign of success in an industry. Such an approach had apparently already been made to Fuller by 'the representatives of one of the big automobile financial Corporations' who wished to acquire a majority shareholding. Aldred and Fuller both warned Johnson that an attempt to secure control of the American company would be made, and that 'the day must come when an attempt will be made to secure control of the English company'. The reason for this was the dependence of Springfield on the co-operation of the English Rolls-Royce company.

Johnson was also optimistic about the future of Springfield, believing that sales would increase and that every car sold would sell more cars. Surprisingly enough, he approved of the purchase of Brewsters.

The works were employing a thousand men at the time of his visit, and he thought that this might well increase by a thousand per annum over the next ten years. Morale at Springfield was high and he thought that the English management should feel encouraged by an offer of $29 a share for the Rolls-Royce holding of the Springfield common stock which Arthur Gibbs had received. This offer meant that the holding, which had never been valued in the balance sheet, was worth £102,000 if the English company had accepted it. Early in 1926 the English board contemplated selling out, an offer of £178,000 having been reported to the board on 25 March. Mackenzie was mystified by their intentions and on 26 February he wrote saying that he could not understand why the English company was thinking of selling. 'On the other hand', he wrote, 'I do not believe for one moment that the present value of the common stock is anything like the figure to which it has been advanced by the Aldreds pool, which of course controls all quotations. It has never impressed me well for them to push up quotations so rapidly and so far.' Apparently nothing further came of this idea, for the English company held on to its holding.

In 1926 Springfield finally switched to the 'New Phantom', the Springfield name for the Phantom I, losing nine weeks' production in doing so. Despite the changeover in production, involving tooling costs of some $450,000 and other complications, this was the most successful year financially which the company ever enjoyed. The total profit, as published in the Annual Report, was $737,000, leaving $524,675 after paying bond interest and taxation. This cleared an accumulated deficit of $238,354 and left a final profit of $368,281.

In December 1926 Fuller wrote to Basil Johnson, who had succeeded his brother as managing director at Derby, asking for a letter from him for purposes of publication, stating that the Springfield and Derby products were identical. The reason, he said, why this letter was necessary, was that 'certain English coachbuilders, customers of yours, have been very active in this market recently making representations to the effect that the production of Rolls-Royce of America is not comparable with that of the English Company.'

The disappointment and chagrin which must have lain behind such a letter is easily understood. The American company was peculiarly vulnerable to such trade slander. They could not sue the coachbuilders without bringing the whole thing into the open and making their position appear quite ludicrous. They could only rely on the fullest possible co-operation from the English company to prevent the somewhat slender psychological foundations of their market being under-mined in this way. The evidence all points to the fact that the direct interest of the English company in its subsidiary, if it can be so called, was too small to create that degree of whole-hearted and effective co-operation which was necessary if the American company was to prosper. Lack of mutual confidence in such matters can make all the difference between success and failure. The key considerations are not economic factors but human relationships.

Though 1925 and 1926 had been much more encouraging years Aldred and Fuller were becoming increasingly dissatisfied with the existing financial and administrative organisation of the company, whose activities and initiative were hamstrung by the rather unimagi-native control exercised from Derby. Several courses of action were open at this stage, but all presented considerable difficulties. If Derby had been prepared to sell its holding of common stock[3] and thus lose all effective influence on Springfield, there is no doubt that the Aldred group would have taken over complete control with the intention of developing the company on different lines. But Derby could not readily acquiesce in the unrestricted use by a completely independent com-pany of the name Rolls-Royce in the United States, whatever the financial compensation. There is little doubt that the Aldred group would have been ready to transfer their financial responsibility to Derby had the English management been interested in taking it over. This they were not in the least interested, nor, as it happens, capable of doing at this particular time.

A third possibility which had suggested itself to Aldreds was the acquisition by American financial interests, amongst whom the Aldred group would naturally predominate, of a majority holding of the stock of Rolls-Royce Ltd in England. This seemed to Fuller to be a logical way out of the impasse and a method of bringing about that fusion of interest and policy whose importance for both companies the English management did not seem able to appreciate. Such a development would naturally have meant that the control of the English company would have passed into the hands of Aldreds.

While Claude Johnson was on his last visit to the United States Fuller had approached him with this suggestion, which he put forward quite openly. Johnson was not in the least enthusiastic. It is easy enough to understand why this should have been so. Having already participated in one battle to prevent the control of the English company passing into the hands of Canadian financial interests controlled by Lord Beaverbrook, it is unlikely that he would be ready to assist actively in the transfer of control to the United States, whatever the intrinsic merits of such a development may have been. His reaction was that of a parent to whom it has just been suggested that he should turn over control of the family fortunes to the prodigal son.

When Johnson returned to England in December 1925 he left Fuller and Aldred in no doubt on his views about the suggestion. The latter however was not easily deterred, especially in view of the losses which Aldreds stood to incur if the current policy was continued. He left for England on 27 March and on his arrival went straight to Derby to meet some of the English directors. On 4 March Fuller dined with Claude Johnson for the last time. One week later Johnson died suddenly and unexpectedly from pneumonia, and Rolls-Royce Ltd lost its first and most brilliant managing director. This was a tragic intermission in the negotiations, and it must have been with some considerable reluctance that the other directors continued to discuss a course of action to which they knew 'CJ' had been so strongly opposed.

On 16 April Fuller met Lord Wargrave and Basil Johnson and discussed with them the possibility of Rolls-Royce selling its holding in the American company. Aldred was prepared to purchase half the holding for $50 a share on condition that he received an option on the balance for five years at $75 per share. A few days later Fuller met Lord Beaverbrook and Arthur Gibbs but once more the negotiations were inconclusive and, after several further discussions with Basil Johnson, Fuller agreed, on 23 April, to drop the idea. He left for the United States the following day and on arrival gave an enthusiastic press interview on the American company, indicating that despite failure to achieve the original objective of his visit, Fuller still had confidence in the American company. The idea of acquiring control of the English company as a last desperate measure to secure for the American management the necessary degree of autonomy in its policy and operations was not completely dropped, however, and when things were beginning to look very serious in 1928, Fuller made one more attempt to put this plan into operation.

Negotiations for the sale of the Derby holding continued throughout 1927, but in December Fuller wrote saying that Aldred felt that he had already sunk enough money into Springfield and was no longer interested. The October 1927 accounts revealed an even more discouraging situation. In January 1928 Fuller again wrote to England and pointed out that there were few potential buyers of the American stock, which he considered completely worthless and of use only to someone 'who has an appreciation of the potential value of the Rolls-Royce name and prestige'. Fuller had approached General Motors, Henry Ford, Studebaker and Dodge Brothers without any success whatever. In his own words all took the view that 'the Rolls-Royce car was not worth the price, and that in the way it was designed and constructed it could not be built, even in quantities, at a price . . . which would enable it to become a profitable thing. From the point of view of Aldred & Co. we have but one desire, and that is to see the bondholders and preferred stockholders who paid one hundred cents on the dollar for their security get an ultimate return on their money.' The American management had obviously reached the stage when it was able to consider a policy of cutting its losses.

Fuller also gave an interesting forecast of the plans of some of the American company's principal competitors. The Marmon Company was planning to produce 80,000 cars at a gross invoice value of $46 million ($575 per car). A director of the Marmon Company by the name of Williams had been considering a project to market the Rolls-Royce through his agencies and the formation of a syndicate with Aldred to acquire 9000 of the Derby shareholding (which now stood at 17,800) provided Derby was willing to sell out at $25 per share, with a two-year option on the balance at $50 a share. Basil Johnson cabled his agreement to this scheme on condition that the Marmon Company did not in any way suggest that the manufacture of the Marmon car was associated with the name of Rolls-Royce. Shortly afterwards, in April, he visited the United States and sent back the gloomy prediction that the Springfield factory would have to close unless American orders increased. 'The only hope,' he said, 'is that they can buy from Derby at a price that will enable them to keep afloat.' This suggestion marks the beginning of the end at Springfield.

The Marmon project did not materialise and there was still no talk of Aldred himself selling out. Basil Johnson thought that the strain of the past few years was begining to tell on Fuller who could, said Johnson, 'talk and think of nothing else whereas his brain and energy could be used far more usefully with their numerous other concerns to make far greater amounts of money. Fuller says it is entirely a matter of pride with both himself and Aldreds and they will do anything to prevent their names being connected with failure.'

In March 1928 there were 108 unsold Phantom chassis and orders were averaging no more than 5.5 cars a week. Yet the Annual Report for

1928 seems to indicate that some recovery had taken place, a gross profit of $496,700 having been made before allowing for taxation and bond interest. In his report Fuller stated that current production both at Springfield and Brewsters was proceeding 'on a larger scale than ever before and that the management planned to increase this rate in 1929'. But despite the profit no preference dividend was paid owing to the 'imperative need to conserve working capital'. It is significant that the goodwill of the company was still valued in the balance sheet at $1,414,000.

In October 1928 Fuller visited England for the purpose of making one final effort to secure financial control of the English company and to explore further the possiblity of purchasing chassis and parts directly from Derby. The problem of converting the English chassis to left-hand drive was of course one of the principal obstacles to this scheme. Derby was again just about to market a new model, the Phantom II, which involved Springfield tooling up to produce the identical car if the factory wished to continue producing cars at all. On 8 November Fuller cabled Aldred that the English board had 'formally resolved not to permit any chassis type other than those made at Derby' and advised Springfield to continue with the existing chassis and also 'make a study of the result of reducing the price to $9,000 with a production of six hundred cars a year'. From this it can be inferred that Fuller had ideas about an American *version* of the Rolls-Royce and that he attempted to persuade the English board that the salvation of the American company lay in this direction.[4] This he was unable to do. At a conference with Basil Johnson, Captain Turner and Arthur Sidgreaves, the policy of continuing production at Springfield was thoroughly examined and Fuller was ultimately persuaded of the futility of continuing the production of complete chassis. He finally agreed that the American company should cease production and convert itself into a selling agency, but this decision was not put into effect for some time.

The American company had not the capital to contemplate retooling for the Phantom II, estimated to cost some $1,000,000, nor had the American management sufficient confidence in the car to encourage them to find the financial backing to do so. For these reasons primarily Fuller decided to continue producing the Phantom I in order to use up existing stocks of material and enable the manufacturing side of the company's activities to be closed down gradually.

The second attempt to secure control of the English company was on a more serious scale and was made with the full knowledge of the English management and board. Various important shareholders were approached, and considerable quantities of stock were actually purchased by Aldreds. The project was also discussed with the heads of several important financial houses in London but the capital of the English company was very large by this time and the shares too widely and tightly held for the scheme to materialise. There was also an understandable reluctance on the part of important English stockholders to part with their holdings, knowing full well that it would result in the control of the company leaving England. In view of the ultimate fate in store for Aldreds itself, it is most fortunate that the scheme did not succeed, for even had it done so it is doubtful whether the American company would have recovered at this stage.

Royce, who undoubtedly treated quality as an absolute and not a relative phenomenon, had frequently expressed concern over the quality of the Springfield car. He was therefore strongly in favour of the new scheme for sending chassis (the first order contemplated was for 200 chassis) at a $22\frac{1}{2}$ per cent discount, the same figure as that given to the largest London coachbuilders. Fuller was not certain that this discount would allow Springfield to make a profit on the car and the available figures reveal that the car had to carry a very heavy burden of charges even after arriving in the United States.[5]

The English board was astonished at the figure for selling costs.[6] They pointed out that the corresponding figure for the English chassis was £140, one-seventh of the American figure. An agreement was finally reached on the basis of a discount of 25 per cent, and shortly thereafter the manufacture of three experimental left-hand SS chassis (the new Phantom about to be marketed in England) was started in England. No sooner had Fuller returned to America than new complications developed. The first came in the shape of a suggestion from Springfield that Derby should delete from the chassis certain important parts which could conveniently and profitably be manufactured in the American factory. The second was a letter from Fuller saying that the price of the English chassis was 'altogether too high!' The English board asked him what he thought a reasonable price would be. His reply was not exactly encouraging. 'It would be impossible,' he said, 'for you to make a price which would permit us to pay the duty etc., and come within a commercial possibility of reselling at a profit.' Considering the severely depressed market conditions with which Springfield had to contend in 1930 and 1931 this was no exaggeration.

Fuller nevertheless thought that to close down the Springfield works completely would be 'a confession of failure' and in consequence the production of the old-type Phantom chassis continued at Springfield for some time after the agreement to import from England had been concluded. In consequence the stock of obsolete chassis accumulated steadily.

It a letter written to Sidgreaves on 3 September 1929 Royce expressed grave doubts about the whole situation at Springfield. Though Royce and Fuller were very friendly, the latter having stayed with him at Le Canadel on several occasions, Royce showed little understanding for the plight of the American company. Highly critical of what he always referred to in jovial conversation with Fuller as 'your cheap and nasty American cars' (he did not mean the Springfield Rolls-Royce), Royce consistently refused to visit the United States and see for himself. This attitude was all too prevalent in the British motor industry at this time. Royce was content to sit in judgement on the American company, and on this occasion he donned the black cap.

> It appears to me that they have created a disastrous situation for which I fear there is no cure . . . We did our utmost to stop them from this stupid enterprise, which is exactly the opposite to my recommendations. I said 'avoid obsolete stock at any cost: rather starve your market and slow up your work'.

Although Royce concluded that it was quite futile to spend further time or money on the American company, the English board was still not prepared to cut its losses and withdraw quite so precipitately. On 18 February 1930 an agreement was concluded whereby Derby would manufacture and ship to Springfield 200 left-hand-drive Phantom II chassis, the payment for which had to be guaranteed by Aldreds, who were most reluctant to do so. The price finally fixed for each chassis was £1330. An important feature of this contract was a clause stating the Derby would be entitled to export chassis direct to American customers or dealers on the condition that a substantial payment was made to the American company for each chassis so exported.[7] By failing to maintain preference dividends, the parent company had lost control of Springfield in the early twenties. Its influence over policy nevertheless remained. The Derby board did not relish the prospect of the American company going into voluntary liquidation (something which they could not prevent) and thus opening up the possibility of the name and goodwill being sold to a competitor. This would have posed a serious threat to the future position of the British company, not only in the United States. Consequently, the board decided to seek the legal advice of eminent counsel (among them Sir Stafford Cripps, K.C., Mr Newton Crane, K.C. and Mr Arthur Barrat). Their answers were not altogether reassuring, though Cripps maintained that, under English law, the agreement between Rolls-Royce and its subsidiary would be interpreted as being strictly between the two companies and that it could not be construed as being binding on the English company and the original American company's successor except at the express desire of the English company. Under American law, the position was more obscure. For some strange reason, the American board never realised the very great value of the legal right of access, which they then possessed under the terms of the original agreement, to all the Rolls-Royce designs and technical information, including aero-engines, and in consequence the danger of these falling into the hands of competitors in the United States or elsewhere never materialised.

On 14 November Fuller had written to Sidgreaves informing him that the American board's decision whether or not to continue production at Springfield depended primarily on the outcome of the tariff discussions then proceeding in the Senate. But the sands of world economic prosperity ran out before this particular problem was decided. The stock market crash on Wall Street completely paralysed the market for high-priced luxury goods.

Mackenzie commented on these developments in a letter written on 11 November 1929:

> The stock market situation has long been a source of anxiety, and the speculative element, aided by funds from every direction, has gone entirely beyond any control. The Federal Reserve and the more conservative banks have been fighting the situation for many months but with practically no success. When the change came everyone was surprised at its suddenness and immensity. The ultimate effect of the stock-market break will, I am sure, be of benefit to business . . . but at present . . . the whole automobile market is in a demoralised condition.

Mackenzie advised Derby that the American board intended to close down the Springfield works and retain only a skeleton staff. Half the sales organisation was to be 'eliminated' and Aldreds were preparing to advance the company another half-million dollars. Fuller had previously advised England by cable that Aldreds had 'sensed the fact that this break was coming and prepared for it successfully as a banking house'. At this date there were 125 finished and 63 unfinished chassis in stock at Springfield, and sales had completely ceased. He thought the likelihood of the tariff being reduced very great and on 2 December cabled England that the American board had finally decided to discontinue chassis manufacture at Springfield and to import the left-hand-drive chassis from Derby. He urged Sidgreaves to visit Springfield and see conditions for himself, but the latter was unfortunately unable to leave England until early in the following year.

Fuller had struggled gallantly with Rolls-Royce of America. He had persuaded a number of able men to serve on the board which, in[8] 1928, was virtually a Milner kindergarten of the business world. But no board, however eminent its members, could have saved the American company at this stage. In a detailed and carefully worded memorandum written on 19 September Fuller set out some of the many reasons why they would not have been able to do so. During 1929 the liabilities of the company had increased substantially. The inventory in the chassis division had increased by $776,000, trade debtors by $139,000 and the notes payable by $225,000. All the available profits had been absorbed by the new programme launched in that year. To make matters worse the news of the English SS chassis had leaked out in the United States. On the problem of prices he compared the Rolls-Royce with the Lincoln at $4400 and the Packard at $1985, both of which had 8-cylinder engines, 'which to the public', he said, 'mean more than six'. As Fuller clearly implied, the successful businessman is usually one who takes the public as he finds it.

> How long [he asked] will the Rolls-Royce command a price for its product of not less than twice and in the average case three and a half times that of other automobiles, which are perhaps on the whole better constituted for American traffic conditions than the very large car which we have to sell? . . . Does it not appear that the situation in the United States is entirely different from what it is in England and that the whole problem is one which is not only tremendously difficult at the moment, but likely to become increasingly so with the enormous resources and the ability of the American manufacturers constantly giving the public greater value by improving their product and selling it at a lower price?

Fuller asked Sidgreaves to send over some of his best men to America to examine the situation, which he considered affected the future of both companies. 'For them simply to look at the picture from the standpoint of their preconceived ideas of the Rolls-Royce position in England would not, in our opinion, be ultimately satisfactory to anyone.' This comment is significant, for it is quite obvious that the whole problem of production and sale in America was looked at by Derby officials from the point of view of what would, or should, have been done in England under similar circumstances. They considered that the failure of Springfield had occurred simply because the American management had not carried out to the letter the Derby manufacturing methods and sales policy. This view simply cannot be sustained.

The basic economic and psychological differences between the English and American markets were never properly understood in England. In England the large high-powered car was looked upon, and to a certain extent still is looked upon, as a sign of wealth and social prestige. The English management realised that a limited output and the high price which resulted were essential features of the market environment. In the United States it was less necessary to observe or display social distinction and, even as early as 1928, the high-powered car was looked upon as a necessity and regarded almost as the birthright of any reasonably successful American citizen. Several manufacturers competed strenuously for the privilege of supplying him with this product at a lower and lower price, and took great pride, not only in the mechanical qualities of the vehicle, but in achieving an optimum combination of a mechanical efficiency and quality at a certain cost. Both were the essential ingredients of success in the U.S. market.

Even in the middle twenties, the American tended to consider the automobile essentially as a means of transportation first and not as a passport to some form of social distinction. The price of the Rolls-Royce was, to many Americans who should in theory (as a given proportion of the number of people with incomes over a certain figure) have bought them, quite irrational.[9]

There was, and there still is, in addition to all this, an element of positive pride in the make-up of the average American which derives from the knowledge that manufacturers in the United States have turned out cars which in general lack nothing except the finish, longevity and name of the Rolls-Royce. About the first of these qualities he is not in general greatly concerned. He does not, as does the wealthy European, look upon a car as a subject for the connoisseur. Longevity is a positive disadvantage in a country where general approbation is bestowed upon an individual who possesses the newest and latest model. There remained, therefore, little more for him to buy than the name Rolls-Royce. For this, he was asked to pay some $8000–$12,000 more than the most expensive American-built car. This was a substantial premium for the magic of a name.

As Johnson himself observed, the wealthy American does not like being 'looked upon as a pretentious ass' by his neighbours and associates, and it is therefore hardly surprising that repeated efforts to make the actual market for the Rolls-Royce in the U.S.A. conform with the theoretical market have met with so little success, despite their ingenuity and persistence. Fuller's concluding comment in his memorandum sums up the whole position. 'There is in America', he said, 'a demand for the very highest grade product which can be produced, but at a price which seems to be warranted by the character of the product itself in comparison with competitive articles.'[10]

It comes as no surprise, therefore, that Fuller should have suggested in his memorandum that the English company should take over the whole concern at Springfield. He had good grounds for thinking that direct and immediate responsibility for Springfield would have brought home to the English board much more forcefully and effectively the fundamental difference between the two markets.

Many of Fuller's remarks were confirmed by Sidgreaves, who made an extensive tour of the American automobile industry on his visit early in 1930. He was very favourably impressed by the new American cars, particularly the 16-cylinder Cadillac and the Studebaker, and considered that in general their springing was better than that of the Phantom. He was also of the opinion that Rolls-Royce would have to adopt the synchromesh gear change then being widely introduced in the United States. After inspecting the research and experimental side of the Studebaker plant he observed that 'the amount of money which they spend annually on this department seemed fabulous', and added that the tests to which the Studebaker car engine was submitted were 'considerably more severe than the 100-hour type test of our aero-engines'.[11]

Sidgreaves thought that the results might have been different if Fuller had had the courage to carry out both phases of his 1929 programme (increasing output and lowering prices). But this comment merely confirms Fuller's complaint that the English board was too strongly conditioned by the environment of the English market to understand the problem of selling the car in the United States. In discussing the various factors which had contributed to the failure of the Springfield company he mentions the list price of the car as being of primary importance and adds, 'I am sure that had the English company possessed territory of equal size, population and wealth, the price of the 40/50 chassis would have been reduced years ago.' This underrates the ability of the Springfield management. Their very keen desire to make a success of the enterprise is amply confirmed by the fact that Aldred and Fuller continued to support the company financially long after it would otherwise have gone into liquidation. On 11 November 1929 Aldred advanced the company $500,000 without which it would have been quite unable to meet even its immediate obligations. This advance was made after the decision had been taken on 21 October to cease production with the completion of the 2900th car.

Sidgreaves reported that the current price of the Springfield car was $18,770, an amount which included $3750 for selling expenses and the loss on used cars, and $1766 for profit (about 10 per cent on gross costs). The allowance for profit was of course invariably not realised in actual practice. In 1929 the average invoicing price had been $15,704, a discount of 25 per cent on the selling price being given to the dealers. As Sidgreaves rightly observed, the basic price at which Derby could offer chassis for resale would make little difference to the Springfield selling price, since the other expenses amounted to the staggering total of $12,443 per chassis.[12]

Although the new tariff had finally fixed the import duty at thirty-three per cent *ad valorem* while Sidgreaves was in America, he thought that Springfield would still be able to realise a profit of £353 on each imported chassis. Selling expenses feature very largely in all these calculations and it is not without interest that the average figure for selling expenses was $1,060,000 per annum, roughly four times greater than the original estimate of $288,624. Sidgreaves also discussed the possibility of importing the 20/25 chassis with Fuller, but the latter considered that the car was hopelessly underpowered for American conditions and that there would be no market whatsoever for it.

6 'A Single Firm Against a Nation'

Late in 1930 Hives went over to examine the situation at Springfield, and on his return advised the board that the main machining shop had been dismantled and the machines sold in conformity with the earlier decision to cease manufacture. He nevertheless believed that the Springfield organisation was well equipped to act as a selling agency for the English company. They would continue to make bodies for the English chassis, most of the Brewster machinery having been moved over and installed at Springfield. After affirming that 'the American market is really in our own hands', Hives went on to enumerate some of the difficulties which he foresaw in exploiting it. Prices in the United Kingdom, he said, were twice the pre-war prices, while those in the United States were half the pre-war level. For this reason he considered that a vast selling organisation would be required. This had already been built up by Springfield and he proposed that it should not be abandoned.

A visit to the New York Show did not encourage him. 'When you see a Cadillac, Packard, Lincoln with a custom built body, as regards general lines, appearance and finish, we can show them nothing very much better. As regards price, one almost hesitates to make a comparison.' The Cadillac was selling for £1500, the Packard and Lincoln for £1100 and the Rolls-Royce for £3500–3600. But despite this Hives concluded optimistically that 'there must be some solution whereby we can sell our products in this huge market.' The solution did, in fact, exist, and Royce himself recognised it, but the English organisation was not yet ready to adopt the radical methods – however logical – which the solution demanded.

Hives considered that there was a market for from four to five hundred cars per annum at a price of about $8000. He suggested that this could be achieved by utilising more fully the engineering developments, technical knowledge and manufacturing facilities at Derby, by importing selected major units into the United States and

71

employing to the full the remaining Springfield facilities, and finally by reducing sales expenses per car by increasing the sales volume. These suggestions seem impressive, but in reality they beg the whole question. In particular, how was the last suggestion to be achieved? The problem was really insoluble within the conceptual framework in which it was considered and discussed, and it is not surprising that Hives was not able to suggest any permanent solution.

In the course of this tour Hives also visited several other factories, and on these he made a number of pertinent and relevant observations:

> When visiting factories in the U.S.A., it is interesting to note how everyone talks costs. If one is talking to engineers they will always end up the description of a part by saying how much it costs. If you walk round the works and take special interest in a part the man in charge of that section will tell you how much it costs.

He confirmed this impression on a visit to the Chevrolet plant of General Motors. Mr Taub, the engineer showing him around, appeared, he said, 'to get all the thrill out of his job by endeavouring to reduce costs'. He noticed that the inspection in American plants was very thorough, and was impressed by the fact that the Chevrolet development department had put a Phantom I through all their tests. The same firm informed him that they would be unable to make the *shaft* of a Rolls-Royce shock-absorber for the price of the *complete* Chevrolet shock-absorber. At the Cadillac works Hives was impressed by the design of the drawing office, into which, if desired, a complete car could be brought and studied in between the drawing tables.

This report was as usual sent to Royce on Hives' return to England, and provoked an unusually interesting series of comments which have, in view of the urgent importance of a fuller understanding of the American market generally, a wider relevance than the immediate problem to which they referred.

> I thank Mr. Hs.[1] for his very able and complete report. To make cars at Derby and to sell them in the United States (by RRAL) and enable them to make a profit is very difficult, and perhaps impossible (*something like a single firm against a nation*).[2]
>
> I am quite in agreement with Mr. Hives that the time has come when we must study cost with the greatest possible vigour, and we are all agreed that it is possible to make great economies without loss

of perfection, which as before must be our very first requirement; but we might sacrifice 1% of perfection for 10 in cost.

There is no doubt that many people are, and have been, watching Rolls-Royce very closely as a standard of perfection etc., and are often trying to make a cheap edition of our work. Naturally they are taking parts from others also: we are not vain enough to think that we are the only good pebble on the beach.

We also know that after we have achieved a certain degree of perfection it is very often possible to redesign for economical production without losing much in efficiency, but through want of capacity and the difficulty of changing we do not do so. Generally also we do not get the final requirements until we are well on with production – (also for the reason of having too much in hand).

It must be remembered that we have a great deal of work of a very highly technical character and it must be realised that while we must economise to reduce our establishment charges from their very high ratio to output, we must not reduce our technical capacity. We know that it is possible to do more with the same expenditure, but that is not the wasteful part of our expenditure.

We are thankful that the aero-engine prospects are bright but while these are promising us support we ought to set about trying to make the Company's operations more efficient – i.e. while there is time, and we can, because if we were to save all the direct labour cost our productions would still be too costly to compete with the U.S.A. Either we have to increase our productions or to decrease our establishment charges, *because no matter how good our work is technically we cannot expect to get the present prices*.[3]

So we must look forward to the fact that we must part with our productions in the near future for considerably less money, so that to get the present turnover we must be doing 100% more productive work.

Materials in England are higher in price than in the U.S.A. This supports my statement that with us it falls more heavily upon our Company *because the whole country is less efficient*.[4] We have always found this forced us into making many things that similar people in the U.S.A. bought from specialists. This is still glaringly forced upon us.

To conclude, we must thank Mr. Hives for his excellent report with which we thoroughly agree. I suggest strengthening our purely technical staff, which one thinks is far better than the average of

> British Companies, and shows that our apparent extravagance is really our strength, and that economies must be made in other directions, and by increasing the efficiency of the technical staff, which I am pleased to say I think far better than even a few years ago.

This report is particularly significant for it reveals that the management of at least one British company appreciated clearly, as early as 1930, the relative insecurity both of the firm's and the nation's economic future. There was no crisis in the 1947 sense in that year, but the foundations of the crisis were already laid. Royce possessed a shrewd insight into economic as well as technical matters, and a few weeks earlier in a letter to Sidgreaves on the subject of the 20/25 car he made it quite clear that he had no illusions about the relative merits of British industry. In the seventeen volumes of his memoranda which have survived it is the only occasion upon which he used capital letters.

> You know how terribly anxious I am to get this model right as quickly as possible, and put it into mass production so that we can sell at such a price as to be able to make enough in number to be profitable.
>   MY GREAT MOTTO FOR GREAT BRITAIN AND OURSELVES IS MASS PRODUCTION WITH QUALITY. UNLESS WE DO THIS WE ARE FATED SO LET US DO IT BEFORE IT IS TOO LATE, BECAUSE AT THE MOMENT ENGLAND CANNOT TRULY BOAST OF EITHER.

The lessons of the Springfield disaster were not altogether lost on the English company. They were not, however, as is the English way of things, applied with any undue haste, and the Second World War intervened just as one of the principal developments was about to start.

The position at Springfield deteriorated steadily during the latter part of 1930 and the early months of 1931, as the figures in Appendix VI show quite clearly. Fuller made repeated requests to Derby that they should slow down the rate of delivery of the 200 chassis ordered under the agreement previously mentioned. To this request Sidgreaves replied that time was of the essence of the contract and that the spreading of manufacture and delivery over a longer period than that originally agreed upon when the price was fixed would substantially increase their production costs and involve the English company in a loss. This attitude is quite understandable. On 27 May 1931 Fuller cabled England that the position was quite hopeless, and it was obvious from his cable that the American company could not last much longer.

> The extraordinary conditions due to drop in security prices and cutting off dividends have caused a buyer's strike on luxury articles which has reduced our cash position below safety-point to meet current obligations including necessary furnishing of bodies to mount on chassis already received . . . we request moratorium which will relieve us necessity further payments to you until Company's cash position improves . . . we are boldly announcing Phantom II.

The English board suggested various schemes to help Fuller out, but the situation was past repair, and in June Fuller wrote asking if it was not time to reach a final settlement.

> Would you not be much happier [he asked] if an arrangement could be made which would be equitable to all concerned whereby you take over the sale of your product in America?

The prospect of regaining complete freedom of access to the American market was one which immediately appealed to the English board. Springfield was prepared to offer an unconditional release from the agreement in return for financial support. This the English board would not give. Nevertheless a new agreement was signed in July which brought the date of release very much nearer. Of the 200 chassis, 32 had been delivered since March 1931, and Derby agreed to store 20 until the end of July. In this agreement it was expressly stated that Springfield would be unable to pay for the remainder of the 200 chassis, and this was thereupon reduced to 125, leaving 73 chassis in all still to be delivered, at the rate of six a month. As soon as these had been delivered the English company would recover unrestricted access to the American market unless Springfield ordered a minimum of 100 chassis per annum. The agreement also specifically precluded Springfield from continuing the manufacture of complete cars and entitled them to manufacture only such parts as were approved by Derby.

This agreement did not meet with the immediate approval of Aldred & Co., who were required to endorse it. In a letter to Sidgreaves Mackenzie said that he thought that the strain was beginning to tell on Fuller and that Aldreds were frequently emphasising what a great load the management of the company had been to them. Shortly after this Fuller resigned and was succeeded by Inskip. Before doing so, however, he announced his intention of appointing a bondholders' committee.

Fuller had had to battle against very heavy odds, and it is unlikely that the company would have lasted as long as it did if he had not taken over in 1925. He was a man of considerable charm and ability, and undoubtedly had a real enthusiasm for, and an understanding of, the Rolls-Royce ideal. His influence in financial and commercial circles in the United States, where he was a Director of a large number of successful and important companies, was considerable. Where he failed it was unlikely that many others would have succeeded.

In October Inskip wrote informing Derby that the sales of the Phantom II had been negligible, that the Springfield organisation could not possibly pay its way, and that he advised the English company not to insist upon Aldreds implementing their guarantee. He thought that Aldreds would probably react to such a move by dumping the cars, which they could then acquire on both the English and American markets for whatever they would fetch. Inskip was still sufficiently optimistic to express the opinion that the American company would survive if reorganised on a new basis.

The situation at Springfield became fairly widely known at this time through the efforts of a discontented bondholder who saw in the company's misfortunes an opportunity of recovering his losses. This individual professed considerable moral indignation at the state of affairs at Springfield and attempted to force the company into receivership. But he saw no inconsistency between this attitude and a prior attempt to persuade the officials of the company to purchase his bonds at a figure several times their market value. This they refused to do, but the situation was extremely precarious, especially as Aldreds were themselves about to feel the full impact of the depression. In March they had written to England pointing out that the guarantee would prove a 'boomerang' if Derby took it up, and on 26 May a deputation called on Mackenzie to inform him that the Aldred organisation was insolvent and in the hands of its bankers. All the company's investments had been surrendered, and Mackenzie was asked if he would request Rolls-Royce to relieve Aldreds of a guarantee which would involve the partners of the firm in personal bankruptcy if it were enforced. Mackenzie considered that the sale of the Springfield property would have a very bad effect, and advised Derby to consider the offer made by a Mr Manville to put up $500,000 to form a new company. This individual had apparently been sufficiently farsighted to convert all his securities to cash in 1929, and had even gone to the extent of withdrawing his cash from the banks and holding it himself.

> I might further add [said Mackenzie] that Mr. Inskip has some other wealthy people who have expressed a very keen interest in going into a pure sales agency for Rolls-Royce cars. I believe that the bondholders' committee will be agreeable to accepting very drastic terms either for their bonds or for the inventory of the cars here. My thought has been that it might be possible to buy the bonds at some very low basis and use the bonds to pay for the inventory, and then, having the new Company with inventory purchased on such a basis, we would be in a position to do business in these very troublesome times.

The English board had some difficulty in following the intricate evolution of events at Springfield, and did not comment on any of these suggestions. They replied that they could not possibly contemplate the non-enforcement of the Aldred guarantee, and threatened to issue a writ. Legal action was postponed from time to time by Springfield paying for small batches of cars, but this position could not be maintained indefinitely, and the case eventually came up for hearing in May 1933. It was decided in favour of the English company after very little discussion. Aldreds and Springfield were given a fixed time within which to make payment of an amount of $53,588, and this sum was finally paid. In February 1934 Inskip was offered and accepted the retail agency of the English cars on the basis of a 20 per cent discount on individual chassis and 15 per cent on standard bodies and accessories. Within the short space of twenty years the wheel had turned full circle.

The Springfield company continued a precarious existence as an independent concern for some time, at first under its original name. It was precluded by the terms of the 1931 agreement from actually manufacturing, and was limited, in the event of England recovering legal right of entry to the American market, to carrying on 'any business whatever having no connection with the products of the English Company . . . under some name other than Rolls-Royce'.

Springfield was in no hurry to change the name for obvious reasons, and the English board had once more to threaten legal action before it adopted the name of the Springfield Manufacturing Corporation. This company continued to manufacture, after reorganising under the Bankruptcy Act, until 1936 when it was finally wound up and the plant sold to an individual by the name of Winslow, who purchased the assets of both the Springfield and Brewster plants for a comparatively small sum. The Brewster Company survived for several years as a profitable aircraft firm, but the Springfield plant was sold to two other concerns and the factory ceased to operate as a complete unit.

The conclusion of this unfortunate venture, though of particular concern to the English management at the time, has an amusing sequel. The Springfield management, now operating completely independently, and being unable to dispose of its out-of-date Phantom I chassis, or a sufficient number of Phantom II chassis to meet even its overheads, decided to purchase Ford V-8 chassis and fit them with Brewster bodies. The assembly of the Brewster car — a desperate and not unimaginative attempt to save the situation — was, in fact, the American company's last major effort to avoid extinction as a manufacturing enterprise. These cars, of which one hundred and thirty-five were assembled, were sold from showrooms which still traded under the name of Rolls-Royce. They were considered to be a vehicle in the luxury class (selling at $2800 to $3200) and were quite popular. Although the chassis was purchased from the Ford Motor Company for a very small sum, the body was still too expensive, and the output too small to make the car an economic proposition. It was nevertheless widely advertised, and it was obvious from the advertisement that the association of the name of the car with the name Rolls-Royce was quite deliberate. The news of this venture, trailed by the usual rabble of wild rumours, was published in many papers all over the world as heralding an alliance between the Rolls-Royce and Ford Motor Companies. Inskip had announced to the press that the new model was in production at Springfield, and as this contravened the applicable terms of the 1931 agreement, the English board approached their legal advisers in New York to see what could be done. Walmsley, the counsel briefed by Mackenzie, considered that an American court would award Rolls-Royce damages, but considered that the extent of the damage would be difficult to prove under the American common law. He advised the English company to advertise the fact that the new car was nothing to do with the Rolls-Royce, and this course was adopted.

Henry Ford was very amused by this incident, and welcomed the gratuitous boost to its reputation which the world's most common car received from its strange and brief alliance with the world's most uncommon car.

Thus ended, in ignominious legal bickering, financial controversy and personal animosity, the attempt of a great British motor firm to manufacture in the United States and to exploit what were to be the boundless possibilities of that market. It was undoubtedly a hard lesson for the English management, which had approached the venture from the outset, with a few exceptions, in a spirit of narrow and obstinate dogmatism. But it is also an episode of unusual interest to the student of industry who has so often been taught to conceive of the market as a prize easily won by those who can force their entrance with the crowbars of price and advertising and establish a permanent tenancy by following simple and obvious policies of production and sale. The Rolls-Royce attempt to manufacture in the United States is an example of how resources can be misdirected and policies misjudged. It disproves the claim that a manufacturer can make the public, or any section of it, buy what he wishes to sell merely by following advertising and sales policies which have proved successful in other markets. The public, particularly in the realm of expensive durable consumer goods, has a collective obstinacy and individual eccentricity undreamt of in those philosophies of the market economy which construct theoretically exact and precise formulations of its behaviour applying to all fields, or even to classes of products. Such theories do grave injustice to the vast uncompromising mass of reality, a mass which includes such large elements of human idiosyncrasy and prejudice.

The Springfield management started with practically every possible advantage – an excellent plant, good financial backing, and an article whose name conferred upon it tremendous prestige, although the latter tended to arouse mixed reactions in the United States. The name also conferred upon the product a reasonably wide price margin within which questions were not likely to be asked. The American company was able to draw on the accumulated experience of the Derby management, as well as that of its own men who had been closely connected with the Eagle spares programme during the war and of a fair number of men specially brought over from England. Its market lay within the largest upper-income group of any country in the world. The whole project was conceived and initiated by one of the most able businessmen of his generation in England and was finally put in the hands of a group of Americans who, almost without exception, distinguished themselves in American industry and finance. From all accounts the staff and works force was capable and enthusiastic.

Yet failure was inevitable because of the rigid conception which the English management held of American market requirements, and the extent to which, in the early years in particular, the control exercised from England hamstrung the local management on its output and quality policies[5] and even on important questions of detail. The axiomatic conception of quality being in inverse proportion to quantity in the manufacture of the motor-car was possibly more legitimate in 1920 than it is at the present day, but it was even then rapidly ceasing to be true, as the virtual mass production of the Eagle aero-engine itself by Rolls-Royce had shown. Had the American management enjoyed from the start the freedom of action and independence of judgement which higher commanders in war inevitably delegate to their local commanders where conditions are unusual and difficult, there is little doubt that Springfield would soon have expanded production to the order of four or five thousand cars per annum. The price of the car – which would have been an American Rolls-Royce catering for American and not British tastes – would then have dropped to a figure which would not have offended the American conception of value for money. The marque would have developed differently from the English car, probably more standardised and less highly finished. It would certainly have been cheaper. It would almost certainly have offended against many maxims which Derby held sacred. But if the *spirit* of quality engineering had pervaded the American organisation (and there is no reason to suppose that it did not) it is more than likely that, encouraged by friendly competition with the parent firm in England, the American factory might well have been able to make a considerable contribution to joint problems of design and manufacture, and the American car provide a stimulus to the Derby design and production staffs. In addition, it is likely that the perceptibly American Rolls-Royce which Springfield would eventually have produced would have established a reputation of the type which appeals to the American buyer – that the car was a better car for half the price.

Had the English management really wished to make a commercial success of the American company, and thereby create a substantial asset in the ordinary stock which it held, it should have done everything possible to encourage such an attitude on the other side of the Atlantic. At the same time it would have been quite entitled, and indeed, obliged, to make the most strenuous efforts to ensure that the Derby Rolls-Royce still maintained those qualities which appear necessary in the English market in which it had established such a high and deserved reputation. It is difficult to see how the position of the English company could have been fundamentally prejudiced if such a policy had been pursued.

Springfield was not set up, as it should have been, to create an American Rolls-Royce for the American market, designed, especially in the superficial details, to appeal to the *American* sense of quality and value for money, knowing that this sense is conditioned by factors, such as the mass production of high-horsepower cars, which were then non-existent in England. It was established, as the early agreement shows, to manufacture the British Rolls-Royce in the United States, and the greatest care was taken to ensure that the car would be identical in all respects. In fact, the English management considered that identity of product was the only insurance of commercial success and this was a fatal mistake. It is quite conceivable that had the Springfield factory been set up as an extension to the Derby works, but designed in all important respects to meet the scale of the American venture, the operation would have been economically justified, even ignoring the reduction in overheads which would have taken place. It would probably have been successful because the American customer would still have been prepared to pay for an imported Rolls-Royce, about which there hung all the usual fascination of the imported product. What he was quite definitely not prepared to pay for was a local *reproduction* of the genuine article, however perfect. And the experience of Springfield shows that while a reproduction might well be almost perfect, it could not be so in the mind of the customer. What is quite astonishing, however, is the eventual reputation which the Springfield-built Rolls-Royce Ghost and Phantom acquired among the 'cognoscenti' of the marque. It is now considered to have been amongst the best ever built and the sale in 1977 of a Brewster-bodied Ghost of 1923 vintage for £38,000 at auction suggests that, at least within the perspective of the twentieth century, there is little to choose between the craftsmanship of Springfield and Derby.

In a very real sense the venture failed because it was not appreciated that the simple term 'market' described a very complex phenomenon. A commodity which sells well in one market will not sell well in another, however much the sales are forced, for much the same reason that propaganda which succeeds in one country falls completely flat in another if literally translated. Springfield was an attempt at the literal translation of the spirit of quality so carefully nurtured at Derby. In a democracy in which the economy is based on private enterprise, purchasing power shares with the vote an ultimate and inalienable sovereignty. Those who attempt to disregard this, whether consciously or unconsciously, invariably come to grief, either as governments or producers. There are few exceptions to this rule.

7 The Years of Peace, 1923–34

The impression is widely held that the years before the depression were years of calm and prosperity, a gilt if not golden age of British industry. The previous discussion of the many vicissitudes which accompanied the attempt of Rolls-Royce to manufacture in the United States might well have given the impression that in England the parent company, secure in the possession of its partial monopolies over the expensive tastes of the wealthy and the patronage of the Air Ministry, trod a relatively stable and secure path, enhancing from year to year its reputation, its reserves and its economic security. Since it was one of the few companies in the automobile or aircraft industries which paid a dividend throughout this period it is not surprising that this should be so. The world does not normally look behind the facade of success. When the achievement is almost unique it is more satisfying to human nature to attribute this to unusual good fortune or privilege rather than exceptional endeavour.

During these years Rolls-Royce certainly enjoyed two unusual advantages, though both of them had been earned by strenuous efforts. At the end of the war the Air Ministry decided to adopt a policy of distributing aircraft and engine orders amongst a number of selected firms. This, as the turnover figures reveal, was of very little direct financial value to Rolls-Royce in the early twenties, though it certainly became of considerable value from 1924 onwards. It had nevertheless a commercial value since the technical reputation of the name was kept continuously before the public through the publicity given to the activities and record-breaking endeavours of the Royal Air Force. In the penumbra of this reputation that of the car was less exposed to the merciless light of competitive publicity which had played upon it before the war. There is very little security for the producers of any product for which technical pre-eminence is claimed.

The second advantage was closely related to this. The firm had always spent heavily to ensure the genuine goodwill of its customers, and had established a clientele for its products whose members were usually loyal to Rolls-Royce if their pockets permitted them to be so. This loyalty was strong and must be adjudged a factor of considerable economic strength in the difficult years now under discussion.

These factors certainly mitigated, but they did not, as some seem to imagine, eliminate the hostility of the commercial environment, though it might be said that this environment was increasingly hostile in the interwar years to the structure of the industry rather than to any single unit within that industry. The design and production of the first 'small' 20 h.p. Rolls-Royce car is an indication of the increasing preoccupation of the firm, as of the industry as a whole, with the problem of cost. The motto 'regardless of cost' was buried very shortly after the war but for many years the industry was not particularly concerned with the whereabouts of the grave, or the nature of the epitaph. Even in the middle thirties when the problem of cost became acute for Rolls-Royce, occupying the continuous attention of several of its ablest engineers, the onset of rearmament made it possible to treat the problem in a relatively leisurely fashion and to avoid the decisive and rigorous measures which its solution demanded.

The production of the Goshawk was the first sign that the old policy was no longer effective. It was realised that the production of the quantity of 40/50 h.p. cars which the firm had come to regard as saleable would no longer, even if supplemented by aero-engine business, guarantee a reasonable margin of profit. To some extent however the decision to produce a smaller car was in fact a decision to let the larger problem go by default. The necessary volume of sales to provide an economic turnover was to be obtained by competing for a share of a new market – with the 20 h.p. quality vehicle – in which the firm had not previously ventured, or thought it necessary or desirable to venture. It was in effect merely a method of postponing the basic problem of the cost of the 40/50 h.p. chassis. This problem can best be represented as the division of the difference between the price of the 40/50 h.p. and the price of the most comparable vehicle in quantity or mass production (in England or the United States respectively), between features of the Rolls-Royce which could not be found on any other car (including the cost of such features as the guarantee) and the difference in the quantity produced or the efficiency of production. In the days when most firms in the British motor industry were operating under more or less identical cost conditions and producing an approximately similar number of cars the discrepancy in price could quite fairly be attributed to the first factor. The proportion attributable to the second factor would gladly be paid by the customer because the value of quality and reliability was substantially greater to him than its cost of production. And since in its early stages the quantity production of the automobile contributed more problems in mechanical reliability than it offered obvious advantages in the way of economical production, advantages which the manufacturer rarely had the time or inclination to seek and exploit, Rolls-Royce could fairly claim that its production policy was basically sound and would stand the test of time. The fact that the post-war attempts of one or two British firms, amongst which Harper & Bean was the most conspicuous, to imitate the mass-production methods of the American automobile industry, had failed conspicuously, served only to strengthen the dogmatism of those who regarded quality and quantity as incompatible objectives. The majority of the firms comprising the industry settled back, albeit with less comfort than before, into their old ways, and one of the industry's leading journals was not inaccurate in its criticism when in 1929 it saw fit to comment that

> The greatest efforts of the automobile engineer in the manufacturing field have been towards producing existing orthodox designs at lower and lower figures. Little or no attempt has been made at considerable innovation with the object of greatly reducing manufacturing costs . . . A comprehensive survey of any assembled chassis will provide ample evidence of the fact that the possibilities of designing for production have not yet been seriously exploited.[1]

Rolls-Royce was probably least conscious of the problem of economic as opposed to technical efficiency in these terms. Consequently the design, production and introduction of the 20 h.p. car involved no major changes in the basic postulates of the firm's economic policy. The target price was to be obtained by building a smaller car which was less expensive mainly *because* it was smaller and its production required less material and labour on that account.

In a memorandum written on 1 November 1920 when the project was in its early stages of serious consideration, Royce made it quite clear that his intention was to design a car whose cost would be 75 per cent of that of the large car. His approach to the problem accepted the existing situation and raised no complicated issues.

It seems manifest to me that a small output at Derby will not allow the Rolls-Royce Company to exist. So that supposing there is not a sufficient market for the big car, or that we shall be spoiling our markets by flooding the big car markets, the prospects of aero work being limited, our best field appears to be in the smaller car market. Owing to our reputation we ought to be able to sell a high quality small article at a figure above what it costs. It would be dealt with in the same Sales, Design and Test organisations and so contribute towards the standing charges, which would otherwise on a small output ultimately become too large.

In concluding this memorandum, however, he made his prejudice quite plain. 'I would like it clearly understood', he said, 'that I should not for a moment recommend a smaller model if we could fill the Derby factory with the large model.' All seemed agreed that this could not be done and the possibility of reducing the price of the 40/50 h.p. chassis by either increasing the quantity produced or redesigning for production, or a combination of both, was never seriously considered. There is no actual evidence that it was considered at all. The design of the small car was thus completed and after the prototypes had undergone the usual extensive trials and modifications the production orders were issued on 13 July 1922. Through uncertainties of one sort or another the first twenty cars were all produced without jigs or tools, and their cost must have therefore been greatly in excess of the estimate. The car was announced to the public in October 1922 at a price of £960, and its immediate success was very considerable. By the 21st of the same month orders for 223 cars had been received, and it was decided that this warranted the ordering of material in batches of 250, a quantity considerably larger than had been customary.

Material for the large car was being ordered in batches of 50 at this time, a policy which was estimated by Wormald, the works manager, to have increased the cost of the chassis by £15. The promising rate of orders for the Goshawk, however, was not maintained, even though 562 chassis in all were actually sold in 1923 as compared with 415 Silver Ghosts. The small car nevertheless made a substantial contribution to the turnover of the year (20 h.p., £500,000; 40/50 h.p., £660,000) and undoubtedly was the principal factor contributing to the increase in total turnover from £1,055,000 in 1922 to £1,800,000 in 1923. In all, 1200 of this particular model were produced before it was succeeded by an improved model early in 1926.[2] The basic design continued in production until the end of 1929 when it was succeeded by a slightly larger car of 20/25 h.p. rating. The basic design of the Silver Ghost continued in production until the introduction of the Phantom I in 1925, a total of 3360 having been produced since the end of the war, an average production of just over 500 large cars per annum, or 700–800 in all after the introduction of the Goshawk.

The general pattern of the company's activity at this time reveals some interesting features. The trade discount on chassis, averaging 11 per cent of turnover from 1920 to 1922, 18 per cent in 1925, and 17 per cent in the following three years, was a heavy burden both on the company and the final buyer. This discount was unavoidable while chassis continued to be sold through the normal trade channels. Most of the chassis were invariably sold through appointed agents and in this respect the pattern of trading had changed little from that developed before the war.[3] The question of trade discount seems to have been accepted almost without question as an inevitable cost of production but its sheer magnitude and relation even to major items of cost such as labour, materials and overheads, invites criticism of a distributive system which, at least on superficial examination, appears to be so expensive. In the year 1926, for example, just over 1000 chassis in all were sold by the company. The discount granted on this volume of sales, valued at £1,415,000 and costing £1,220,000, was no less than £258,000, a figure which gives a rough average of £258 per chassis.[4] Before final judgement could be passed on this figure the proportion represented by actual service, spares, and real costs of distribution (transport, storage and finance) would have to be known. It is conceivable that this figure might represent quite a high proportion of the total, depending primarily on the extent, in quality and time, of the service provided by the agent. But there are reasons for suspecting that such a large total could not be entirely justified in this way. Since Rolls-Royce is by no means unique in having to carry the burden of trade discounts and since the position in the British car industry remains substantially unchanged, it would appear that the distributive efficiency of the entire system – based on a multitude of expensive showrooms, salesmen, servicing equipment and stores – merits serious investigation.

There are two basic questions which might be asked. The first is whether this system is in the least necessary actually to distribute the vehicles when new – there being strong grounds for believing that either for individual firms or for the industry as a whole it could be achieved through a substantially smaller and less costly organisation. The second is whether the service actually provided bears any relation to the proportion of the retail purchase price which is represented by the discount and whether the customer would, in fact, were he given the choice, consider that the benefits received were worth the price asked. There are few things more insidious than a custom so well established in a trade that its mere existence is considered ample justification to those who benefit from it, while the public at large is unaware that it has lost some freedom of economic choice.

The answer to these questions may be different for the present time and for the inter-war years. Though a system which wastes resources is never justifiable, it is easier for an individual firm operating under strongly competitive conditions in a buyer's market to employ an existing apparatus of distribution, however costly, which almost guarantees a certain number of sales, than to shoulder the risk of marketing the entire output directly. Even had Rolls-Royce decided on purely economic grounds to market its own production directly, a policy far more feasible in England than in the United States, this would have placed the company at a peculiar disadvantage if the policy had proved a failure, as is often the case with unilateral action on the part of a single firm, or a policy which depends for its success on a change in consumer habits.

The question of trade discount was raised, from a very different angle, at sales conferences during the latter part of 1923. There had been a noticeable decline in sales, which was attributed by the works manager, Wormald, to a number of causes. These included the political situation, the usual bad season of August and September, the prospect of the Olympia Show and publication by other manufacturers of reductions in prices 'which give the public the idea that we might be reducing'. Keener competition and the demand for front-wheel brakes also played a part, as well as what Wormald described as 'a big one — the fact that we have let go the business with the "sporting" type of owner-driver to a large extent.' Rumours that Rolls-Royce might be producing a new type of chassis on the lines of the '20' were rife. Wormald also felt that comparatively small discounts affected sales, as did 'lack of output from the works during the best selling period of the year . . . when we are getting an average of six chassis per week and selling eight; consequently having no stock cars to sell all through the summer.'

The decline of sales was more specifically attributable to the poor follow-on in the reception of the 20 h.p. Goshawk. This failure Wormald attributed to Rolls-Royce's disinterest in the 20 h.p. ('for fear of its effect on the 40/50 h.p.'), to a decision not to show the car at Olympia, to its high price, and to the limited size and weight of the coachbuilt bodies that the chassis would carry. Strong competition was also being experienced from Sunbeam and Lanchester.

A detailed calculation was made[5] on the effects of increasing the trade discount as one possible method of stimulating the dealers but this policy was considered too costly for the results that it might possibly achieve.

At first the Goshawk was something of an ugly duckling within the organisation. It was conceived as a product of commercial necessity rather than the outcome of technical evolution. Some hoped that a return to more 'normal' conditions would enable the company to dispense with it altogether and concentrate on the large chassis. Johnson had always been afraid of spoiling the market for the large chassis by producing a small car which did not offer a sufficient price differential. There were many other arguments in favour of continuing a one-model policy. This policy was reflected far more in the concentration of design and experimental effort than in production economies, but this was becoming increasingly necessary if technical excellence of the product was to be maintained, particularly in face of the sheer volume of specialised research and development which the mass-production manufacturers in the United States, and the mass-production component manufacturers which supplied a substantial proportion of the whole industry in Great Britain, were now undertaking. Royce was in consequence always pressing the board for a larger allocation of funds for experimental work. His views on this subject were elaborated at some length in a memorandum from Le Canadel written in November 1926.

> I would like to emphasise that I consider that the experimental expenditure should be made as liberal as the Directors think possible, because our only hope of continuing to be successful appears to be in the flexibility of our system of production, so that we can improve whenever we know how, and so be without fear of becoming fossilised by the production bug. Had we been low-cost specialists in any way on the lines of the Americans, we should naturally have been obliged to have other views; but in England, with our small output, our only chance is that our production shall stand out by all round perfection, rather than price, and the Company must be satisfied if they can make small and safe profits (safe because they are likely to continue).

Royce was always consistent on this topic. E. A. Claremont once said of him that his heaven would be a place where he could produce one car at a time and in which no two cars need ever be exactly alike. Royce always regarded production as an instrument, never as a consequence, of design. Production efficiency, as an end in itself, was something which he, in common with a great many others who were handicapped by the traditional outlook of the British automobile engineer, was prepared to leave to the Americans. 'Mass production' and 'flexibility' he regarded as antitheses almost synonymous with 'quantity' and 'quality', and though economic conditions were not exactly easy, there existed no urgent imperative to explore production possibilities even within the given structure of the industry. The Derby production engineers were not trained in a tradition of cost-consciousness, that characteristic of the American engineer which so impressed Hives on one of his early trips to the United States, but the small quantities going through the factory, and the irregularities of production which the system of ordering in small batches closely geared to sales made necessary, presented Wormald with a good many problems which could not be strictly labelled as cost problems, though failure to solve them was certainly reflected in higher costs.

Towards the latter part of November 1923, the output of the 20 h.p. was reduced to eight chassis per week. A few weeks later it was decided to reduce the output of the 20 h.p. still further and to increase that of the 40/50 h.p. This led to an indignant outburst from Wormald. 'We will of course', he said, 'make arrangements to do this. It is however very unfortunate that for many months now we have been up and down so much with our output owing to Sales instructions. This sudden stopping and starting is most disastrous to stability. Our workmen lose heart and interest and generally the works have got an attitude of ''here today and gone tomorrow''. Indeed, we have become known as the ''Stop 'em and Start 'em works''.' It was difficult, however, to introduce the element of stability which Wormald required with such a small volume of production, and for some years the rate of production at Derby was very closely geared to the barometer of sales. The Sales department would not accept, as it were, the economic responsibility for whatever the factory decided to produce. The whole organisation was constructed on the basis of the principle 'made to order'.

No startling changes of policy, technical or commercial took place between 1924 and 1927. Chassis output continued relatively stable, being divided between the large and the small car in much the same proportion. The introduction of the Phantom I in 1925 stimulated the sales of the larger car in that year, but the total turnover of the firm continued at an average of just over two million pounds. Chassis production accounted for an average of £1,300,000 of this total, but the contribution of chassis production to gross profit was certainly not in this proportion.[6] Aero sales, though much smaller in volume, made an almost equal contribution. Over the period 1924–8 chassis sales, forming on the average 72 per cent of the turnover, contributed 60 per cent of the gross profit, while aero sales, forming only 22 per cent of the turnover, contributed 39 per cent of the gross profit.

It cannot be concluded from these figures that chassis production was 'subsidised' by aero-engine production. Such a conclusion could only be legitimately drawn if the average rate of profit on chassis production was less than the average prevailing throughout the industry in the production of a similar type of car, measured over a period of years, and if the average rate of profit on aero-engine production was in excess of the average prevailing in the aero-engine industry in the same period. Only under such circumstances could it be said that the customer of the one class of product was subsidising the customer of the other. Even if the chassis division was making less than average profits, or for that matter a net loss, there would be no question of the one section subsidising the other unless aero profits were above the average. In this context, however, the term 'subsidy' is too imprecise. Where two major products are made in the same factory, particularly if they are extremely complex mechanical products such as automobile chassis and aero-engines, the precise allocation of cost normally conforms to conventional cost accounting practice rather than careful theoretical calculation.[7]

In an organisation such as Rolls-Royce at this time, where a very considerable proportion of the total cost of either product was represented by an allocation of an estimated share of overhead expenditure common to the production of both major products, any attempt to judge, in the strictly economic sense, the independent profitability of either product is beset with very great difficulty.

An Air Ministry assessor, zealously safeguarding the expenditure of public money, would conceivably have concluded that the precise allocation of costs to cars and aero-engines was a comparatively simple process, given the refinements of cost accounting technique available even at this time. But where the two major products were produced in the same factory and depended heavily on common services, such as design, development and sales, this would have been difficult enough, even without the complicating factor of economies of scale. The casual employment of the term 'subsidy' in this or in any other similar context invariably assumes that the production of the 'subsidised' article could be suspended without any important effects on the costs of production, and thus on the profitability, in independent production, of the 'unsubsidised' article. Even where there are two completely separate organisations based on separate factories, a stage in the evolution of the firm's organisation which was not reached until after the Second World War, the question of the relative profitability of joint and independent production is not easily solved if a large volume of overheads is shared by the organisations. Under these circumstances, however, there is a natural tendency towards an increasingly precise allocation which makes it possible to define the issues more simply.

But during the twenties the question of the relative profitability of the two activities of the company was not regarded in quite the same light as in the later thirties, when the profitability of chassis production had become an acute problem. There is no doubt that this is at least partly attributable to the fact that in the twenties there was no clear division from the point of view even of administration, organisation, design and research, between chassis and aero-engine production. The need for such a division was not strongly felt and the production of aero-engines was still to some extent regarded as a profitable sideline of chassis manufacture. It was not until rearmament brought about a thoroughgoing change in the whole administration that the concept of two divisions became clearly established, and with it an increasing consciousness of both the nature of the dependence of the two spheres of production in the past, and the advantages which this gave, and of the necessity for further evolution in the direction of administrative, functional and financial independence.

It is not without significance that throughout the twenties and early thirties the problem of the relationship of the two spheres of production was never formally analysed. Until 1938 no attempt was made to allocate non-manufacturing overheads (i.e. overhead expenses not included in the manufacturing cost of aero-engines or chassis) between the two divisions. No attempt was made to assess accurately the economic contribution of the various items of turnover, and though the relative importance of chassis and aero turnover was understood, the management did not have or demand the analytical information which would have enabled them to anticipate the trends which were to lead inexorably to the more serious position of the later thirties. The most elementary statistical and economic analysis was not employed, and the management was content with the knowledge that the operations of the company as a whole were profitable.

The published balance sheet and profit and loss account which characterised British industry between the wars was a primitive and uninformative document. In the case of Rolls-Royce, these documents make it impossible to make any useful analysis of the profitability of different sectors of the business. It is nevertheless possible to reach the qualified conclusion that the price charged for aero-engines was substantially in excess of actual cost, and that, as will be appreciated from a subsequent discussion, the profitability of chassis production was not as great as that indicated by the figures, though this was due to an error of judgement which affected both spheres. But it cannot be concluded from this that an independent organisation not concerned with chassis manufacture could have provided these engines at a substantially reduced figure. Even if this conclusion is not accepted — and proof either way is admittedly difficult — there can be no doubt that the contribution which the company and its technicians were shortly to make to the national prestige and aeronautical reputation of Great Britain in the course of the Schneider Trophy competitions heavily outweighed any element of concealed subsidy, whether it was incurred at the time or previously as part of a policy of keeping the organisation in being.

The average annual profit for the years 1923–5 was £162,000. It was considered at the time that the actual average figure was slightly lower than this after making a variety of internal adjustments which it was not considered necessary to include in the published figures. A physical stocktaking held on 28 February 1925, the results of which did not become known until August, revealed a grave miscalculation as a result of which the book stock was overvalued by a quarter of a million pounds. This was the direct result of the introduction of an excessively complicated stock system by a new accountant whom Johnson had persuaded to join Rolls-Royce shortly after the war. The foremen disliked it and gave it no support. Captain Turner, who was officially in charge of the Aero Sales Department, but had always taken a close interest in the financial affairs of the company, was the first to suspect that something was wrong, and on his recommendation Johnson brought in a firm of consultant accountants which examined the whole position and discovered that the actual earnings for the four years were considerably less than expected.[8]

The discovery that the production of the Phantom I and the Goshawk had cost some £100,000 more than anticipated was a serious matter and called for drastic action. A rigorous economy campaign was introduced and was followed by a reduction of salaries from a total of £245,000 in 1925 to £163,000 in 1926. Wages fell from £831,000 to £780,000, but this reduction was by no means proportionate, even if allowance is made for the slight increase in turnover.

A net profit of £100,000 was declared for 1926, a reduction of £65,000 on the previous year. The published balance sheet reserves were drawn on to the extent of £76,000 and by the employment of these exceptional measures it became possible to base the balance sheet on physical stock. The mistake was successfully repaired, but it is both of interest and significance that no mention whatever was made of the entire episode in the customarily discursive, eulogistic and uninformative directors' report and chairman's address. This was quite in accordance with the tradition of commercial secrecy so well established throughout British industry at this time. While there may be some advantage to management in being able to conceal miscalculations of this nature, if adequate reserves have been created, the modern view that the published accounts should reflect past performance and current financial strength as accurately as possible does represent a considerable advance over the attitudes prevailing in British industry in the mid-twenties.

The years 1925 and 1926 had imposed a great strain on the senior executives of the company. Claude Johnson, who returned from the arduous negotiations in the United States at the end of 1925, had shouldered most of the financial worry created by the revaluation of stocks. His brother, whom he had made general manager under him in January 1926, was unaware of the general state of affairs, and when Claude Johnson died unexpectedly in April, Basil was somewhat shocked by the complex situation which he had inherited. As soon as he became fully acquainted with the situation, he appointed an Economy Committee to run the severe economy campaign which the disturbed industrial conditions of 1926 (the year of the General Strike) and the difficult internal financial situation made necessary. Since the latter was of course a closely guarded secret the measures adopted were considered by many to be unduly severe, and Basil Johnson himself incurred considerable personal unpopularity in consequence. The strain of carrying out an extremely difficult task under these conditions proved too much for his health. He suffered a severe breakdown and was advised by his doctors to retire completely. This he did in September 1928, recommending as his successor Arthur Sidgreaves, then general sales manager. Sidgreaves was relatively junior at this time but his rapid promotion, though unexpected, was an excellent thing for the company and proved the wisdom of Basil Johnson's recommendation. Sidgreaves had been associated with Basil Johnson for a considerable period, first as sales manager of Napiers before the war, then as senior officer in charge of the White City Engine Depot which he had taken over from Johnson when the latter had been recalled, at the Admiralty's request, to deputise for his brother when he left for the United States to organise the Eagle programme.

The chairman of the board, Lord Wargrave, invited Johnson to remain as vice-chairman, but Johnson felt that this would not be fair to Sidgreaves, who would have felt restricted by the presence on the board of a previous managing director. Since his doctors were insistent that he should reduce his activities to a minimum he was content to retire completely. As so frequently happens in such cases, Basil Johnson's somewhat unexpected retirement, preceded as it was by a series of administrative measures which would have incurred personal unpopularity for anyone who had the misfortune to have to introduce them, gave rise to the legend that Basil Johnson lacked the personality and ability of his brother. The board probably found it convenient not to deny this since it would limit the possibility of any residuum of the unpopularity of the economy campaign attaching to themselves. But the legend is not supported by the facts. After the war Basil Johnson had taken an increasingly large share of the burden of administration from the shoulders of his brother and after Claude's death in 1926 he bore the full weight of a very serious situation, which he handled with competence and integrity. He had the misfortune to suffer the consequences of a situation for which his brother had very largely been responsible.

The company nevertheless did not suffer greatly from the change in chief executive, which had repercussions throughout the organisation. Sidgreaves was a shrewd and able financier and administrator who displayed that quality, so essential in all senior executives, of being able to employ the knowledge and weigh the opinions of his assistants without feeling that this undermined his authority or prestige. He was not an engineer by profession, but a lifelong association with the industry had developed in him a considerable understanding of the relationship between technical and economic problems. He was not long in office before he demonstrated considerable acumen and intiative by bringing about the purchase of the Bentley Company, which had, at one stage, looked like becoming a serious competitor.

At the end of 1924, Royce, who had been giving Elliott and Rowledge an increasingly free hand in the field of aero-engine design, decided that the company was relying somewhat unduly on the existing designs of aero-engine. The Eagle and Condor were still being developed, the Condor having been employed for a series of novel experiments with turbo-superchargers. This was the era of the flying-boat and the Condor acquired fame through its use on the giant flying-boats produced by Dornier-Wal, and on the Supermarine flying-boats used in the Royal Air Force and by Sir Alan Cobham on his famous flight around Africa. The Condor was also the engine used in the ill-fated airship R.101.

The comprehensive study of aircraft engine design which Royce and his assistants began in 1924 soon convinced him that the Condor and the Eagle were obsolete and that there was little scope for their further development. His decision to abandon the Condor was reinforced by the decision of the Air Ministry that the engine was too difficult to produce. At this stage strong transatlantic influences were brought to bear both on the Air Ministry and on the aero-engine designers through the remarkable victories of Curtis-engined aircraft in the 1923 and 1925 Schneider Trophy races. These aircraft were powered by the Curtis D12 and a developed version of the D12 known as the V-1400. The D12, which developed 400 h.p. for a displacement of only 1205 cubic inches (compared with the 525 h.p. of the Condor I from 2138 cubic inches), was brought to England in 1924 by C. R. Fairey, who had acquired a licence to manufacture the engine. Around it the Fairey Company designed and manufactured a reconnaissance bomber known as the Fox which had a general performance equal to that of contemporary single-seater fighters. The Hawker Hornbill, powered by the much larger and heavier Condor IV developing 700 h.p., was only slightly faster than the Fox.

Though the Air Ministry refused to bring the Fairey Company into the exclusive 'family' of government-supported engine-builders, the advent of the D12 exercised a strong influence on official engine policy. Before 1924 the Air Ministry had favoured the air-cooled radial for single-engine fighters. The Curtis D12 completely reversed this trend. Though no support was given to Fairey's endeavour to establish himself in the aero-engine business, several engines were bought and tested at Farnborough and a number were installed in the Fairey Fox. The Air Ministry became convinced that an engine of this type should be developed in Britain and since Napiers were regarded as being in the medium-power class the first approach was made to this firm. Napiers unwisely refused to undertake the work, since the then managing director, H. T. Vane, failed to recognise that the 'Lion' was reaching the end of its career. The Air Ministry in consequence turned to Rolls-Royce, who gladly undertook the development of a similar type of engine. When asked to undertake this development Royce's first thought turned instinctively to the Eagle design. The original Eagle had run through eight marks and was in regular use on the London–Paris service. His idea was to obtain more power from this engine by increasing the number of cylinders to sixteen. This engine, which in no way resembled the original Eagle, was to be known as the Eagle XVI. This redesign was a long-term project, however, and since the Air Ministry's demand was somewhat urgent Royce reverted to the idea of modifying the Eagle VIII 'to suit temporarily'.

The Eagle type of engine was still based on cylinder blocks built up from separate steel forgings for each cylinder, whereas the Curtis D12 was the first successful example of a V 'monoblock' engine, in which the cylinder blocks are machined from six-cylinder aluminium alloy castings fitted with steel liners. It soon became obvious that something more radical than a redesign was needed but Royce was convinced of the urgency of producing an engine forthwith.

By this time he was well aware that a great deal of attention was being paid to the problems of aero-engine design in France, where the two-speed supercharger was developed, and America as well as in Britain. In a minute from West Wittering, he expressed his concern that this order had found Rolls-Royce inadequately prepared.

> If we cannot or will not do this (modify the Eagle Mk. VIII) the probable alternative is that an order for Curtis engines will go to the U.S.A., which would be extremely dangerous and a national calamity and disgrace. Our Eagle XVI might, if proved to be superior, regain the position, and we have many friends who will rejoice if we can succeed in achieving this. By making our old Eagle do the work, it would in fact be an enormous triumph for us, and give us breathing space to produce the Eagle XVI, so we ought to stir our souls to get through.

In fact, the Eagle XVI was designed and produced, but it remained an experimental engine since some of the basic characteristics of the design imposed too great a limitation on development. A sample of the D12 had meanwhile been sent to Derby by the Air Ministry and in July of the same year (1925) design work commenced on the 'F' engine, later named the Kestrel, which was eventually produced in considerable

8.   The Rolls-Royce Kestrel aero-engine

quantity for the R.A.F. This engine was the first Rolls-Royce engine employing the aluminium monoblock casting; and it was the basic design which was scaled up for the 'H' engine, later named the Buzzard, which was intended as an engine for large flying-boats and which was later transformed by intensive development into the magnificent 'R' engine that won the Schneider Trophy outright for Great Britain three times in succession. The Kestrel was designed to produce 480–500 h.p. and its output was eventually increased to 750.[9] The Buzzard was designed originally to have an output of 820 h.p. and in the final version of the 'R' used in the 1931 race this was increased to the phenomenal figure of 2300 h.p. developed in the actual flight.[10] On one occasion this engine developed 2780 h.p. at 3400 revolutions per minute and a boost of 20¼ lbs – figures which were considered outstanding even at the end of the Second World War.[11] In the construction of these engines the development work which the firm's distinguished research metallurgist, H. C. Hall, had put into aluminium alloys in the late twenties, was used in the later stages to very great advantage. This research, which resulted in the development of the 'RR' series of alloys, paid very rich dividends, financial and technical, to the company. Their production, which was licensed to High Duty Alloys Ltd in 1929, eventually became the source of a substantial royalty revenue.

Though Royce was ably assisted by Rowledge, Hives, Elliott and others in this work, the conditions under which the Schneider Trophy work was carried out, and the general uncertainty of the Air Ministry policy at this time, imposed a considerable strain upon him. That the Air Ministry was being peculiarly exacting in connection with the 'F' (which was not called the Kestrel until 1931) can clearly be seen from the following minute written at West Wittering in October 1927 and addressed to Basil Johnson:

> Apparently the British Government seem to be doing their best to crush us under difficulties. I do not think they actually mean it, but they either want F.11 in the best form we can turn out, or they don't want it and only want us on the bigger engine.
>
> Now they appear to ask us to do more and more, and so put off the time for giving us orders.
>
> We do not mind all this for racing and competitive conditions, but that our salvation and every day bread and butter should depend upon it appears to be wrong, and it looks as though there are too many of us in this aero business, and that we should do better by giving such talents as we have, and the capacity of our factory, to our automobile work, as it appears to be a job of sweated slavery to meet first one condition and then another, apparently putting off the reward until we are no longer in existence . . . it would appear that the Air Ministry and their staff have not the sympathy they should have with the people creating the goods; probably this is the same with all the critics. There is my grouse: I hope it may help your defence.

The designers were not all of one mind on the subject of the most suitable type of engine for the Schneider Trophy. Rowledge thought that a 16-cylinder type was the most suitable but Royce stuck grimly to his favourite V-12 layout. Though the subject was under discussion throughout 1928, the final decision to scale up the Buzzard was not taken until quite late in the year and the design work was not started until November. In the light of subsequent developments Royce's faith in the intrinsic merits of the V-12 layout seems to have been amply

9.   The Kestrel-engined Hawker Fury

justified. But he was unusually accommodating on the subject of the V-16, which he considered should be made, if only as an engine for the Schneider Trophy. In a minute from Le Canadel where he was spending the winter, as usual, Royce recommended that the design should continue but that the V-12 'F' should also be scaled up.

Without doubt this is the most useful engine for the Schneider Cup and therefore if we can be in for winning this for Britain this engine should be made by us if only for that purpose. When it has been made, and its virtues and troubles found, we shall be able to judge if it is a better engine for our trade than the 12 cylinder V.

Shortly after writing this, he made up his mind finally against the 16-cylinder and cabled Johnson that 'after a long and careful thought my decision is definitely for 12 cylinders unless our technical staff and Ministry officials unanimously think otherwise.'

The success of the Schneider Trophy engine naturally brought Royce very considerable fame and in 1931 he was offered and accepted a baronetcy. This was a cause of considerable satisfaction to him but he wore the honours lightly. Success had been too strenuously earned for this to be otherwise and his greatest rewards were found in simple things – excellence of design and quality of manufacture. His health began to fail fast in 1931, and he did not welcome the prospect of another Schneider Trophy race. He felt that these had more than served their purpose, at least as far as the firm was concerned, in much the same way that Claude Johnson had once felt that there was little to be gained from further participation in the Tourist Trophy races and reliability trials before the First World War. Royce was always acutely conscious of the principle of diminishing returns in all spheres of life, as his attitude towards the final race makes quite clear. But this was the race in which Lady Houston's generous gift of £100,000 had made it possible for Great Britain to compete, an action which imposed a special obligation on all concerned. Though the burden of work had, as far as possible, and as far as was consistent with Royce's acute sense of what was 'going on', been removed from his shoulders when his illness made it imperative that this should be done, he still carried the burden of responsibility mainly because he wished to do so and because, like

10.   The Rolls-Royce 'R' engine

so many men who have carried it all their lives, he would have been lost without it. In July 1930, he discussed the 1931 race in a letter to Sidgreaves.

> It was agreed with you that we all wished there would be no race in 1931, and that we had derived considerable benefit from last year, and my impression was that we should get some benefit from future development work, but nothing like the same amount ... We might publish that we do not feel justified in attempting to derive any benefit at the expense of such a costly enterprise as regards risk of life and money cost, and we definitely should not do so for our own benefit. We feel, however, that if pressure is brought to bear upon us by the Government or elsewhere we feel it is our duty to do our best to uphold British prestige.

British prestige was conspicuously upheld at Cowes in 1931, and though, as Royce suggested, Rolls-Royce did not learn as much from the last race as it had done from the first and the second, the experience which the firm acquired in developing the maximum output from the V-12 engine was to stand Great Britain in good stead in a contest on whose outcome a great deal more than the fate of a silver trophy was to depend. The Schneider Trophy races also exercised a marked influence on the future of British aero-engine development. The supremacy of the liquid-cooled in-line engine and of the Rolls-Royce liquid-cooled engines in particular was firmly established. The services were also convinced by the success of the 'R' that the ground-boosting of service engines was now a feasible proposition, requiring only the large-scale production of high-octane petrols. To Rolls-Royce the races offered one conspicuous advantage. The 1929 race marked the end of the Napier Lion and the Napier Company ceased to be a serious competitor until the 'Sabre' entered the picture towards the end of the Second World War.

The late twenties and early thirties were the years of record-breaking endeavours on land, sea and in the air, and the 'R' engine played its conspicuous part in all three spheres. Sir Henry Seagrave and Sir Malcolm Campbell, whose exploits lent a certain colour and excitement to years otherwise far from colourful for those who were struggling to survive the depression, both used the 'R' engine in their cars. The prestige of the company grew steadily throughout this period and the decline in turnover was not as serious as might have been expected in a company whose products were in some senses a super-luxury both for

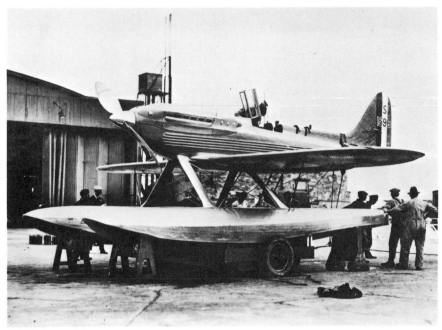

11. The Rolls-Royce 'R'-engined Supermarine S6B seaplane, Schneider Trophy

the individual and for the state.[12] The recovery from the dangerous situation which had first revealed itself in 1925 had been rapid and complete in the following three years, and in 1931 Sidgreaves found himself in the fortunate position of being able to mobilise sufficient liquid reserves to achieve an important extension of the company's sphere of operations.

8 The Acquisition of Bentley Motors

There was one consequence of the company's decision not to participate in trials and competitions which had not altogether been foreseen. In becoming 'respectable' through the production of a sedate and dignified vehicle, Rolls-Royce had, to a very large extent, as Wormald pointed out in his report on the 20 h.p. sales position, forfeited the interest and custom of the class of driver who was probably best typified before the war by the Hon. C. S. Rolls himself. Johnson seemed to support this policy, for he strongly opposed any attempt by the company's designers or officials to produce cars for the enthusiast. The minutes of the board meeting of 11 July 1922 contain the amusing comment that 'there was creeping in from all sides of the Company a desire to increase speed and power at the expense of silkiness.' This temptation had to be strongly resisted.

But the enthusiast is never denied the object of his enthusiasm for very long and if Rolls-Royce were not prepared to supply this class of car there were others who considered that the risk was worth while. During the First World War W. O. Bentley had acquired a considerable reputation as the designer of the Bentley rotary aero-engine. In 1912 he and his brother, H. M. Bentley, had acquired control of a firm by the name of Lecoq and Ferri Ltd, who were concessionaires for a little-known French car called the D.F.P. The name of this company was changed to Bentley & Bentley. Its registered objects were to sell and manufacture motor-cars, but the war broke out before any considerable progress had been made. Immediately after the war, in January 1919, a new company, Bentley Motors Ltd, was formed to purchase from the old company the design of a car. Yet a third company was formed in July 1919 and purchased the assets of the second company for £30,000. Its management remained in the hands of the Bentley brothers, who registered it with a nominal capital of £200,000 of which £69,400 had been issued by the end of 1920. Backed by this organisation Bentley proceeded to design and build experimental chassis, a small number of

12. W. O. Bentley

which were sold for the first time in 1921. These very soon acquired a considerable reputation as fast and reliable high-quality sports cars. Production increased and in 1924 the company's output (322) was over a third of that of Rolls-Royce.

In the following year Royce, who rarely paid much attention to the commercial activities of other companies, indicated that he considered the position worthy of some consideration. In a minute from West Wittering written in October he elaborated his point of view.

> Regarding the Bentley, the makers are evidently out to capture some of our trade, but we do not think we can learn much by buying a car because we can see in which way it can be better than we are – that is – for high-speed performance, because it has four valves per cylinder. It would appear more costly than ours to produce for equal silence. We have the advantage of better machinery, staff and plant: they get much of their work done outside, but at the same time we are under heavy expenses.

Conservative as he was, the idea of the Bentley appealing to the sporting owner worried Royce somewhat and in November of the following year (1926) he wrote from Le Canadel that he would like to design 'a high-speed sports car, not expecting much in the way of sales, but for the good quality of ordinary sales'. And again in the following year one of the officials visiting Le Canadel wrote back to Derby that Royce was 'very keen on seeing a very smart sports car of some kind on our stand at Olympia'. Royce was not a man who ignored a challenge on his own ground, but the board held firm for other reasons. The Bentley Company was catering for a precarious market and provided the competition did not become too severe Rolls-Royce was quite prepared to let others shoulder the risk of producing this type of car.

The experience of the Bentley Company (the details of which were unlikely to have been known by the Rolls-Royce board at this time) proved the wisdom of the decision not to compete. In 1924 the company made a loss of £56,700, and in the following year it was liquidated and reorganised. The precarious state of affairs which existed at the end of 1924 can easily be appreciated from the fact that loans amounted to £43,000, almost a third of the issued capital, while goodwill and experimental expenditure were valued in the balance sheet at £82,000.

It is unlikely that the company would have obtained the capital to continue in production had it not been for the commercial philanthropy of the millionaire racing driver Captain Woolf Barnato, the son of the diamond magnate, who invested nearly £143,000 in the reorganised company, £107,000 in shares and £35,000 in debentures. This gave the organisation a new lease of life and it continued in production until 1931, when it was again forced into liquidation. In these years it produced an average of just over 300 cars per annum. Since the company was catering for the specialised market it was quite unable to restrict its production to one basic type. But even for a firm of this nature, the proliferation of chassis types was remarkable and indicates a failure to appreciate the relationship between design, uniformity, production-efficiency and profit. The figures in Appendix X show 1929 to be the only year in which the company made a reasonable profit.

The position of the Bentley Company was in many ways typical of the British motor industry at this time. In 1927 the industry produced 160,000 cars and 150 separate models. Seventy-five per cent of this production was in the hands of three firms and the general structure and strength of the industry was a cause of some concern to those who took the national viewpoint. 'It is usually assumed', said *The Economist* in its review of the industry,[1] 'that the motor industry, being of recent development, is in every respect up-to-date, and does not stand in need of overhauling, as do the older coal and cotton industries. To those in close touch with the industry it seems that no other industry stands more in drastic need of rationalisation in every sphere of its activities.' The article pointed out that the cost of selling was almost as great as the cost of production, a fact which is amply confirmed by the Rolls-Royce figures given earlier. It concluded that 'the vast potential market awaiting the British motor industry within the Empire alone cannot be regained by the haphazard and inadequate efforts of 50 small or moderate sized firms from the hold of such rivals as Ford and General Motors.'

The figures in Appendixes X and XI reveal quite clearly the reasons for the Bentley failure, which was hastened by the onset of the Depression. Practically every year a not inadequate manufacturing profit was eliminated or turned into a substantial loss by the weight of indirect expenditure which it had to absorb. This was almost equalled by the volume of discount allowed to the trade, but both figures are a reflection of the same situation. In the years during which the Bentley Company was in production, the indirect costs averaged 34.7 per cent of the direct costs of production. Of this total of indirect expenditure 27 per cent represents sales expenses and racing, 18 per cent experimental work, 21 per cent administration expenses, and 14 per cent the cost of running a separate servicing organisation for a few hundred cars. All these figures illustrate the struggle which faces a specialist low-output manufacturer such as Bentley when the firm attempts to escape from the strait-jacket of indirect costs. Criticism of the structure of the industry as it existed in 1929 would be of no more than historical interest were it not for the fact that neither the industry nor its problems had altered much by the end of the Second World War.

The management had been able, partly through the close contact which Rolls-Royce had maintained with American industry and partly through strongly sustained powers of self-criticism, to form a clear idea of the position of the company in the industry. Hives' discussion of the relative strength of the quantity producer in the United States, which had caused Royce to formulate his maxim of 'mass production with quality',[2] and the bid which the Bentley Company had made for the quality market, caused much thought to be given to future policy. Several possibilities had been turned down in 1929. In March S. F. Edge had made a proposal that Rolls-Royce should assist in the manufacture of A.C. cars, but this was not approved. In November of the same year the board gave serious consideration to a proposal that they should purchase the control of Barkers, a well-known firm of coachbuilders which had always been one of the principal outlets for the company's products. This too was rejected after careful investigation. The next proposal that was received however excited considerable interest.

On 11 June 1931 Sidgreaves received a long letter from J. K. Carruth, the managing director of Bentley Motors. Carruth had been appointed managing director by Captain Woolf Barnato in December 1930 in the hope that he might be able to salvage something of the very considerable amount of money which Captain Barnato had invested in the company. It seemed unlikely that Carruth could do very much and he considered that outside assistance would have to be sought. The letter suggested that Rolls-Royce might be interested in an amalgamation.

Carruth's original report to Captain Barnato (written before the approach to Rolls-Royce was made) reveals the desperate situation in which Bentley Motors found itself. Even the small profit shown for 1930 would have been turned into a substantial loss if an adequate reserve had been made against the general stock position, but it had been decided to show a small profit 'so that we may not have further embarrassment from the creditors'. The company was entirely dependent upon the production of new models to meet current cash requirements. Carruth attributed the failure of Bentleys to the production of undeveloped models.

Broadly speaking, our main troubles in the past can be traced to the delivery of new models to the public before adequate tests of production have been made. Let me at once emphasise that I do not for a moment suggest that this course has been deliberately adopted from choice. Too often the till has been empty and, in such circumstances, I readily admit how easy it is for a harassed management, beset by many difficulties, to fall into such an error of policy. But it is an error of policy, and may even be a fatal error of policy.

This interesting statement indicates the strong propensity to search for a *single* reason for failure in a complex situation where it may in fact be quite beyond the control of the management, as was undoubtedly the case with Bentley Motors at this time. Carruth suggested that the company should base its future policy on an increased production of the 8½-litre model. The implementation of this policy would have required £77,000 which he suggested should be obtained by an issue of preference shares which would be taken up by Baramans Ltd, a finance house which had already lent the Company £70,000. These funds were not forthcoming from the sources on which Bentley Motors had relied in the past, and it had thus become necessary to approach former competitors.

In his letter Carruth pointed out that the 8-litre had been a success, and that 'one of the problems was to keep the works going satisfactorily while the new 4-litre was being prepared and progressed.' The company had 100 chassis in various stages of completion in stock, and Carruth pointed out that these would probably be completed under any circumstances, even in the event of Bentleys being put into receivership. In the latter event they might very well be sold at very low prices and this implied a threat to Rolls-Royce which he was quite frank in stating:

In considering this position it would appear that either contingency must have a very grave effect on Rolls-Royce and as the total trade creditors of Bentley Motors are only about £15,000 with, possibly, contingent liabilities for unexpired contracts, which could be settled, in my opinion, for not more than £20,000, it seemed to me that ordinary business prudence demanded that details of this position should be disclosed to you before anything further is done. One can imagine the immense benefit which could accrue from a working arrangement between the two companies.

To implement this agreement Carruth suggested that Rolls-Royce and Bentley Motors should arrange a common sales policy, a common service policy, and partially integrated production policy which would involve Rolls-Royce manufacturing two-thirds of the components which Bentley Motors normally purchased from outside. Rolls-Royce would also obtain the services of W. O. Bentley as a designer. He considered that with Rolls-Royce 'having a large say in the future of the Company, it need only be a question of time until the models of each Company cease to compete, and are definitely designed to cater for different aspects of the luxury market'. In conclusion, Carruth pointed out that he was primarily representing the interests of Captain Barnato, who controlled most of the loan and share capital and was 'prepared to go a long way to maintain the name of Bentley'.

There was no attempt to hide the fact that the Bentley Company was in serious difficulty but it is significant that Carruth's scheme envisaged not only the separate corporate existence of the two companies, but the independence of Bentley Motors as a manufacturing organisation. The merger would yield no economies other than those provided by a common sales and service policy and the slight increase in Rolls-Royce's manufacturing turnover. The proposal shows clearly how little had been learnt from failure and how limited was the general appreciation of the problem facing motor manufacturing firms of this size.[3] It illustrates, in a very different sphere, the truth of Churchill's comment that 'the human mind, except when guided by extraordinary genius, cannot surmount the established conclusions amid which it has been reared.'

The proposal was discussed at length by the Rolls-Royce Board on 16 June and on the following day Sidgreaves replied that Rolls-Royce were interested but required further information, particularly on creditors and sales. This was immediately forthcoming. A first mortgage of £65,000 on the assets was held by the London Life Association and a second mortgage of £35,000 by Captain Barnato. Suppliers were owed £19,700 for supplies already delivered, and orders for material to the value of £92,000 had been placed. Carruth considered that the last item could easily be reduced to £20,000. The overdraft of £91,500 was guaranteed by Captain Barnato and Baromans Ltd. The sales of the 8-litre car had averaged six a month since its introduction and those of the 4-litre nineteen a month.

This information, which added little to the figures contained in the accounts, was sent to Captain Turner for his opinion. This was very adverse. Turner pointed out that if the tangible assets were worth their book value the whole of the preference and ordinary capital had been lost. The balance sheet certainly presented a sorry spectacle. Of liabilities totalling £477,939 no less than £282,186 represented loans of one sort or another. £171,320 represented the issued capital, and the balance of £24,433 sundry liabilities. This was covered by tangible fixed assets valued at £98,827 and current assets, consisting very largely of stocks and work in progress, valued at £217,674. The balance of £158,919 was composed of three items, a loss of £92,000, goodwill and experimental expenses valued at £47,000, and preliminary expense and underwriting charges valued at £19,500. There was thus good reason for Turner to doubt whether a realisation of the assets would provide a sum large enough to repay the loans and mortgages. He considered that the current assets were almost valueless and that the £35,000 which Carruth had suggested would be sufficient to tide the company over was totally insufficient and would probably be lost to Rolls-Royce unless secured by a mortgage having first preference. This judgement was to prove substantially correct since the Bentley assets realised just over £140,000 when the whole organisation was finally purchased by Rolls-Royce and the manufacturing organisation completely dissolved.

The board again considered the proposition on 23 June, and decided against it. In his letter to Carruth the following day Sidgreaves pointed out that they had found the position to be 'much more adverse than we formerly understood'. The main points of Captain Turner's memorandum were reproduced but the essence of the problem was the opinion held at Rolls-Royce that £40,000 would not keep the Bentley Company in existence. The obligation, if undertaken, would involve a steady drain on Rolls-Royce's liquid resources which the management could not contemplate.

> The main point however is that assuming it did [i.e. that Carruth's estimate of liability worked out correctly] the most favourable aspect is that £42,000 is required forthwith to meet these two liabilities. This point is important because, you will remember that in our conversation you mentioned that if we were prepared to put up a sum of between £30,000 and £40,000 you thought we could be given control. In our view however such a sum would only be a temporary

palliative, as apart from the liquidation of stocks, there would be no other cash available for current expenses.

In conclusion, Sidgreaves pointed out that the debenture holders could call in their money and place the company in liquidation at any time, and that the board therefore felt that they could take no action.

This letter terminated the negotiations between the two companies. From the financial angle especially the cons had heavily outweighed the pros. Control of the Bentley Company, though a most desirable development, was not worth the burden of the grossly inflated liabilities which Bentley Motors had incurred. The management nevertheless had the satisfaction of discovering that a competitor of some consequence was no longer in a position to compete. This in itself was a discovery of some considerable value.

Shortly after the conclusion of these negotiations the principal mortgagee, the London Life Association, called in its loans and forced the company into insolvency. A receiver was appointed and the due process of law could no longer be restrained. The demise of the Bentley Company soon became an open secret in industrial circles, and several concerns became interested in the disposition of its assets. Amongst these by far the most important was the aero-engine firm of Napiers, which, following exactly the opposite policy to that of Rolls-Royce, had abandoned the motor-car business entirely for aero-engines after the First World War and was now particularly anxious to remedy this mistake and to secure the services of a first-class designer. This seemed an excellent opportunity to do so, and Napiers entered into a conditional agreement of sale with P. T. Frere, the receiver acting on behalf of the mortgagee, the London Life Association. Under this agreement Napiers intended to purchase the entire assets of the Bentley Company for £84,000. The court made an order for sale on 20 October and the conditional agreement of sale, which had to be confirmed by the court, was made on the following day. An agreement was conditional because of the duty of the court under such circumstances to ensure that the maximum amount is obtained for the assets of the insolvent concern.

News of this development reached Sidgreaves, who immediately decided that Rolls-Royce should endeavour to prevent this from happening. The reasons for his decision are obvious and need no elaboration. Had Napiers acquired the Bentley assets and re-entered the motor-car field in this way, this would have presented a much more serious competitive threat than that which would have arisen as the result of the disposal of the Bentley stock of chassis.

The Company's solicitors, Claremont Haynes, were instructed to outbid the Napier Company in court but it was realised this would be a much more expensive business if it was known that they represented the Rolls-Royce Company. It was thereupon arranged to appoint agents who would not be associated with Rolls-Royce in any way and the British Equitable Trust were briefed to act in this capacity. In this way anonymity was preserved and Rolls-Royce succeeded in purchasing the entire Bentley assets for £125,175. This gave Rolls-Royce the right to use the name Bentley and the Bentley trademarks, though it was discovered that the latter, though valuable, had never been registered by the old company. After some slight difficulties had been overcome, both were registered.

This was an astute move on Sidgreaves' part. Even had Rolls-Royce made no use of the name to re-enter the sports car field the venture would have been both financially and commercially profitable. This development led subsequently to some regrettable and costly legal controversy arising out of the fact that W. O. Bentley, in the sincere belief that he was legally entitled to do so, allowed his name to be used by the Lagonda Company, whose staff he joined as a designer in 1936. But this episode occurred after the Second World War and thus falls beyond the scope of this narrative.

W. O. Bentley, after a very short stay with Napiers, was eventually persuaded to join Rolls-Royce by Sidgreaves, though questions of temperament and prestige made this a somewhat difficult arrangement on both sides. Bentley wanted an independent design and drawing office at Rolls-Royce, but this was obviously out of the question, and he was finally given the somewhat nebulous post of technical adviser to the managing director. This meant that there was unfortunately little scope for him to do creative work and finally in January 1936, by mutual consent, Bentley left Rolls-Royce to join Lagondas.

A new company, Bentley Motors (1931) Ltd was immediately formed and registered by Rolls-Royce as a fully-owned subsidiary under whose name it was intended to market a new type of Bentley sports car produced at Derby but having many of the characteristics which the public had come to associate with the original Bentley car. This promised increased turnover for the Derby works, a possibility which was regarded with considerable favour at this time. It is unfortunate however that Royce, who had wanted so much to design a sports car, did not live to see his policy come to fruition.

9 Improving the Breed

QUIDVIS RECTE FACTUM QUAMVIS HUMILE PRAECLARUM[1]

Between 1928 and 1932, Royce devoted most of his attention to the Schneider Trophy engines and to the 'F' or Kestrel engine for the R.A.F. He was also toying with the idea of producing a small radial engine suitable for small private aircraft.[2] It is not surprising that he should have come to the conclusion that the basic V-12 type of liquid-cooled engine, on which he had worked for some fifteen years, had been fairly fully exploited from the design point of view, if not from that of development, and since very considerable progress in radial engines was being made by Bristols and Armstrong-Siddeley in England, and more especially by Wright and Pratt & Whitney in the United States, the temptation to shift his attention to this type of engine is understandable.

In March 1930, he pressed this point of view on the Board:

There is no doubt that there are several plane builders who will not touch water-cooled engines owing to the difficulties of installation, and I fear somewhat the same may be said of pilots, owing to water leaks, corrosion, freezing, boiling, loss of water and control of water temperatures.

My impression is that for simplicity and first cost we should consider the question, and I recommend that we make an experimental air-cooled engine of the greatest perfection, both in design and workmanship . . . Our engine must be superior to what is at present being made, or there will be no excuse for our making it, and asking for a higher price . . . per horse power . . . It is to be regretted that we have spent so much time on the small V-12, water-cooled, and that so much good work has been done, but we hope it will be useful for other purposes supposing we find it is required, as indicated many times in past years, i.e. increasingly so if supercharging is demanded.

Royce was also devoting a considerable amount of his attention to car design, especially to the study of gearing. The main advances in car design in the late twenties had been made in gearing, and of the various alternative schemes which had been developed Royce preferred the epicyclic gearbox. Synchromesh gears, which had just been developed in the United States, and were being widely introduced, did not impress him at first, but eventually in 1932 he agreed that they were superior to the system employed by Rolls-Royce and recommended their adoption.

13. The Rolls-Royce Phantom II

In 1928, Royce was occupied principally on the Phantom II replacement for the Phantom I, which had been in production since 1925. In March of the same year one of the younger engineers who had joined Rolls-Royce as an engineering apprentice and had shown conspicuous ability, W. A. Robotham, stressed in a report that the development of the Phantom II was a matter of some urgency. 'Owing to the improvements made by our competitors — amongst them Buick and Sunbeam — we must really push forward our own progressive development . . . we must get better performance and greater simplicity, i.e., better value for cost.' It is always easier to obtain agreement on present facts than on future policy and Royce was not unduly dogmatic in this respect. But it was almost impossible, as Robotham was to discover in later years, to convince its protagonists that there was a causal connection between the persistence of unpalatable facts and the policy which lay behind them. Royce was quite frank and even vigorous in his concurrence with Robotham's point of view:

> I have long considered our present chassis out-of-date. The back axle, gearbox, frame, springs, have not been seriously altered since 1912. Now we all know it is easier to go on the old way, but I so fear disaster by being out-of-date, and having a lot of old stock left, and by the Sales falling off by secrets leaking out, that I must refuse all responsibility for a fatal position unless these improvements in our chassis are arranged to be shown next autumn, and to do this they must be in production soon after midsummer 1929. I will take moral responsibility for the risk, and think it is far less than having old stock (to wit the aero-engine position two years ago) and other risks of our present situation.

Royce, though he would probably have been the last to admit it, was becoming increasingly susceptible to transatlantic influences at this time.[3] The engineering merits of what he always tauntingly referred to as 'cheap American cars' were not lost on him, even though the competition from these vehicles was not as serious as would have been the case had the average motor-car purchaser always behaved in an economically rational manner. It was, of course, part of the industry's policy to withhold information which would encourage rational market judgements, particularly when the progress of mass-produced vehicles had begun to press hard on the quality differential. But Royce always realised the precariousness of this situation, which also conflicted strongly with his sense of fundamental honesty. This comes out very clearly in a minute which he wrote in April 1928 from Le Canadel on the subject of instrument boards.

> It is astounding that we, charging the very top prices cannot give as good a scheme as Citroen and Chrysler, and I am looking upon it as my duty to make our scheme so attractive in appearance and price that our Sales cannot do otherwise than adopt it. It should be realised that it is the first principle of good trading *to give good value for*

money, and if you are posing as making the best, see that your buyers get it, and do your very utmost that the customers, for your good, are not overcharged by the retailers.

We must knock over any conditions that get in our way. When you are sure that the scheme is as good as can be made – I mean all round, appearance practical, and minimum cost – we should next decide if it is *desirable at this cost to the customer*.[4]

The Phantom II was produced in time for the 1929 Show at Olympia, but the orders received immediately after the introduction of the car indicated that a rather bleak period lay ahead. Only 113 cars were ordered in the first four weeks compared with 145 Phantom Is in the same period in 1925. Though it was not realised at the time, this was the first indication of a significant change in the character of the market for chassis. The chassis turnover for 1929 (a year in which the financial period was extended to 14 months to bring the former into line with the calendar year) only just exceeded the figure for 1926 even though a slightly larger number of chassis were produced. It was the last year in which sales of the large and small car were to be in the ratio of three to two. In 1930, the 40/50 h.p. market virtually collapsed, only 423 being sold compared with 648 in the previous fourteen months and an average of 546 per annum during the period 1924–9.

The sale of 20 h.p. chassis also declined substantially, the total reduction of chassis turnover being over £420,000. This was more than compensated by an increase of £150,000 in aero turnover which yielded an additional gross profit of £90,000. Total manufacturing profit thus actually increased in 1930, but this year marked the beginning of an ominous trend. During the period 1924–9 chassis manufacture had averaged 73.1 per cent of total turnover and had contributed 63.6 per cent of the gross manufacturing profit. In 1930 chassis turnover declined to 66.7 per cent of the total, contributing only 59.3 per cent of the total profit, and in the following year the recession turned into a slump. In this year only 440 chassis in all were sold, 76 of these being left-hand-drive vehicles produced at no profit for the American company. Turnover declined to little more than half the total of the previous year, and the contribution of chassis manufacture to gross profit was reduced to 21 per cent. There is no doubt whatever that the Kestrel contract, which almost doubled the aero turnover in the same period, made it possible for the company to continue in production without a serious drain on its reserves. On any basis of calculation

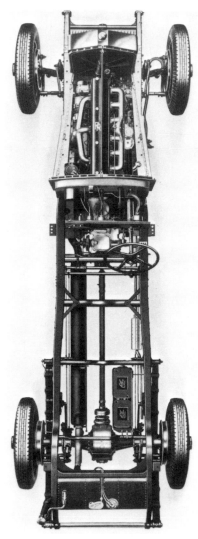

14.   The Phantom II chassis

15.   The 40/50 h.p. Phantom II engine

the company would have been unable to realise or declare a real profit on chassis manufacture alone in 1931 and 1932. There was a substantial recovery in the prosperity of the chassis division in the following two years, but it proved short-lived, and the depression may thus be said to have made Rolls-Royce economically dependent on aero-engine production for the remainder of the period under review (with the exception of the two years 1933 and 1934). The writing on the wall had, however, appeared well before 1929. Taking the period 1930–4 as a whole, chassis turnover averaged only 51.1 per cent of the total and contributed only 35.3 per cent of the gross profit, while aero turnover increased to 38.8 per cent of the turnover and contributed no less than 64.5 per cent of the gross profit.

In 1933, a year in which trade was recovering generally, the Rolls-Royce-designed 3½-litre Bentley was put on the market, and the sale of 540 of these, plus 890 of the 20/25 h.p., more than compensated for the decline in 40/50 h.p. sales, which amounted to only 239.

Considerable publicity was given to the new Bentley by E. R. Hall's successes with this car in the Tourist Trophy races in 1933 and the two following years. He had the unofficial backing and support of the company in these endeavours, unofficial because Rolls-Royce had no

16.   The Rolls-Royce-built Bentley 3½ litre Coupé de ville

intention of participating in competitive events. In this case however a certain flexibility of outlook served its purpose by demonstrating to the public that there had been no change in the character of the car now produced by Rolls-Royce under the name of Bentley.

The decline in Phantom sales and the obvious unprofitability of chassis production in 1931 and 1932 were a cause of some considerable misgiving. The inevitable comparisons were made with transatlantic practice and the almost equally inevitable conclusions were reached that nothing very much could be done within the restrictive orbit of established policy, though it was not expressed in this fashion. The Sales Division had always been afraid of the influence on the large car sales of a smaller one, for which almost as much had to be claimed in view of the fact that its price was not substantially below that of the Phantom. What had started as a 20 h.p. car became a 20/25 h.p. car, and finally a 25/30 h.p. car, in response to the demand for more power and greater weight-carrying capacity. In a letter to Sidgreaves Royce commented that this was always so: 'History generally has been that everyone makes a big car or little model and gradually enlarges it until they ultimately start a new and smaller one to fill its original place.' Royce said that he would prefer to reduce the size of the Phantom rather than increase the size of the 20/25 h.p. but this was not considered desirable, and the Phantom II replacement, the Phantom III, on which design work began in September 1934, showed a clear failure to appreciate the economic significance of the events of the previous four years. The Phantom III was designed round a V-12 engine, a magnificent but complicated piece of mechanism. It proved to be the largest and most costly car which the company had ever produced. To a considerable extent it reflected the situation that something like this had to be produced if the company's claim that it produced the finest car in the world was not to become a shallow and costly pretence. Royce, whose death occurred before work on the Phantom III started, summed the position up very accurately when he remarked, in giving his comments on the 1930 Show, and the price of American cars, that 'we have to pay for our reputation as well as live up to it.' As will be seen, the Phantom III was a high price to have to pay.

To some extent the decision to build a V-12 engine in the Phantom III was influenced by American luxury practice. The trend in the United States, even in mass-produced vehicles, was towards a larger number of cylinders. Both Packard and Cadillac had a V-12 and a V-16 on show at the 1930 Olympia. In the same year Daimler produced a V-12 engine coupled with a fluid flywheel and preselector Wilson epicyclic gear-box. By the standards of technical advance in the twenties this was a somewhat spectacular development which set designers thinking in terms of gears and transmissions and was followed by the development of synchromesh and independent suspension in the United States.[5]

In 1934 Robotham made a technical tour of the American automobile industry and in his report commented on the trends in that country. Independent front suspension and synchromesh were coming in to stay and most firms were paying a great deal of attention to weight reduction. There was in consequence a tendency to merge the body and chassis into one unit, a development which was also aimed at silence and smoothness. Performance was defintely subordinated to these two criteria, a policy which Robotham supported. He pointed out that most producers relied on a large body of specialist firms, including the luxury producers such as Cadillac and Packard, and that Rolls-Royce was the only firm in the world which still produced its own electrical components. He was convinced that it was the policy of purchasing components from specialists which enabled these two firms, whose output of the V-12 class of car was only some 400 per annum, to market these cars at £1400. Robotham was impressed by the amount which most firms spent on development and by the standard of their accep-tance tests. He recommended that Rolls-Royce should either spend more on design and development or concentrate the existing design and development effort by incorporating a large number of proprietary parts in their chassis.

There was thus an increasing realisation within the organisation that the margin of merit was diminishing rapidly, if it had not already disappeared. In a strong memorandum written in 1933 Hives was bluntly critical of the whole position.

> We do not consider the Phantom or the 25 h.p. good enough . . . It is a fact that where we are selling cars against competition there is no outstanding merit in our cars to make a customer desire to possess one. The reputation of Rolls-Royce was built up on silence and smoothness: there are a number of other cars now which are most silent, have less vibration, and a better peformance. There is no doubt about this and it is a point which can easily be confirmed by trying our competitors' cars . . . The fact that we are selling a large number of cars at the present time does not alter the position technically . . . My own view is that we are not prepared and are not shaping the right way.

Hives attributed the commercial prosperity of the firm to a doubly protected home market – protected by a high tariff and the desire to 'buy British'. This was all serious enough, but as Hives ruefully concluded, 'the alarming point is that in spite of us charging fabulous prices there remains very little profit.'

Hives was critical of the waste of experimental expenditure on the production of a number of small cars intended as replacements for the 20/25 h.p., which were scrapped because there was little prospect of producing them at a price much lower than that of the Bentley $3\frac{1}{2}$-litre.

Early in 1935 Sidgreaves, who had himself just returned from a visit to the United States, added to the chorus of self-criticism. 'I feel', he said, 'that not only are we not progressing but that we are definitely going back – in other words we are being surpassed by the Americans in particular respect of those features on which our name and reputation have been built up.' Sidgreaves was also critical of the aero-engine position where he felt that the air-cooled engine was gaining the lead.

These critical memoranda asked more questions than they answered. There was general agreement as to what was wrong, there was somewhat less agreement as to why it was wrong, and still less agreement as to what was to be done. There was a tendency to search for one principal cause or group of causes. The more fundamental questions which should have been asked were avoided. Policy was sacrosanct and no one seemed to dare question, even to himself, whether or not these developments were a symptom of industrial obsolescence, of the inadequacy of the whole structure of the British vehicle industry in a competitive world market or of the confusion between the demands of technical superiority and economic vitality. It had once been sound commercial policy for Rolls-Royce to sell technical superiority. The firm could now no longer claim, even to itself, a degree of technical superiority for its cars which would justify its attempting to base its whole production and marketing policy on this factor alone. This was attributable primarily to the stabilisation of chassis design, for stability of design favours the mass-production unit. If the exclusiveness conferred by legal devices such as patents is disregarded, technical advance must inevitably spread throughout an industry. Where, in addition to these factors, adverse to the technical superiority and economic security of the specialist firm, the economic strength of the mass-production firm enables it to devote tremendous effort to design and development as well as productive efficiency, the viability of the small organisation comes to depend increasingly on its ability, through the relative flexibility of its productive mechanism, to improve and incorporate technical advances which are made throughout the industry. But when an industry as a whole ceases to make any important technical advances, the disadvantages of the small organisation tend to overwhelm the advantages which its smallness might otherwise confer. It is forced to emulate the methods of the major units or go out of business. There remain, of course, opportunities to cater for genuine quality (mainly of materials and finish) but the struggle against the cost disadvantage of small-quantity production of the basic components which are more or less standard on all vehicles leaves little margin for extravagance in this direction. If the market itself is being affected by heavy taxation of large incomes it is not surprising that the small unit should find itself in grave difficulty.

Industrial history exhibits many examples of the reluctance of individuals to admit the necessity or decide the character of major changes which must inevitably destroy the comfortable security and familiarity of existing forms and institutions. Even when a sequence of undeniably adverse events threatens this security both the formal and informal organisation of an institution reveal a remarkable power of inhibiting the formulation of policies which will completely alter its character. Those institutions which survive are those which nurture within themselves individuals whose independence of judgement and outlook enable them to perceive the necessity for change and adaptation, especially when this is more than marginal in extent. To achieve this, men must feel able to speak freely without prejudice to their position. This was certainly possible within Rolls-Royce at this time.

The pace of technical advance in the early thirties tended to focus criticism on the design and experimental department. There was some justification for this but the failure of the design and experimental staff to maintain the great margin of supremacy in the technical excellence of the chassis was attributable to the fact that the department was badly organised and tried to do too much.[6] There was a strong case for separating chassis and aero-engine design into two separate departments. The specialisation in both fields made increasing demands on designers and engineers and there are always few men of Royce's calibre whose natural engineering competence enable them to make a contribution at almost any point. This did not reflect a decline in the average level of ability so much as an increase in complexity, but while Royce was alive his status as Chief Engineer made it difficult to introduce the changes which logic dictated. The manufacturing side of the experimental department also handled both chassis and aero work and it was not until rearmament was in full swing that it became imperative to separate these activities.

The changes which were required in the whole organisation by what were virtually worldwide developments in the technique of automobile manufacture were much more fundamental than those which the firm was in fact able to introduce before the outbreak of the Second World War. They required throughout the firm an attitude of mind very different from that which had prevailed in the twenties. Royce had probably done more than most to develop a conservative attitude, but he cannot altogether be blamed for the failure of his successors to understand the consequences of changes in the structure of the industry which, as his minutes reveal, he himself understood remarkably well, even though he would not accept their implications.

It has up to this point been both possible and desirable to discuss the history of aero-engine and chassis production together. Both were considered as more or less interdependent activities by the management, both products were produced in the same factory and designed and built by the same designers and engineers.

The year 1935 marks the point at which it ceases to be desirable or possible to treat the development of the firm in this integrated manner except from the point of view of the overall financial and economic results. In 1935 Rolls-Royce became primarily an aero-engine firm. Though it did not abandon chassis production, its history from this point onwards in primarily that of a major aero-engine manufacturer. The following chapter will discuss development of chassis production policy, and the formulation of a solution for the various problems which this chaptor has discussed. It will conclude, for the purposes of this study, the history of chassis production, which was not restarted until 1946.

10 The Battle of Costs

The discussions which have already been summarised in the previous chapter reveal that the design staff and senior executives of the company were well aware that progress in design and in mass-production manufacturing techniques, both in Britain and the United States, had seriously undermined the economic security of the chassis division. The price which the company was paying, and asking, for its reputation was undoubtedly excessive, not because of any deliberate policy but simply because of the production economics involved in the manufacture of a small number of cars. Yet the management, though fully aware of the fact that the chassis division had not paid its way during the depression, and that it appeared unlikely to do so in the future, made no attempt to measure the relative strength of the two branches of production until 1938. Many important items of expenditure which could without much effort have been allocated with some degree of accuracy between chassis and aero production were combined and deducted from the gross manufacturing profit of the two divisions.

The illusion of independent profitability was thus maintained. This is probably attributable to the fact that the company was prosperous and that turnover and gross profit showed every sign of increasing as the rearmament expansion continued. Moreover those executives primarily responsible for policy in both divisions were at this time very fully occupied with the production problems of the aero division. This preoccupation showed no signs of diminishing and had it not been for the persistent attention given to the problem of costs by several of the chassis division engineers and officials who were not really responsible for policy it is unlikely that the concept of rationalisation would have developed, and still less likely that the company would have had the confidence to return to chassis production in 1946.

W. A. Robotham, now Chief Designer of the Chassis Division, was primarily responsible for the vigour with which the cost problem was attacked and for the eventual modification of the conservative design and production principles which had previously defied all attempts at reform.

In his reply to Sidgreaves' memorandum[1] he pointed out that if the Americans were ahead this could be attributed to only two things. Either Rolls-Royce technicians were technically incapable or the overall policy directing the efforts of the various divisions was unsatisfactory. He suggested that the company should make far greater use of proprietary parts and concentrate design and development effort on major items. General Motors, with a capital one hundred times as great as Rolls-Royce, employed a proprietary carburettor, the Stromberg, over which the Wraith carburettor could claim very little advantage. He advocated a greater degree of decentralisation in the design department which experience had shown to be capable of achieving surprisingly good results when presented with 'a limited and fixed objective'. The decision to abandon the development of one of the experimental small chassis built in the early thirties he considered to have been ill-advised, and concluded that 'in the past policy has delayed improvements far more than the technical capacity of the factory'.

There were four directions in which policy could have developed at this time. The first would have involved planning for quantity production, with an output of from five to ten thousand chassis per annum. Historical tradition exercised the most powerful veto over this possibility. Figures of this magnitude were not seriously considered until just before the outbreak of war, when the 'rationalised range' concept had been fully developed. The second possibility was to reduce costs by purchasing proprietary components from specialist manufacturers wherever possible. This also went strongly against the grain but was seriously considered and partially adopted. The third direction from which the assault on cost could be supported was design, which had hitherto ignored for all practical purposes the criterion of manufacturing economy.[2] The fourth possibility was to reduce other components of manufacturing cost – material, machining, assembly. Material costs were to receive the closest scrutiny of these three, but the very substantial items of cost not directly attributable to manufacture or development were either completely disregarded or regarded as a fixed and irreducible minimum over which the chassis cost committee – even though this committee included the managing director – had no control. An even more surprising omission is the fact that no consideration whatever was given to the policy on which the company had originally established its reputation and its economic prosperity – the policy of producing one chassis. Three vehicles were now being produced, the Phantom II 40/50 h.p., the 25/30 h.p. and the 3½-litre Bentley. All were shortly to be replaced by slightly larger vehicles with an improved performance.

The proposal to purchase proprietary components was strongly opposed by Wormald, who had been with the company from the earliest days with Royce and had been elected a director in 1929. His personal stature as works manager was considerable and though a socialist by political conviction his technical and administrative policies were most conservative. 'It is questionable', he said, 'whether we can purchase outside units of Rolls-Royce design and specification in the quantities we require at as low a cost as we can produce them ourselves.' Aero-engine sub-contracting experience he considered to have confirmed this point of view. It is clear from his use of the phrase 'Rolls-Royce design and specification' that Wormald did not appreciate the fact that the component firm derived its main economies from the production of standardised components. He was a diehard exponent of the old tradition of copying and improving the best. 'There is only one reason', he said, 'why we ever recommended adopting a bought-out unit and that is because we have not had a satisfactory design of our own.' This controversy arose mainly over the proposal to buy carburettors and clutches from specialist producers and Wormald did not accept the fact that, however desirable it might be for Rolls-Royce to design and develop every component on the car, such a policy was now beyond the financial and technical resources of the organisation. In an industry which was becoming increasingly specialised it was impossible for a unit with an output as small as that of Rolls-Royce to compete without taking advantage of the specialised facilities which the industry as a whole had created.

The situation was in a sense paradoxical in that those units of the industry which produced the largest numbers and could most afford to manufacture their own components relied heavily on the specialist manufacturer of components. Those firms which could least afford to do so, if only from the point of view of manufacturing economy, had allowed themselves to grow into a position in which their reputation was to some degree associated by their customers with the fact that their components were non-standard. There was therefore some opposition to the proposal on the grounds that, if the change were made, the customer would be dissatisfied whether or not the proprietary article was technically superior to that which it had replaced. This argument applied more to the conspicuous items on the chassis but these, generally speaking, were precisely those items on which considerable economies appeared to be obtainable without a drastic reorganisation of design and production methods.

The new policy was applied very tentatively on the Bentley $4\frac{1}{4}$-litre and the Rolls-Royce Wraith which were put on the market in 1935 and 1936 respectively but the possibility of further substantial economies in this direction had by no means been exhausted by the outbreak of war. Early in 1936 Hives, who succeeded Wormald as general works manager in October, pointed out that the decision to purchase radiators from a specialist manufacturer had saved thousands of pounds and eliminated numerous complaints. There had been some criticism from the design department of certain other items which had either been standardised or were on trial in experimental vehicles, but he felt that once the firm had adopted a proprietary article it should make the best of it. He supported the policy mainly on the grounds that it facilitated a very desirable concentration of design effort and remarked in a minute on the subject that Rolls-Royce 'had dropped so far behind with major components such as frames, springing, engines, steering, brakes, etc. that wherever we can get help outside we have got to take advantage of it in order to be able to tackle these major problems.'

It was clear from the start that this policy was a palliative rather than a cure, designed to reduce or at least to stabilise the cost of the chassis to whose production the company was already fully committed. The analysis of material costs and of production methods also offered some immediately realisable advantages, but it soon became clear that a more radical departure from existing practice would be needed if the company was to achieve the necessary manufacturing economies within the limits of small-quantity production. Not only did Rolls-Royce produce a small number of cars in all; this small total now comprised three basically different types of vehicle all of which shared an almost negligible quantity of common components. After wrestling with this situation Robotham came forward with the concept of a 'rationalised' range of cars. If it was undesirable or impossible under existing circumstances to limit the number of types the least that could be done was to endeavour to redesign these types so that they could all be built up from the same basic components, utilising identical accessories where these bore no necessary relation to the size of the vehicle. The near similarity in size of the Phantom, the Wraith and the Bentley – the smaller cars having increased steadily in size as Royce had predicted – and their marked dissimilarity in manufacturing requirements suggested that considerable economies might be obtained in this way.

Robotham considered that the policy of producing two chassis, the one scaled down by about eight-tenths of the other, was 'altogether too extravagant from the production design and development point of view' and resulted in a 'frantic scramble to keep the whole range up to date'. He suggested that the two chassis frames, brake gear, steering axles and suspension layout should be identical, the increased accommodation on the Phantom being obtained by increasing the length of a standard frame. The original scheme contemplated that the two cars would have different engines and gearboxes and also envisaged the development of a similar scheme between the 20/25 h.p. and the small Bentley. The latter required a different frame, suspension and steering to provide the peformance expected from a sports car, but this would be suitable for a small Rolls-Royce. This car Robotham considered could be placed on the market at £990 if it was given a steel body.

This proposal amounted to yet another revival of the 'small-car project' and in his defence Robotham argued that the large-car market was steadily declining in importance and that even the Spectre (the name of an experimental 25/30 h.p. car which was designed as a replacement for the original 20/25 h.p.) would find a much smaller market than expected. Compared even with the Phantom III, which appeared late in 1936, it could not possibly claim to be a small car. Its production would, moreover, have dissipated development effort which should have been directed at features which could not be 'bought off the shelf' and Robotham concluded that if the experimental department were relieved of the obligation to handle clutches, carburettors and electrical components it would 'undoubtedly handle the programme of the four cars outlined above with far greater ease and efficiency'.

Though he knew better than to expect an enthusiastic reception for a scheme which, for Rolls-Royce, was relatively far-reaching and aroused Sidgreaves' scepticism, Robotham perserved with the development and advocacy of this policy. He proceeded to turn the energies of the design and development staff towards two objectives. These were the reduction of the cost of manufacture of the existing types and the development of an entirely new range of cars similar in size and catering for the same sectors of the market but employing identical components in their construction wherever possible. The attainment of both objectives was to be assisted by a rationalisation of production and manufacturing methods wherever these proved to be feasible.

A number of further investigations into material and component costs showed that further economies were attainable in various directions. Proprietary starters and dynamos were tested out on experimental cars and it was found that the difference in cost between these and the Rolls-Royce components was equal to the cost of the chassis frame. The Rolls-Royce shock absorbers cost £7 18s 6d compared with £3 for the proprietary substitute. The exhaust system cost £12 13s 6d while an American type of exhaust system could have been produced, even in Rolls-Royce quantities, for just over £1. The American-type exhaust might fail in two years whereas the Rolls-Royce was unlikely to fail under five, but, as Robotham pointed out, the customer would be better off in ninety-nine cases out of one hundred if he employed the less costly system and replaced it if and when it failed. 'This', he said, 'is how the situation is treated by every other car manufacturer. We are beginning to think that this is a rational outlook.'

In the case of certain major bought-out components such as crankcase castings and crankshafts, which were obtained in an unfinished state and machined at Derby, it was found that production economies were directly related to quantity and that major reduction in cost could only be obtained by increasing the quantity purchased, which would induce suppliers to install machines of increasing complexity and cost. An eight-cylinder crankcase, for example, would cost £4 14s 0d produced as a sand-casting on the floor, £3 15s 8d as a sand-casting on an automatic machine, £2 2s 9d as a die-casting (involving a tool cost of £350), and £1 8s 6d in pressed steel (involving a tool cost of £550). This particular case illustrates the very substantial economies which were obtainable for comparatively small increases in output. For a production of 212 crankcases it would have been cheaper to employ the third rather than the second process, and for a production of only 785 it would have been cheaper to employ the pressed steel method. Since production was unlikely to exceed 400 per annum, the third method would have involved the risk of ordering a two-years' supply of each type which might have become completely redundant in the event of the failure of the model concerned.

In the case of crankshaft forgings it was found that although the price paid for these by Rolls-Royce was more than twice the estimated cost of production with the latest American type of equipment, the capital cost of erecting a suitable plant to supply Rolls-Royce aero and chassis forgings was £25,000.[3] This outlay would have been completely recovered in just under two years on the basis of a production of 7500 crankshafts per annum but had chassis crankshafts alone been considered this period would have been about three times as long. The matter was further investigated by R. H. Coverley, who had recently joined the chassis division and discovered that the suppliers were not entirely to blame for the high cost of Rolls-Royce forgings. Rolls-Royce crankshafts had integral balance weights, and the wear on the dies employed in their production was considerable. Check-pieces were demanded from each shaft and the wastage of material was as high as 50 per cent. The English Steel Corporation informed Coverley that they employed their best men on this work, which was separated from their mass production lines, and that these men were paid 20 per cent more than their other employees. Most manufacturers were content to use .40 carbon content steel, costing £22 per ton, whereas Rolls-Royce demanded a high-grade V.C.M. steel, costing £43 per ton. The English Steel Corporation pointed out to Coverley that the total Rolls-Royce order amounted to some 4000 crankshafts per annum whereas one of the larger producers of popular cars ordered 170,000 per annum. One possible alternative, which had been widely adopted in the United States, was a patent hardening process which brought the carbon steel crankshafts almost up to the V.C.M. standard, but even this process did not permit the recovery of the capital costs over the production of such a small number of chassis.

In the case of rear axle shafts it was found that all firms quoted the same price whether the order was for 500 or 1000, indicating either that there were no production economies to be obtained within this small range of increase or, what is more likely, that the suppliers did not intend to pass them on. In the case of many other smaller components die-casting would have made possible considerable economies, but the tool costs could not be recovered over the quantity for which the dies were likely to be used. In most cases, the cost of dies alone could not be recovered unless there was a minimum production order for 2000 standardised parts.

The question of body production raised several important issues. The first attempt to produce something approaching the standard body of the mass-production firms was made with the introduction of the Bentley. In the twenties and early thirties, the firm had produced bodies for about an eighth of its total output of chassis. The average turnover from this was less than £100,000, on which the gross manufacturing profit (calculated in the same manner as that of chassis production) averaged about £7000 until 1930, after which it fell to £4000, a figure which was not improved despite the increase in body turnover resulting from the manufacture of standard bodies for the Bentley. It is unlikely that this figure was large enough to absorb even a proportionate share of the unallocated overhead expenditure of the chassis division, quite apart from the very considerable design and development expenses which were associated with the production of bodies. After the introduction of the Bentley about half the total sales of this car were made with standard bodies, the total output of bodies being in the vicinity of 300 per annum. A small manufacturing profit continued to be made on the Rolls-Royce bodies, but the Bentley bodies were produced at a loss.

The majority of Rolls-Royce and Bentley chassis were fitted with coachbuilt bodies by several well-known coachbuilding firms, the most important of which were Hoopers, Park Wards, Thrupp & Maberly, Barkers and Windovers. These firms specialised in the production of custom-built bodies which catered for the individual tastes and eccentricities of the rich. They built bodies primarily on the Rolls-Royce class of chassis and the output of the entire group before the Second World War averaged little more than 1500 bodies at most. Each body was a hand-made affair, usually of composite wood and steel construction. They were exquisitely finished; their construction exhibited the very highest standards of craftsmanship. But the same forces which had already made their influence so strongly felt on the manufacturers of high-priced chassis were also operating in this field. Mass-production techniques of body construction had developed bodies which were, in many respects, technically superior to the custom-built body. The very large price differential could not be justified purely on technical grounds.

Such industries doubtless arise and survive because economic man is not a rational animal and will sometimes pay very heavily to acquire and exhibit such desirable badges of wealth, distinction or success.

The production of a standardised body for all or nearly all the Rolls-Royce and Bentley output would obviously have had a significant impact on the profitability of the chassis division. A number of the design staff also felt that it would be increasingly difficult to uphold the technical reputation of the entire car, however excellent the chassis, unless the body could be kept up to the same standard. Most of the Bentley bodies were sub-contracted to Park Ward, and it was felt that as a mere trade customer Rolls-Royce had insufficient control over the work of this firm. Robotham considered that it would ultimately be necessary to manufacture the great majority of Rolls-Royce and Bentley bodies at Derby in the interests both of economical production and design. 'We find it difficult', he said, 'to understand any policy that does not ultimately lead to us producing our own bodies. Many features . . . only give satisfaction if engineered in conjunction with a chassis . . . heaters, radios, noise insulation.' The solution of this problem was again found to depend on the relationship between the cost of dies and the production quantities over which it was possible to recover the capital outlay. The cost of the white unfinished body shell by Park Ward's construction methods was £70. The next type of body (all steel front-end and centre pillars die-pressed, panels semi-pressed by hand and reinforced with timber) would have involved a tool and die cost of £20,000. An output of 727 bodies of one type would have made it economical to employ this method which reduced the cost of the shell to £42 10s 0d. The third type of construction (all-steel front end and centre panels, all panels die-pressed and reinforced with timber) would have involved a tool cost of £55,000. A minimum production quantity of 1600 would have been necessary to recover the capital cost of this method, which reduced the final cost to £36. The final possibility was an all-steel shell similar to that employed by the largest mass production manufacturers. The die costs for this method were £76,000, but the cost of an all-steel shell produced in this way was only £28 and a minimum of 1800 bodies of one type would have had to be produced.

Several interesting points emerge from these figures. In the first place, the maximum rate of reduction in cost is obtainable with a surprisingly small increase in the quantity produced. (Assuming that a coachbuilder such as Park Ward was already producing 300 bodies per annum this figure would have had to be increased to just over 1000.) At this point, a similar increase in output would have achieved a reduction in cost only one-fifth as great as that achieved by the first change in method. The final method required only a relatively small increase in quantity (200) to make possible a greater saving (£8 per body shell) than that brought about by increasing the quantity produced by 900.

A further point of some significance is that once a firm has committed itself to, say, the second method, the increase in output required to justify scrapping the existing dies and adopting the third method is very considerably greater than the quantity required to justify the adoption of that method at the outset. In this case it would be 8400. If the third method had once been adopted it would require a further increase in output of 9500 bodies to justify a change to the last method. From this it is obvious that mass-production techniques should not be adopted in small doses.[4] This is a lesson which had not been learnt by the British motor-car industry in the first half of the twentieth century. The majority of firms preferred to proceed, at immense cost, from one stage to the next rather than take the risk of jumping the intervening steps. Many considerations other than cost have naturally affected these decisions but it seems fair to conclude that some of the most important factors in cost reduction have generally not been appreciated and that firms have lacked the capital or the nerve – both are equally necessary – to reorganise their production to take full advantage of mass-production methods. Many appear to have stuck half way in a position where the capital cost of further cost-reduction schemes seems disproportionately great.

In a memorandum on this subject Robotham remarked that 'it is difficult enough to get results even when everyone is clear about the objective.' Where there is no clarity of purpose the outcome of most policy discussions will be an explanation if not a justification of the *status quo*. Future uncertainties and the facile hope that a succession of minor alterations will combine to make a major improvement generally provide a ready excuse for the industrial Micawberism that has inflicted so much of British industry since the Second World War.

'What we think is lacking', he continued, 'is a co-ordination of the original programme, the basic design, the manufacturing facilities available from past experience and the proposed selling price of the article in order to reach some well-defined objective with the ultimate product.' Such a degree of co-ordination could not have been achieved on the basis of the inadequate knowledge of real costs with which the management was content in the inter-war years.

The management was obviously not ready to adopt any scheme as radical as these figures implied but when, late in 1938, the possibility of acquiring the coachbuilding firm of Park Ward presented itself, the board decided that this was desirable not only from the point of view of technical control and cost reduction but also because of the scarcity of skilled coachbuilding labour. Such labour would have been difficult to train within the organisation had Rolls-Royce finally decided to embark on some more ambitious scheme. Park Ward had an authorised capital of £100,000 of which only £45,105 had been issued, the stock being almost entirely controlled by a small group of shareholders who managed the business. The company was in difficulties and had made a loss of £2658 in the first six months of 1938. The overdraft facilities were just about exhausted and the company would probably have gone insolvent had Rolls-Royce not intervened. This would have interferred seriously with the output of Bentley bodies and in view of rearmament committments it would not have been possible to bring this work into the Derby factory, even if the management had wished to do so. A controlling interest was therefore purchased for £30,000 and shortly afterwards the remaining Park Ward shareholders were induced to accept Rolls-Royce stock in exchange on an agreed basis, the total cost of the transaction being £82,000.

This acquisition was quite incidental to the development of the rationalised range. It did not facilitate any important changes in production methods or policy, partly because of the physical separation of the Park Ward factory, which was in London, and partly because the declining market in 1939 and the outbreak of war suspended serious work on all chassis plans and projects for five years.

Those most concerned with this project could easily have admitted defeat and used the imminence of war as an excuse for shelving plans which appeared increasingly unlikely ever to be put into operation. They refused to do so, even though mitigating circumstances were plentiful, and continued development work on the rationalised range until the outbreak of war. The partial application of some of Robotham's ideas had brought about small, but not negligible gains. The unexpectedly high cost of the Phantom III and the steadily declining demand for all high-priced cars gave added impetus to the formulation of a production scheme which would enable the chassis division as a whole to operate at a profit.

The Phantom III was a serious disappointment from the cost of production point of view. While the chassis was still under development in May 1935 Sidgreaves had been informed that it would cost less than the Phantom II, a car which is still regarded by many as one of the most superb examples of automobile engineering ever produced. It was also expected that the Wraith would prove cheaper than the 25/30 h.p. car; but neither expectation proved correct. The main reasons for the increase were the very heavy development charges incurred on a completely new type of V-12 engine and independent suspension, and a rise of approximately £100 in labour cost per chassis. Little attempt had been made to produce an economic design, since the car was conceived in 1933–4 before the management had begun to investigate the real causes of the loss incurred in chassis manufacture. The Phantom III was the result of an all-out attempt to regain technical supremacy rather than an attempt to control cost.

One of the most serious aspects of this discovery was that the costing control did not provide the relevant information until several months after the company had fully committed itself to production. This prompted a pertinent comment from Hives. 'I have always held the view that accountants make just as many mistakes as engineers, but that it is very much more difficult to find them out.' The inadequacy and delay in the presentation of accounting information necessary for production control purposes was one of the principal reasons for the decision to employ the services of a firm of consultant production engineers.

To a very considerable extent this confusion arose from the long-established tradition of secrecy which had taken such a firm hold of the organisation that not even those executives who should have known what was happening had more than a vague idea of the realities of the situation. This was undoubtedly due to the fact that there was a quite evident 'guilty conscience' about the fact that the rates of profit were so markedly higher in the aero division. It was felt that this would be difficult to justify to the Air Ministry. The management can hardly be blamed for this, since it is more than likely that the Air Ministry officials would have jumped to the conclusion, had they been presented with this information, that the aero division was 'subsidising' the chassis division. But, as Hives pointed out, this was no excuse for the management confusing itself. 'I have a feeling', he said, 'that our accountancy feel that as long as they can confuse the accounts so that the Air Ministry cost officials cannot understand them, they are doing very well, but unfortunately we suffer from the same confusion. Personally, I doubt whether they do deceive anybody. I look upon the Air Ministry cost people as something like the Income Tax people – they have so much experience of people trying to confuse them that they know all the answers.'

One of the most frequent explanations of the high cost of the Rolls-Royce chassis had always been that it was far more complicated than any other chassis, and that this complication was necessary in the interests of mechanical reliability and efficiency. There was some evidence to support this argument[5] but investigation soon revealed that complication of design could be held responsible for only a very small proportion of the cost differential. It was certainly no justification, argued Robotham, 'for the fact that we cannot produce cars at the price at which they are sold and yet make a profit'.

The search for further causes of high cost was accentuated by the steady decline in demand which took place from 1937 onwards and by the fact that although the turnover of the chassis division in 1937 exceeded that of 1929, the gross manufacturing profit was barely half that achieved in the earlier period. The chassis division as a whole undoubtedly made a net loss, and though increasing taxation and the threat of war were partially to blame for the precipitous decline in orders in 1938, there was little doubt that a permanent shrinkage of the market had taken, or was about to take place. Though the Bentley had made a good name for itself and a large contribution to turnover, its contribution to manufacturing profit declined steadily from 1936 onwards. It was obvious that the existing state of affairs could not continue indefinitely. Had the company as a whole been dependent on chassis manufacture alone the financial position would have been very serious indeed by the beginning of 1938, as the figures in Appendix XI clearly reveal.

Under Robotham's leadership, the Experimental Department had laid the foundations for a scheme of production which was potentially economic during the years 1936–8, but despite this intensive effort, the target of £950 per chassis was not in sight. The design and development staff had just about exhausted the possibilities of cost reduction on the various aspects of production which came under their influence or control. A completely new range of six rationalised chassis (one of which was left-hand-drive) employing common components had been developed in two years at a cost of £9500 per model, a set of figures which compared very favourably with that of the previous seven years, in which only three models had been evolved at an aggregate cost of £66,000 per model. The greatest reduction in cost on the new range had been achieved on materials,[6] but calculations soon showed that this was insufficient. The Bentley V (the large Bentley which was to succeed the 4½-litre) came nearest of the chassis in the rationalised range to the target figure, and an analysis of its production costs supported the view that very little further reduction in cost could be expected from attention to design.[7] While the direct production cost of the car was £614, this figure was increased to £1022 by indirect expenses amounting to no less than £408, of which £377 represents sales expenditure (an item which included a large amount of administration expenses as well as advertising) and the inevitable trade discount.

These figures were disturbing, for, as Robotham remarked, 'we have eliminated all extravagances from the Bentley V except the servo gearbox (the servo accounting for only 7 per cent of the gearbox cost) and . . . have nothing that is not included in some American $1500 specification.' Nor could refinement be blamed for the high cost of the chassis since it was estimated that the three features peculiar to Rolls-Royce products – the servo, the side-change mechanism and governor control – accounted for only 2 per cent of the cost of the chassis. High finish accounted for 7 per cent. A programme to reduce the excessive number of pieces and machining operations was expected to yield no more than a 5 per cent saving in cost.

In further pursuit of this will-o'-the-wisp of high cost an attempt was made to explain the difference in price between the SS Jaguar, a sports car which had just appeared on the market and had caused much comment, and the Bentley 50 – the production Bentley 4½-litre. The market price of the Jaguar was £450, that of the Bentley £950. The Bentley had servo brakes, one-shot lubrication and lubricated road springs, features which were not supplied on the Jaguar. The Jaguar had an adjustable steering wheel which was not provided on the Bentley. The Bentley engine was 10–15 per cent more costly because of design and materials, but the frame was produced by the same makers and was cheaper. The Jaguar exhaust, on the other hand, was more costly than that on the Bentley. It was decided that an allowance of 25 per cent of the difference in price for design differences in favour of the Bentley would be generous. Alloy steel and aluminium employed in the Bentley engine accounted for 3 per cent of the factory cost of the latter. The Bentley crankshaft was twice as expensive although it was made of the same material and was a less complicated design. The Jaguar body cost £80 to manufacture and the total weight of the car was 150 lb lighter than that of the Bentley, the saving in weight being entirely justified. The remaining 70 per cent difference in price could not be explained except by what the report described as 'good manufacturing technique backed up by sound purchasing of fabricated parts'.

All this was informative but not exactly encouraging to those who had been struggling with the problem for several years. Few lines of attack were left open. It was considered that a reduction in the standards of silence and durability might yield a saving of 10 per cent, but this was contrary to practice and policy. There was still scope for further use of proprietary components, but under normal conditions an extension of this policy would take work out of the factory.

The pressure of aero-engine rearmament work on the resources of the Derby factory was undoubtedly an important factor in the evolution of chassis production policy during this period. Had the management decided to adopt a quantity production scheme its implementation would have been exceedingly difficult and would probably have involved the erection of a new factory. Hives would have welcomed such a step, for he had long felt that a good many of the Derby traditions were a severe handicap to any management attempting to take advantage of new manufacturing techniques. The erection of a completely new factory for chassis manufacture would have been a bold step at this stage since there was obviously no guarantee that the Derby factory would continue to be fully occupied by aero work. Chassis manufacture was coming to be regarded, rightly from many points of view, as of secondary importance. It is not surprising, therefore, that those who were attempting to lay the foundations of a completely new system of production should have been discouraged by the somewhat passive reception of their plans and ideas. In some firms the effects of war were felt long before 1939.

Much of this work on costs was nevertheless valuable and instructive. It eliminated waste and extravagance in many processes and methods where it was not previously thought to exist, but there was no escape from the main implication of each and every investigation. Low cost could not possibly be obtained without quantity production. This conclusion was strongly supported by a comprehensive analysis of the operations of the chassis division in 1937 – apparently the first of its kind – which was carried out by R. H. Coverley. This report stressed many of the factors which have already been discussed but concluded that production policy could not escape the main share of the blame. Frequent design modifications introduced to stimulate sales had increased the already heavy expenditure on jigs and tools to a point where there was no hope of recovering it over the quantities for whose production they would be used. From 1935 to 1937 jig and tool charges had cost £247,554, an amount which had to be recovered over the production of only 4094 chassis. The Phantom III jig and tool costs alone amounted to £182 per chassis. To liquidate these costs at the rate of £50 per chassis would have required the production of a further 1400 cars. To reduce this figure to £10 per chassis, production would have had to be increased to 9200.

Coverley attributed the profitability of the chassis division in the 'good old days' – a fact frequently used in support of the argument that there was nothing wrong with the *status quo* that could not be cured by gentle modification – to four factors. These were the considerably lower overhead charges per chassis, lower development expenses per chassis due to concentration on one type, much lower sales expenses and lower guarantee costs due to the lower mileage covered during the guarantee period.

Coverley also emphasised that there was no point in ignoring the mitigating fact that the 1937 chassis was a much more complicated and efficient mechanism than that produced in 1920, and that this had to be paid for. High manufacturing cost was not attributable to lengthy process times. Information from sub-contract work showed that manufacturing process times in Rolls-Royce plants compared very favourable with those elsewhere. Substantial cost differences arose from 'frequent dislocation of machine equipment employed on small quantities in the course of manufacture'. Coverley recommended the determination of an annual sales policy well in advance, fixed production schedules, and a careful control of jig and tool costs to ensure their liquidation within a given time over a calculated number of chassis.[8]

Not one of these measures would have had much effect on indirect expenditure, which in 1937 was calculated to amount to £308,038. This figure comprised £86,000 for development expenditure, £60,000 for guarantee expenses and £161,000 for sales expenditure. The inclusion of the whole of the last figure (which was the total for both chassis and aero divisions) was an elementary accounting error, but if it is divided in proportion to chassis and aero turnover, a total of £70,000 is attributable to chassis manufacture, reducing the total indirect expenditure under these heads from £308,000 to £217,000. The total cost of chassis manufacture in 1937 was £1,482,964 of which £1,194,572 was allocated in the financial accounts before obtaining the gross manufacturing profit. The total of unallocated indirect expenditure attributable to chassis work amounts to £217,073, a figure which converts the gross manufacturing profit of £110,583 into a net loss of £106,490 (making no allowance for various small adjustment items which do not affect the order of magnitude of these calculations). The chassis division, taken by itself, was in much the same position as the Bentley Company had found itself in 1929 and for very much the same reasons. 'Uncontrolled indirect expenditures', concluded the report, 'have been the major factors contributing to the uneconomical chassis position with which we are faced today.'

By the middle of 1939 it had become quite obvious that under existing conditions even the rationalised range could not be put on the market at a profit unless production exceeded a minimum of 1500 to 2000 cars a year. And since even this level of production would probably not have enabled the large cars to have been marketed at a price which would enable that number to be sold, it was essential, if the minimum volume of production was to be maintained, to produce a very much smaller car which would retail for about £400 to £500. Robotham therefore recommended that a 2.8-litre 4-cylinder car employing rationalised parts should be designed and developed. 'We have got to go for a lower price class', he argued, 'and to get the price down and make the project worthwhile we have got to appeal to a different and wider public.' Robotham would have preferred to design this car round a standard rationalised four-cylinder engine, but, as he pointed out, the public associated running cost with engine displacement despite the fact that even down to the £200 class of car depreciation was a far more important item of expense and it would have been expensive 'to educate Englishmen as to the fallacy of their views'.

Another possibility which Robotham envisaged was for the company to enter completely new lines of business such as commercial vehicle production, for which a diesel engine was most suitable. These could be fitted to rail-cars, long-distance buses and other similar types of vehicle. Hives favoured this project, but the outbreak of war prevented any work being done on it. The small car, appropriately named the Myth, was completed, but its ultimate fate had likewise to be postponed until the conclusion of hostilities in 1945.

From all this corporate introspection, there emerged a clear and unequivocal choice which Robotham stated as follows. 'Are we to forsake quality for quantity or find some outlet for our energies where quality can be made to pay?' These were not in fact the alternatives facing the management. The choice lay between producing the highest grade of vehicle in such quantities as would enable it to be sold at a price which did not ignore the limited potentialities of an increasingly discriminating market and abandoning altogether the manufacture of chassis of any description. What was clearly required was a completely new conception of quality which took into account the progress of the industry throughout the world, both in manufacturing techniques and in industrial specialisation, the standardisation of design, the substantial and continuing changes in the distribution of wealth and incomes, the political and social attitudes which were both cause and effect of this change, and above all the company's own costly experience during the previous two decades. Adaptation to the environment, which is the only sure guarantee of any form of survival, requires, both of countries and of those economic institutions on which their strength is based, a continual redefinition of principle and policy in terms of present circumstances and future possibilities. Institutions and policies must never be allowed to become ends in themselves. There is a limit to the extent to which the cumulative differential of change can be met by a series of piecemeal adaptations. A bold reformation of policy is often risky and dangerous, but no institution is indispensable in a progressive society, whatever the system of production, and no society in a progressive world in which the independent units are not isolated can avoid the assumption of risk. Societies, or institutions, which seek to avoid it never fail to attribute the consequences of their failure to the malignity of fate.

Towards the middle of 1939, the management seemed to be almost prepared to take the steps which were necessary to give effect to the production plan which Robotham had formulated. These were clearly essential if the chassis division was to make a fair contribution to the prosperity of the company in the event of a serious decline in rearmament orders in 1940 and 1941. The decision as to how many chassis should be produced in 1940 appeared to be controlled by four factors which Robotham enumerated in a report written a few weeks before the outbreak of war. These were the absorptive capacity of the market, the minimum number that must be sold to enable the chassis division as a whole to make a profit, the minimum number 'that the engineering and production department would like to produce with a view to learning how to fabricate at a price that will enable the factory to be kept busy after rearmament ceases' (this was put at 1200), and finally 'the maximum number that Hs. [Hives] would like to make in view of his rearmament commitments'. This figure was put at 1000, a somewhat optimistic estimate in view of the fact that only 597 chassis had been produced in 1938 and less than 400 in the first eight months of 1939.[9] It was estimated that the net profit on a production of 700 cars would be £43,490 and on 1200 £193,900, the increase resulting exclusively from a reduction in overheads per chassis. Robotham was still urging that the small car should be put into production if and when opportunity offered.

Within a few weeks, however, all work in the chassis division was suspended. For a while, until it became possible to absorb their energies in other directions, a small nucleus of the design and development department continued to work on post-war plans. As far as the chassis division was concerned it seemed that Vegetius's epigram could well have been reversed – *Qui desiderat bellum praeparet pacem*. During the first few months of the war – that period so aptly described as the phoney war – there was a good deal of stocktaking and self-criticism, especially in relation to post-war plans. Robotham thought that the war would last four years and that, at its conclusion, Rolls-Royce would become dependent once more on chassis production. He did not envisage the development of a civil market for liquid-cooled aero engines, a prophecy which was to prove substantially correct. The output of 1200 cars contemplated under the rationalised range scheme – the details of which were far from complete – would employ only 40 per cent of the capacity of the existing factory on one shift. He suggested that all work necessary for the introduction of the rationalised range should be completed, that both lorry and tractor manufacture should be investigated, that plans for a really small car should be completed and that a $5\frac{1}{2}$-litre straight eight engine should be developed for the marine market.

Sidgreaves had by this time accepted most of the arguments which had been put forward in favour of increased production of the smaller-horsepower class of car and in a final report presented to the board in October 1939 he concluded that it was 'quite clear that the days of what might be described as the Silver Ghost mentality have gone and that there will have to be an entirely fresh outlook not only on design, manufacturing and production methods but also on sales methods.' He was convinced that the war would completely eliminate the market for the 40/50 h.p. Phantom class of car.[10] Production-Engineering, a firm of industrial consultants, was asked to examine the general situation of the chassis division and to make recommendations for the post-war period. The preamble to this report showed that Robotham's work and the experiences of the previous few years had effected a fundamental change in economic policy. 'The policy in the past has been to design the best car in the world and to base the selling price on the cost at which it can be produced under existing conditions at the Derby factory . . . It is now proposed that the starting point should be the selling price at which there is a market for a car which will still be accepted as better than any other of its class.' This study otherwise did little more than confirm most of Coverley's analysis of the causes of the existing situation but in conclusion several important suggestions were made, amongst which by far the most significant was that referring to the attitude of mind which existed at Derby:

It is apparent that one amongst other reasons why American firms are able to produce motor cars at a very much less cost, in spite of the higher labour rates, is the general attitude of mind on the part of the personnel. It is a positive attitude towards reductions in cost, improvements in method and new processes. It will thus be necessary to use the greatest care in selecting the staff who will eventually be employed on the chassis production side.

The consultants recommended a very careful analysis of overheads, a most obvious and serious deficiency, and that the volume of production should be worked out on the basis of this analysis. The significance, from the point of view of jig and tool costs, of the frequency of model changes was strongly emphasised. The firm had never succumbed to the temptation of either setting, or following, the fashion of an annual model change designed solely or primarily to give the appearance of change. Such a policy would have involved an increase in costs which would have more than offset any sales advantage that might have accrued. The high vulnerability of small-quantity production to uncontrolled overheads had always to be borne in mind but in this case virtue was not altogether the product of necessity. The Silver Ghost and the Phantom had established for themselves the enviable reputation that they were superior to this necessity and even the smaller cars continued in production virtually unchanged for several years. The name had thus become associated with stability of appearance, a stability which was anchored to the shape of the radiator, as well as with continual refinement of performance. This reputation, though fully deserved in most respects, was also most convenient from the production point of view. It nevertheless involved a special type of obligation since both the public and industry regarded the announcement of a new Rolls-Royce as an event of unusual importance. These expectations were not easily fulfilled.

In the later thirties however there was a perceptible retreat from this policy, the result of pressure of circumstances rather than conscious decision, as well as from the more fundamental policy of producing only one basic model which had ensured the profitability of chassis production in the Silver Ghost era. The management seems not only to have accepted this trend as inevitable but to have made no attempt, up to the stage of the final pre-war plans for production of a rationalised range in 1940 and 1941, to revert to a one-chassis policy. There was, if anything, a proliferation of models under the rationalised programme, since it was calculated that the chassis division could not be made to pay its own way on the basis of producing any one single type in the range, large or small.[11] The policy which was evolving would have involved tapping a proportion of the sales in several price classes. The unwritten assumption on which this conclusion was based, and which seems to have been responsible for the development of this manufacturing pattern throughout the British motor industry, was that the limits of a particular price-class were more or less absolutely fixed. Therefore no firm could expect to sell more than a certain percentage of the cars sold in a particular class, or to increase its share of the market in this class if this was already high. Since the industry could not be expected to agree to allocate the different classes of production in a rational manner, one class to a particular firm or group of firms, the safest procedure was to concentrate on that class in which the firm's reputation was strongest and, as an insurance against the capriciousness of public taste, produce several other models in the adjacent classes of production. The possibility that an outstandingly good car, produced in large quantities at a price which established a record for what might be described as all-round value per pound, might easily double or quadruple the number of cars sold in a particular class, at the expense both of the classes above it and of those below it, seems not to have been considered. The statistical characteristics of the market were regarded as given and unalterable. If this is so, as the evidence would seem to indicate, it is not surprising that the management regarded the production of several classes of car as the only means of providing a market for production in sufficient quantity to make the chassis division profitable.

In its final stages the rationalised programme for 1940/41 would have involved the production of no less than six different models. The design of these had been rationalised to the extent that they required only three lengths of frame, one front suspension with two yoke pieces giving two heights of car, three sets of body dies for standard bodies, two specialised body designs, one Bentley radiator, three Rolls-Royce radiator skirts, two engines (six- and eight-cylinder), two petrol tanks and two rear axles. Though the similarity of design features makes this list somewhat less formidable than it sounds, it might be concluded that the rationalised programme had been hoist with its own petard. This was in fact not the case. It was envisaged that the recommended range would enable the firm to gauge customer reactions and that unprofitable models could subsequently be dropped. Though three different engine sizes with nine possible capacities were mentioned it was never contemplated that more than three engines should be included in the production programme. The full range was put forward as a means of combating the day-to-day vacillations of the Treasury on the subject of car taxation. It was designed so that the size of the engine could be altered in a relatively short space of time by an alteration in cylinder bore size which could be adjusted with almost the same rapidity as the horsepower tax.

This apparent 'de-rationalisation' of the rationalised programme was commented upon by the chairman of the board, Lord Herbert Scott, in a letter to Sidgreaves in November 1939. 'It might be well to consider', he concluded, 'whether the original programme of the one model which made the name of Rolls-Royce world-famous would not be a sound proposition to revert to for the initial stages of post-war production. Such a plan commends itself to me because it would give breathing space for our sales, and those concerned to discover the reaction the war has produced on the motor car market due to taxation and other causes.' There was not much time left for consideration of these matters but in the event Lord Herbert Scott's advice was taken, and though the evolution of post-war policy belongs to a future chapter in the history of the company, it is significant that most of the lessons of the thirties were not wasted. A single basic type of six-cylinder chassis was put into production at Crewe in 1946. A great deal of the work and development which had been put into the rationalised range was employed in its design and there is little doubt that the reversion to a single-chassis policy made possible the production of the Rolls-Royce and Bentley chassis at post-war prices which had increased less than most makes of cars produced in the United Kingdom. This remarkable achievement was a tribute to the intensive analysis and imaginative thinking which Robotham, Coverley and others applied to the company's problems in the immediate pre-war period.

11 Rearmament: the Years of Indecision

Within the short space of one year, three events occurred which were of considerable importance. The design work on the Merlin engine, or PV-12 as it was then called, instrument first of survival and then of victory in the Second World War, started in October 1932 as a purely private venture. On 30 January 1933 Adolf Hitler became Chancellor and within a few weeks had inaugurated the Third Reich. In May of the same year Sir Henry Royce died at his home at West Wittering after a long and painful illness which did not prevent him from continuing to work until almost his last day. During his latter years Royce's influence over the policy of the design department was not as strong as it had once been and the general policy of the firm was very largely beyond his influence. The practical direction of design and development came increasingly under Rowledge, who had come over to Rolls-Royce from Napiers. Commercial and administrative policy, over which Royce in the later years of his life had never had a very great influence, was largely directed by Sidgreaves. Royce was succeeded as chief engineer by A. G. Elliott, who until then had been head of the design staff at West Wittering.

The mood of the administration during the early thirties was conservative, both in finance and manufacturing models. The technical pre-eminence which Royce himself had done so much to foster had become somewhat attenuated during the twenties when the volume of aero-engine production had been too small to provide an adequate margin for design and development. But the success of the 'R' engine in the Schneider Trophy did much to restore the legend of the name in the eyes of the public and the Air Ministry. Though Rolls-Royce had been consistently a member of the 'family' for Air Ministry orders, the firm's output from 1928 to 1930 was considerably smaller than might have been expected on this basis of calculation.[1] What may be termed, in a relative sense only, 'quantity production' of the Kestrel engine did not start until July 1930. In the following two years nearly six hundred of these engines were produced, and in 1933 the five hundred a year mark was passed for the first time since the First World War. The output of aero-engines increased steadily each year until the outbreak of war, but this was not the result of a clear-cut Air Ministry policy reflecting itself in a consistent programme of production and development.

Winston Churchill's speeches in the House of Commons were still generally considered to be alarmist and aggressive in the early thirties. The requirements both of a vigorous foreign policy and of national defence were subjugated to the idealism which found expression in disarmament conferences and attempts to limit the military power not so much of Germany as of France. The economic disasters of the Depression and the searing memories of 1914–18 were the main preoccupations of those who commented on public affairs. These catastrophes were attributed to the wilful malignance of national and economic ambition. Political decision, particularly in the realm of defence, was strongly infused with wishful thinking. Optimism sheltered behind the existence of the League of Nations.

The Air Estimates of 1933 and 1934 clearly reflected this state of affairs, though in July of the latter year a substantial increase in the front-line strength of the R.A.F. was authorised by the Government. A report of the Army, Navy and Air Force Committee which the Cabinet had established in 1926 to review Service requirements reveals that in 1933 it was expected that the Air Force would require 12,300 engines

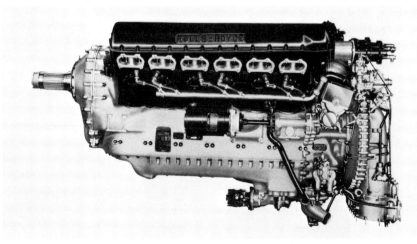

17.   The Rolls-Royce Merlin Mark I aero-engine

in the first year of war. This was clearly beyond the capacity of the existing firms and consequently a suggestion was made to Rolls-Royce that Humbers should produce a small number of Kestrel engines. A meeting with representatives of the Air Ministry was held on 3 October 1934 to discuss the general questions involved. This 'shadow' scheme was opposed by Sidgreaves on the grounds that the money could be far better spent on jigs and tools for the Derby factory which could be employed on finishing and assembling additional parts manufactured by subcontractors. This was the first, and by no means the last, occasion on which Rolls-Royce executives agreed that the productive capacity of the country could be expanded more rapidly and efficiently by the use of the sub-contracting system rather than by the expenditure of large sums of money on the erection of special factories to be run by the motor industry.

As early as 1931 the Air Ministry had considered asking the Daimler factory to undertake the production of Bristol Jupiter engines owing to the low capacity of the parent company, but this proposal had also ended with the acceptance by Daimlers of a large sub-contract order. It is not without interest that one of the grounds of Sidgreaves' protest against the Humber scheme was that this would involve the disclosure of trade secrets in a manner and to an extent that would be bound to affect the commercial interests of the firm. It was not possible, he argued, to train the Humber organisation to build the Kestrel without at the same time disclosing to the firm, which could certainly be consi-dered as one of the company's principal competitors in the motor industry, the technical knowledge and skill which gave Rolls-Royce its pre-eminence. While this was an important consideration from Sid-greaves' point of view, it was secondary to his main contention that a sub-contract scheme was more economical, efficient and flexible, and therefore in the national interest.

It is obviously difficult where a firm's conception of the national interest happens to coincide with the official view of its private interest for the former to argue strongly in favour of the scheme which it proposes. But the next few years will provide a good number of examples where the management's assessment of the national interest – though it frequently happened to coincide with what the firm considered to be the most convenient or beneficial from its own point of view – was often more accurate than that of some Air Ministry officials who felt that this coincidence of interest must bias the judgement of the firm's representatives, and that their payment of the piper involved them in a direct obligation not only to call the tune as to what was produced but to influence the conductor's interpretation of the score as to how it should be produced. This entire period in the firm's history provides a most interesting commentary on the relationship between the independent firm and the State, where the latter started by being an important customer and ended up by being the only customer.

The gradual transition of the firm's interest from the motor industry to the aero-engine industry occurred under the relatively artificial influence of the expansion of military aviation. Whereas in the twenties Rolls-Royce had produced cars and interested itself in the design and production of aero-engines, the thirties saw an exact reversal of this position. A glance at the figures of turnover in Appendix XI reveals that the turnover in aero-engines exceeded that of cars in 1935, the year 1934 being the best year in the chassis division in the inter-war period. A comparison of aero and chassis turnover in the early thirties (Appendix VIII) also reveals that the former was a much more stable source of demand. The remarkable increase in personnel employed in the period 1931–4 from 2900 to 5800 cannot however be attributed to increased aero-engine turnover, since this increased only from £808,000 to £1,828,000. The initial expansion of facilities (mainly personnel, stocks and tools) which the increased demand for chassis stimulated during these years was not, as the later turnover figures reveal, warranted by the demand in subsequent years. But the resources were quite readily absorbed by the increasing demands of rearmament and since the decline in demand for chassis may not unreasonably be attributed to the general conditions which produced the demand for aero-engines this investment cannot be considered as an error of judgement even in the technical sense. It was certainly not an error of judgement in the practical sense.

Thus a considerable expansion in the firm's activity in all fields had in fact taken place before the end of 1934 and in October of the same year two important decisions were taken by the board. The first was the decision to lease and develop an aerodrome at Hucknall as an experimental establishment where flight testing could take place under the close supervision of the firm's own designers and experimental staff. The main objective was to provide a workshop where the problems of engine installation could be studied on flying test beds and on the aircraft concerned. During the twenties the considerable difficulties experienced with the cooling systems of liquid-cooled engines had

18.   The Hawker Henley prototype with Rolls-Royce Merlin Mark I

caused a large number of engine failures. Both in England and America the engine companies had taken little responsibility for the development and installation of these systems. In 1929 Rolls-Royce's Schneider Trophy experience proved that the engine-builder would have to take a much closer interest in installation if the best results were to be obtained. An installation engineering department was consequently established and given the objective of attaining an all-round improvement in liquid cooling. An important subsidiary objective was the reduction of radiator drag, which had reached serious proportions in the Kestrel. All this work required flight-testing facilities and, although the aircraft manufacturers at first resisted what they thought to be an encroachment on their sphere of operations, the value of the work done at the Derby municipal airport and then at Hucknall soon proved the wisdom of this development. This work, which was financed by special Government contracts from the beginning, enabled Rolls-Royce to compensate for the fact that, unlike some of its main competitors, the firm did not manufacture complete aircraft.

The second major development was the decision to co-operate

closely with Vickers in the production of the Spitfire. The latter was not in fact a policy decision but marked a rather significant continuation of a policy of intimate collaboration with the aircraft firms employing Rolls-Royce engines. This was eventually to develop into a new and important branch of the firm's activities — the design and construction of power plants, a term which came to include the engine, its mounting, auxiliary drives and nacelle.

It is significant that both these decisions were made on 26 October. Winston Churchill's amendment to the Address on the subject of the strength of the German Air Force was moved on 28 November and was categorically denied by the Prime Minister, Stanley Baldwin. In March 1935 the reconstitution of the German Air Force was officially announced and on 22 May, shortly after Anthony Eden's visit to Berlin, Baldwin made the famous admission in the House of Commons which may be said to mark the Government's first realisation that wishful thinking and practical politics would have to part company. Though Lord Londonderry, the Air Minister, caused considerable surprise as well as making his own resignation inevitable by attempting to persuade Baldwin to justify the original figures on which he had based his estimate, it would appear that the Air Ministry was not altogether unaware that the 'Treasury fetters', which Churchill described in the first volume of his memoirs, had been broken. At a board meeting on 30 May it was announced that orders for 1998 engines to be completed by September 1936 were expected from the Air Ministry and on the strength of this expectation capital expenditure was immediately authorised of £120,000. This was easily the largest amount authorised since the First World War, the previous largest amount being £55,000 authorised in February 1933. This date thus marked the beginning, as far as Rolls-Royce was concerned, of the period of expansion directly attributable to rearmament for the Second World War. As the Merlin was still in the experimental stage there was no alternative to the Kestrel, which was a proved engine in quantity production, and in 1935 and 1936 over 2500 of these engines were produced at Derby. In a sense this marked a sacrifice of quality to quantity since more powerful engines were known to exist. If it was this consideration alone, however, which as is suggested elsewhere,[2] caused the Air Staff to resist pressure for the immediate expansion of the Air Force after Baldwin's retraction, it will be the first occasion on which those in authority learnt the lesson that the production of large numbers of an untried engine can involve formidable risks. At a later stage in the war

Hives found it necessary to develop with great force the proposition that one horsepower in the air is worth two on the ground. Had his views not prevailed the decisions taken might well have proved disastrous, especially in view of the serious loss which was incurred as the result of applying the opposite policy to the Napier 'Sabre'.

The design and development work done in this period very largely determined the technical limits of what could be done during the war years. This was certainly not appreciated at the time, and it was often not appreciated during the war. It is therefore of some importance to provide a background to the somewhat confused currents of policy which characterise these years so markedly. Though the environment of decision from 1935 onwards might have been expected to be rather simple, it was in fact more complex and it is instructive to examine briefly the nature of the problems which had to be solved at the time.

The national policy decisions on rearmament had of course to be taken by the Cabinet and approved by Parliament. Once made, executive implementation became the responsibility of the Air Ministry, which had been responsible for advising the Cabinet on the disparity between the various air forces and the current and anticipated rates of output of various national aircraft industries which were considered relevant to the strategical situation.

Having determined the R.A.F.'s requirements the Air Ministry had next to determine their technical specification, in itself no easy task. Once these decisions were made the Air Ministry was in a position to formulate precise requirements from the aircraft and aero-engine industry. Each such requirement represented the outcome of a further series of decisions on the rate of expansion required to achieve a given air strength in a certain period, the rate of obsolescence and deterioration of existing aircraft and engine types and finally the volume of production of spares and replacement units required to maintain the air force at a given strength. Since many of these factors are independent the 'fetters of the Treasury' were by no means the only limitations on freedom of action. Nor, as will shortly be seen, do the problems disappear as soon as the orders are given. The volume production of aircraft is one of the most complex of all industrial undertakings and the problems of co-ordination both within the various units of the industry and between them are immense. All the available evidence of two world wars supports the view that they would not be solved by any attempt to integrate the processes of decision and control under a more centralised authority, whether of a private or public nature.

It is nevertheless apparent that in the years immediately before the outbreak of war financial limitations became less important. This is not because the cost ceased to be of any importance but because most other problems tended to be obscured by the sheer physical problems of maximising output. As political crisis succeeded political crisis, the government became more convinced that rearmament was unavoidable and the flow of orders created a new climate of confidence in the industry. The problem of competing ends did not of course disappear with the clarification of the ultimate objective of rearmament. A limited volume of resources had to be allocated by a combination of public and private decisions – a combination in which the former predominated to an increasing but never to an exclusive extent – between the competing claims of production and development, civil and military output. This involved an inescapable choice between larger immediate production and larger future production as well as a subsidiary decision between the flexible layouts required by development and the comparatively rigid layouts required by quantity production. That the management succeeded in retaining this flexibility by diversifying the character of production in the main factories under their control, thereby ensuring that balance between quantity and quality which is the foundation of progress, is probably the most remarkable achievement of the Rolls-Royce group of factories during the Second World War. The relative sacrifice of quantity which this system involves is always more immediately apparent. But the very real advantages of rapid technical progress which a flexible organisation makes possible are inclined to be obscured, especially in time of war, by the more visible phenomena of sagging production curves. Such curves tend to become the main preoccupation of central planning departments, which are naturally more concerned with output than with performance. The war years ahead illustrate the intensity of this conflict in great detail.

The sacrifice of development to production, which usually involves the parallel sacrifice of performance (achieved through constant modification) to production, is of course a particularly pernicious form of living on capital. In the early part of this period, when resources were not fully utilised and the allocation of effort was still largely within the control of individual managements, the problem does not assume the importance which it does in later years.

The evolution of both Air Ministry and Rolls-Royce policy had to be set against this background but the latter will not be fully understood without a consideration of some of the independent factors which influenced the management at this time. The first problem was to sort out specific instructions to manufacture certain engines from numerous official and unofficial estimates of what was likely to be required in the future. These had to be considered in relation to the period of production which was to a greater or lesser extent a contractual obligation, a period which was largely based on the management's own estimates. The management had also to consider the various warnings received from time to time that a large volume of orders was impending and set these against the reductions in orders that were also received. Their own knowledge of the general situation enables them to form an independent judgement of the volume of orders which would be forced on the Air Ministry and from these combined factors to advise the Air Ministry what aero-engine capacity existed and what could be created. This also involved an assessment of the rate of production which could be achieved at the existing Derby plant, with and without the conversion of chassis manufacture. The management had to decide the extent to which existing orders justified the expenditure of additional capital on plant, tools and stocks of raw materials, and the extent to which anticipated orders justified any additional expenditure.

These decisions affected, in their turn, such matters as the division of output between the parent factory, the sub-contracting organisation, and the new factories to be built under the Shadow Scheme. The conversion of plant from chassis to aero-engine manufacture was a particularly acute problem which involved the balancing of such factors as the decline in demand for cars, the relative profitability of aero and car work, the adaptability of chassis manufacturing tools and labour, the cost of converting these resources compared with the cost of creating additional resources. The availability of new plant and machinery was also of great importance. In making such decisions the management refused to take anything for granted and openly questioned the judgement of the Air Ministry on such matters as the absorption of engines into aircraft. 'We find it difficult to believe,' said Sidgreaves in a letter to Colonel Disney of the Air Ministry early in 1938, 'that a serious increase in production of engines at this juncture would assist the aircraft programme because we know and have already shown that even on the present programme there will be many hundreds of Merlin engines over and above the requirements by the end of the present year.' There were also labour problems. Had the aero division employed additional labour while the chassis division worked short time there inevitably would have been friction and unrest.

Such were the problems which faced both the Air Ministry and the Rolls-Royce management at this time. Neither were in a position to act at any time between 1933 and 1939 on the assumption that war was inevitable. The paradox of the situation lies in the fact that had they so acted war might not have been inevitable, but the cost of throwing Rolls-Royce, Bristols and other aero-engine firms into full quantity production could not then have been offset against what is now known to be the cost of not throwing them into full production – the cost of the Second World War. Even had the war been avoided there would have been severe repercussions, bearing in mind the pacifist temper of these years. Those responsible for the initial decisions and expenditure would have been pilloried as irresponsible and extravagant alarmists and most certainly called to account for their actions. It is against this background of the confusion, uncertainty and wishful thinking induced in a peace-loving people by the events of the previous twenty years that the equally confused nature of the relationship between Rolls-Royce and the Air Ministry during this period should be examined.

In September 1935 several estimates of capacity were made in answer to a questionnaire sent out by the Air Ministry. This information was requested at the time of the Abyssinian crisis and since Britain appeared to be taking a strong line it seemed reasonable to conclude that the Air Ministry was making enquiries relating to the possibility of mobilisation. The management was apparently informed that this was not the case, for on one of the documents there appears the significant remark that 'This had nothing to do with Abyssinia'.

The Air Ministry was informed that the Derby factory was capable of producing 180 engines per month on the assumption that car work was completely stopped. This total was divided into 153 Kestrels and 27 Merlins (the drawings for the latter were not in fact released until early in 1936) and the production of spares yielded an additional total equivalent to 40 engines. Total output was limited by the large units of the engine which were not being sub-contracted at this stage. On the basis of a potential volume of orders amounting to nearly 4000 engines per annum these figures of potential capacity revealed a deficiency of the order of 150 engines a month. An estimate was made for the first time of the cost of a new plant to be specially erected to produce the balance of these requirements. This estimate gave a total of £3,300,000.[3] The Air Ministry had discussed the possibility of such an extension with the management but the decision was postponed partially because of the impending discussions of the Shadow Scheme.

An alternative recommendation was then put forward that the Air Ministry should authorise Rolls-Royce to purchase a year's stock of raw material, since its existence would make a great difference to the rate of expansion which could be achieved. This alone would have cost £866,200, a commitment which the firm could not be expected to undertake of its own accord, although a similar independent decision had been primarily responsible for the relatively rapid increase in Kestrel production which took place in 1934. The unsettled state of mind at the Air Ministry could not be hidden from the executives at Derby for in a departmental minute concerned with these calculations there appeared a comment that the scheme then under discussion was much smaller than one discussed a few months previously in which a figure of 10,000 engines in the first year had been mentioned. This was the first occasion on which the Air Ministry requirements and the estimated Rolls-Royce production were drawn up in the form of a programme.[4] This attempted to forecast a monthly rate of production over a period of six months but since car production was not suspended no interesting comparisons can be made. It is nevertheless interesting to compare the optimistic estimate of production confidently expected from a new factory with that actually achieved in the first six months of operation of the new factory eventually built at Crewe.[5] The rate of production of 370 a month was not achieved for twenty-two months.

In the early part of 1936, before Hitler reoccupied the Rhineland, various schemes of expansion were under discussion at the Air Ministry. None of these involved demands which could not have been met from existing capacity, but the serious deterioration in the international situation which took place early in the year led the Cabinet sub-committee on defence to revise its opinion. It was decided that it would now be necessary to initiate the partial operation of the Shadow Factory scheme which was dependent on the co-operation of the motor industry. At this stage the output of liquid-cooled and trainer engines was considered satisfactory and attention was concentrated on Bristol radials where the gap between supply and demand was estimated to be 4000.[6] The first scheme, which proposed the collaboration of the Austin, Daimler, Rover, Standard, Humber, Singer and Wolseley Companies, called for the erection of factories close to the parent aero-engine factories. This was strategically dangerous and also ignored the possibility that the supply of skilled labour would be rapidly exhausted. On these grounds Rolls-Royce opposed the suggestion that they should erect and operate a factory at either Shrewsbury or Liverpool.[7] It was not strongly pressed, however, and the board did not discuss the Shadow Scheme again until 17 December.

The year 1936 saw the general disappearance of the mood of righteous indignation which the invasion of Abyssinia and the reoccupation of the Rhineland had generated in the hearts of the British people. Seemingly secure in the possession of his great majority in Parliament, Mr Baldwin felt able to neglect the pressure which was being put upon him to forestall by abnormally energetic measures of rearmament the grave deterioration in the international situation which only a minority saw to be inevitable. At the head of an all-party delegation to the Prime Minister in July 1936, Winston Churchill urged 'the development of our air power in priority over every other consideration . . . We must accelerate and simplify our plane production and push it to the largest scale and not hesitate to make contracts with the United States and elsewhere for the largest possible quantities of aviation material and equipment of all kinds'.[8]

Baldwin was not persuaded. He considered that the efforts already being made were sufficient and preoccupation with domestic affairs diverted the attention of the Government and the country from the ever-increasing gap in the balance of power. There were consequently no further important developments in the direction of rearmament expansion at Rolls-Royce directly inspired by the Air Ministry in 1936, though important progress was made by Rolls-Royce itself in preparation for the great ordeal which lay ahead.

Earlier in the year the board had decided to negotiate the purchase of the aircraft manufacturing firm of Phillips & Powis (later to become Miles Aircraft Ltd) on the grounds that the close association between an engine and an airframe manufacturer would be to the great advantage of both firms. This was in reality the same motive which had led to the acquisition of Hucknall two years earlier, but the management probably considered that the independent airframe experience available at Phillips & Powis could not rapidly be duplicated at Hucknall. Since there was at this time nearly a million pounds of the firm's own resources available for investment, the proposition seemed unusually attractive. At the board meeting on 3 April it was reported that Rolls-Royce intended to acquire 500,000 $3\frac{1}{2}$ per cent cumulative preference shares in this firm, which would thereupon become a subsidiary of the company. It was stated that the board did not look upon this as an investment in the financial sense but rather as a development expense having as its object the successful development of aircraft for Rolls-Royce engines. A report by the auditors which was discussed in May confirmed this point of view, since they considered that the terms of the subscription for these shares were not justified. The purchase was nevertheless concluded and the firm remained a subsidiary of Rolls-Royce for several years until it was finally sold under very favourable conditions during the war. Although this venture cannot really be judged a great success from any point of view, had it not been for the independent development of Hucknall a closer integration on the technical level might conceivably have developed between the two firms.

Two important domestic changes took place during the latter part of this year. Lord Wargrave, who succeeded Claremont as chairman of the board, died in July after a tenure of office of some thirteen years. He was succeeded by Lord Herbert Scott, a director who had been associated with the company from its very earliest days, and who was widely known in industrial and financial circles in London. He was eventually to become President of the Federation of British Industries and though he never played any important executive role in the company's affairs its interests were his main concern and he made considerable efforts to make himself fully acquainted with every phase of its activities. His political contacts were no less wide than his business contacts and he was frequently able to anticipate developments likely to affect the company. A change of far greater immediate significance took place in October on the retirement of Wormald, the works manager and a well-beloved figure in the company's history. He was succeeded by Hives, on whom the main burden of rearmament and the war was to fall. It was not long before this outstanding executive made his presence felt at Derby.

Kestrel production was at its zenith during this year, and was greatly accelerated in the last few months to clear the way for the Merlin, which was expected to come into full production in 1937. The detailed design work on this engine had begun early in 1933 just before Sir Henry Royce died. The Merlin, like the Buzzard, was an exact scale-up of the Kestrel, which was now considered too small. It was designed to replace a steam-cooled version of the Kestrel known as the Goshawk, on which considerable development had been carried out in 1929 and 1930, and to profit from the lessons which had been learnt from this work. The Buzzard and the 'R' were regarded as quite unsuitable for fighter aircraft because of their weight.

The Air Ministry was kept fully informed of the Merlin plans, which were approved, although no official development funds were available until the first two experimental engines were ready for test in October 1933. The Merlin was consequently designated as a private venture – the PV. 12. The Air Ministry was sympathetic towards the designer's original intention to build the engine as an inverted 'V' but the hostility of the airframe builders, who were shown a mock-up in 1932, caused the firm to abandon this idea. In January 1934 the prospects of the engine were sufficiently reassuring for two aircraft companies – Hawker and Supermarine – to initiate the design of the Hurricane and the Spitfire, two aircraft whose performance throughout the Second World War depended on the development potential which Rolls-Royce was able to extract from the Merlin. One of the two experimental engines passed its first-type test in July 1934 with a rating of 730 h.p. at 12,000 feet for a weight of 1177 lb.

The development of a new type of cylinder-head known as a 'ramp-head' began in the same month. This involved changes in the valve gear and the first engines incorporating this head – the Merlin B – were not ready for test until January 1935. Serious difficulties were subsequently encountered with this head, for which a scaled-up Kestrel head had eventually to be substituted in the Merlin 'G'. Development continued on the Merlin 'C' with separate castings for the crankcase and cylinder block. Flight-testing began in April 1935 in a modified Hawker Hart and these resulted in an immediate change from the original composite cooling system (based on the Goshawk experience) to a pure ethylene glycol system.

So anxious was the Air Ministry to obtain a production engine that it was even prepared to relax its type-test regulations. As a result, the Merlin F, with the ramp-head, was put into production as the Merlin I. Sixteen out of thirty-four sections of the engine were released by the drawing office on 8 March 1936, but because the 'F' failed to pass even the relaxed type-test they were withdrawn shortly afterwards and most of the 180 Merlin Is were produced in the Experimental Department. All of these were used in the Fairey 'Battle' which was a notoriously underpowered aeroplane.

Hawkers were instructed by the Air Ministry to wait for the Merlin II with the Kestrel-type head and 500 sets for this engine were released early in September. The first production Merlin II was delivered in August 1937. It is noteworthy that even at this stage the executive directly in charge of aero-engine production, Mr Swift, was complaining that the rate of modification was excessive and seriously interfering with production. Design work on the Peregrine, a higher-powered Kestrel and the Vulture, an X engine of 24 cylinders in the 2000 h.p. class, was started during this year. Both these engines were to have somewhat chequered careers.

An important conference, with Colonel Disney representing the Air Ministry, was held on 7 December. Hives prepared a memorandum for this meeting at which he stressed the importance of the sub-contract system which Rolls-Royce had developed in the First World War. The best sub-contractors in the First World War were the British United Shoe Machinery Company and the Linotype Company. From these firms Rolls-Royce obtained 'infinitely more help than from any motor car people'. Hives urged that the firm should be allowed to extend its sub-contract organisation and that the firm's own engineers should make an extensive survey of the sub-contract capacity in various suitable firms all over the country.[9] He also pointed out that the good firms were picking and choosing their work, and that it was essential for Rolls-Royce to be in a position to give large and definite orders. Hives further suggested that the Derby factory should be balanced up with tools so that it could be converted entirely to aero-engine production at a day's notice. Colonel Disney approved these suggestions and assured Hives that Rolls-Royce would be allotted the best available firms for sub-contract work. He was informed that a special sub-contract department would cost from £15,000 to £20,000 a year, and that the cost of converting the factory from chassis to aero work would be of the order of £100,000.

A very good indication of the decline in the sense of urgency which had occurred during 1936 is the fact that the total number of Rolls-Royce engines required by the Air Ministry between December of this year and June 1939 amounted to 3540 engines (3521 from January 1937). This figure gives a rate of production of 121 engines per month, or 1400 per annum. The full capacity of the Derby factory alone, with the existing sub-contract system, was stated by Hives in the memorandum referred to above to be 3000 per annum. It would therefore appear that at least in relation to what eventually became in 1940 the most important single weapon in the British armoury – the Merlin-engined interceptor – the statement that it was already too late to retrieve air parity with the Third Reich is not strictly accurate.[10] It is conceivable that a total of 9000 Merlins could have been produced by the outbreak of war had a firm decision to rebuild the Air Force on this scale been taken early in 1936. In fact, between January 1937 and December 1940, only 4771 Merlin engines were produced, including a small number of Merlins built for civil aircraft and for foreign governments. For such a decision to have been effective there would, of course have to have been a complementary decision to expand the production of airframes and other vital ancillary components and it is probable that had the whole of the British aircraft industry made similar demands on the capacity of civilian industry this figure would have to be revised. The fairest comparison between what was done in the 32 months before the actual outbreak of war and what could have been done in this period can probably be made by considering the total production of the Rolls-Royce group in the first 32 months of the war. This amounted to 26,708 engines of all types. By far the majority of these were Merlins. The estimate of a possible 9000 engines does not by this standard therefore appear excessive.

At this conference on 7 December the Air Ministry's requirements were formulated in the form of a programme which endeavoured to predict a monthly rate of production to within one engine over a period of nearly three years. The firm's own estimates of production on the basis of the utilisation of existing facilities were set against these figures which were constructed, on this occasion as they were so often to be in the the future, on the basis of the desirable rather than the possible.[11] The Rolls-Royce estimate predicted the following annual production of Merlins:

        1937   938
        1938   2220
        1939   363 (Jan–May inclusive)
(These estimates both allowed for the completion of Kestrel production — a matter of some 300 engines.)

The Air Ministry programme was severely criticised on the grounds that it was not practicable 'to jump from a comparatively small output from one month to another'. Neither set of figures approximated with any accuracy to the production finally achieved.

The year 1937 saw the initiation of a unique project in industrial co-operation, the purpose of which was to supply the British aircraft industry, and in particular the two firms mainly concerned, with propellers, an item of aircraft equipment which was in such great demand that many had to be imported from the United States. Bristols and Rolls-Royce, the two largest firms in the British aero-engine industry, both under the patronage of the Air Ministry and both competitors, agreed to form a company to be known as Rotol Limited, with an initial capital of £500,000, of which exactly half would be subscribed by each of the two parent concerns. The board was composed of Sir Stanley White and A. H. R. Fedden (then chief engineer) of Bristols, and Sidgreaves and Hives of Rolls-Royce. The first meeting was held on 3 June, the day after work started on a completely new factory which was erected specially for the production of propellers. The history of this concern, except in so far as its financial requirements during the early years of its life were to a very considerable extent provided by loans from Rolls-Royce, cannot be considered here in the detail which the novelty and importance of the experiment would justify; the initiation and development of such a project marks nevertheless a most signal achievement and it would be doing less than justice to those responsible were this not mentioned in the history of one of the principal partners in the enterprise. The existence of an additional propeller factory of the most modern type at the outbreak of war was a factor of great importance in determining the rate of expansion which the aircraft industry as a whole was able to achieve. A very large measure of credit must be given to the purely private enterprise which alone was responsible for this development.

Shortly after becoming general works manager, Hives prepared a report for the chairman, Lord Herbert Scott, which threw a revealing light on the general conditions prevailing in the Derby factory at this time. He was particularly critical of the firm's general competitive and technical position and concluded that the whole works suffered from excessive administrative conservatism, lack of familiarity with new methods and processes, a preponderance of old and inefficient machines and material costs which were 'ridiculously high'. He advocated the promotion of foremen on merit as well as on seniority and suggested that there should be considerably greater factory representation on the policy committee which met on the average once a month. By separating chassis and aero-engine production into two separate divisions, the one under Coverley and the other under Swift, he brought about a change which was long overdue. He encouraged senior engineers and foremen to get away from Derby and see how things were done in other factories and other countries. The factory had relied too much on 'brawn and craftsmanship' in the past and had to acquire new techniques and learn to employ its brains more usefully. A marked lack of effective leadership throughout the organisation was due, in Hives' opinion, to the fact that Sir Henry Royce had always made all engineering and design policy decisions himself. The consequence of this was that initiative had been stultified over a fairly broad front.

Rolls-Royce had in fact neglected the most important task facing the management of any large human organisation – that of ensuring continuity in the quality and efficiency of its leadership. This can only be achieved by creating the conditions in which junior executives can be tested with progressively larger amounts of responsibility and in which their success or failure can be measured by objective yardsticks within the organisation. Most large organisations whose existence depends on the power of effective decision in a constantly changing environment of great complexity experience from time to time the consequences of what Chester Barnard has described as a 'restriction in the circulation of the elite'.[12] If an outstanding individual such as Royce succeeds in creating a virtual monopoly of decision within an organisation then such an organisation will operate under conditions which cause the powers of decision in its potential executives to atrophy. The extent of this weakness does not become apparent until, through death or retirement, it becomes necessary to appoint successors. If the organisation has large reserves and a considerable momentum the effects may not be appreciated for several years or until some crisis arises. In a discussion of precisely the same problem Peter Drucker has concluded, in his study of General Motors, that the efficiency of that organisation 'lies in its having a small number of big businesses to make the money and a large number of small businesses to supply the leadership'. This pertinent observation is not inapplicable to the situation at Derby in 1937. Here was a large and growing organisation whose administration imposed an ever-greater burden on a management limited in numbers and lacking in reserves. Hives appreciated this situation clearly and he set out to remedy it with considerable vigour.

He took immediate steps to separate physically the production of chassis and aero-engines and introduced a new system of responsibility for the ordering of machines in both sections. He considered that there was an excess of handwork in the factory and that far greater use should be made of machines. The operation planning department was separated from the tool design office and was instructed to examine all designs independently as soon as they were completed, the objective of this arrangement being to ensure that more attention was paid to

production requirements. A new rate-fixing department was established which priced parts as soon as they were designed and not, as
had been the case hitherto, after they were in production.

Changes of this magnitude were bound to cause dissatisfaction,
however intrinsically meritorious or justifiable, since they inevitably
disrupted both formal and informal organisations all over the factory.
Hives's approach to this problem is interesting.

> Labour: We boast that we have never had any trouble with labour:
> there is no reason why we should have any trouble as long as one
> gives way to every demand. In negotiations with the Unions all the
> amenities which we have provided count for nothing.
>
> I advocate high wages. We can afford to pay a lot of money for a lot
> of work. At the present time I do not find fault with the workers. My
> complaint is against the organisation which is so bad that it does not
> enable the workers to earn as much money as they ought to. The
> condition I do lay down however is that we cannot tolerate any
> interference from the workers as regards making improvements in
> efficiency and in our organisation. We also do not intend to tolerate
> any interference as regards Works Management.

He was also critical of the scheme of bonus payment then in operation.
Under this scheme the time saved was divided equally between the
firm and the employee, a method which Hives considered to be out of
date. The whole bonus, he thought, should be earned by the employee.
He was equally critical of the yearly bonus scheme which operated for
foremen and supervisory staff, since this was related purely to their
salaries and not in any way to the efficiency of their departments.
Bonus earnings varied between various departments and caused dissatisfaction. The report concluded with a discussion of the firm's
apprentice scheme which he considered a complete failure, since it
gave insufficient opportunity to talent. Hives considered that a greater
effort should be made to obtain young men with a secondary school
education to be trained under an entirely new scheme.

On 18 February Hives received a letter from Lord Herbert Scott
giving him the full backing of the board in his 'difficult job of putting
the Rolls-Royce factory in order'. It was certainly not an easy task, and a
strike in the grinders' shop at a time when the maintenance of
production was of great importance appeared at the outset to be rather
serious.[13]

The grinders had asked for an increase of 10s per week in the basic rate. This was refused on the grounds that it would not be fair to discriminate between grinders and other equally skilled men who were paid the same basic rate. The inevitable result of granting the grinders' demand would have been its extension to these other trades. A conciliatory offer of 2s a week for semi-skilled men was refused.

The dispute was negotiated at first between the local executives of the Amalgamated Engineering Union and the Engineering Employers Federation but they failed to reach agreement and referred the dispute to a local factory conference. This also failed to reach a settlement and the grinders decided to call a strike. It was not recognised by the National Executive of the A.E.U. and caused considerable resentment among the other employees who were somewhat contemptuous of the 'skill' on which the grinders based their demand for a differential reward. The average earnings of grinders at this time were £5 0s 6d per week in the toolroom, a wage which was based on a 61s week of 47 hours plus a premium bonus. The fact that a few weeks before the strike 48 grinders in the toolroom had received an increase of 3s per week may have had some bearing on the dispute.

Hives made a direct personal appeal to the workers to refrain from this action, pointing out that the firm had spent £370,000 on welfare and offering a £10 reward to anyone who could name a firm which had done better in this respect. The reward was not claimed. This was an effective answer to a letter in the local press in which the strikers' representatives claimed that the allocation of funds for welfare was inadequate. This letter also complained about the 'annual summer lock-out' (the August holidays) and the Foremen's Club, but neither of these matters was raised again. The ostensible reason for the strike was the alleged belief of the grinders that the new methods introduced by the reorganisation would affect their pay envelopes. The dissatisfaction certainly expressed itself in this way but the trouble started, as Hives commented in his report, in a shop where there was a lazy supervisor and dirty conditions of work, and this isolated instance would seem to support the general conclusions of Warner and Low that the ostensible reasons for a strike are very rarely the real reasons.[14]

Fortunately, this incident, which created very little bitterness or interference, was settled quite rapidly. It was not altogether without advantage to the Company which was able to carry out a careful analysis of the labour requirements under the aero programme. A considerable surplus of fitters and labourers was discovered and not all of the 3000 men laid off were taken back. One hundred and seventy men who had received bonuses of up to £1000 in 1936 were told that they were redundant and that the firm could only offer them jobs at £4 10s 0d a week. Only one of these men decided to leave, an indication of the very strong social cohesion which existed within the organisation and of the extent to which employment within it could be said to have satisfied non-economic motives. This incident clearly illustrates the total inadequacy of contemporary theories of wages which failed completely to explain such behaviour because of their disregard for the important motives (essentially non-economic) which inspire it.

Hives was sympathetic towards the general demands for higher wages at this time. 'I am hoping,' he said, 'that an agreement will quickly be reached for a national increase in wages for the engineering trades. It must be accepted that the law of supply and demand shall work in both directions. The Engineering Employers Federation do not hesitate to reduce wages when things are bad, therefore at the present time the men have the right to expect an increase.'

He was equally concerned at this stage with the general organisation of the costing system which was woefully inadequate and obsolete. Little attention had apparently been paid to his report on American production written some fifteen years previously, for, he comments, 'whichever way you turn you find an utter disregard of cost-consciousness. At the present time practically the whole of our costs are history.' There was, however, a rapid change of attitude under the new administration, which at first had been so unpopular that some of the departmental heads had asked to be made directly responsible to Sidgreaves, the managing director. They soon revised their point of view as the new system began to demonstrate its efficiency. Hives had set out to create 'an entirely new atmosphere throughout the works based on the motto that we must never be satisfied'. What was achieved at Derby during the following four years could not have been achieved had he not succeeded in this aim. A catholic dissatisfaction coupled with the ability to ensure the co-operation of the great majority of the staff in achieving his objectives led to a series of administrative reforms which played an important part in preparing the Derby organisation for the burden which rearmament was imposing on it.

In 1936 a group of the firm's senior engineers, headed by Swift, made an extensive tour of a number of aircraft and engine factories in Germany. On their return they submitted a series of reports[15] which led the responsible executives at Derby to take a grave view of the situation. Few people were in a better position to compare what was being done in both countries and to assess the potentialities of the British and German aircraft industries. Hives had already expressed some dissatisfaction with the production of the Merlin I, 60 per cent of which had had to be sub-contracted. Lack of skilled labour at sub-contractors had been an acute problem, and Rolls-Royce had itself started a training scheme to overcome this difficulty. Scrap presented a serious problem as is evidenced by the fact that in the production of the first 190 Merlins no less than six cylinder-head castings had had to be made to obtain two good ones for each engine. In the production of the Merlin II the scrap figure was 80 per cent and at the time of this report (March 1937) the figure was 12 per cent to 15 per cent.

At this moment Rolls-Royce received notification from the Air Ministry of a reduction in orders from 3540 to 3120 engines, coupled with a warning that the reduced programme might have to be spread over three years instead of two.[16] It was suspected at Derby that this reduction had something to do with the Vulture engine, which was still in the design stage, and that the Air Ministry had hoped to expedite its development by reducing the volume of Merlin orders.[17] Hives was fully alive to the danger of such a procedure. The vacillation at the Air Ministry, coupled with the reports received on German industry, led him to prepare a thorough analysis of the whole aero-engine and Shadow Scheme generally. Copies were sent to Lord Swinton, the Air Minister, to Lord Weir, and to Mr Fedden, the chief engineer at Bristols.

This report laid great stress on the fact that only a fully developed engine could be 'shadowed' with any success. It marked a change of policy in that the Rolls-Royce management now advocated the shadowing of their own engines for the first time. The letter made it quite clear that Rolls-Royce would insist on the direct management of any factories in which its products were to be manufactured. The limiting factor in expansion was technical skill. 'As engineers we claim that given efficient management, the success of any project is in some ratio to the amount of technical skill put into it. In technical skill I would include designers, technicians, metallurgists, chemists, factory engineers and planning engineers.' The shadowing of the Bristol Mercury radial engine was likely to be a success because a large number of technical man-hours had been expended on its development. This was not the case with the airframe programme. Hives knew that the rate of absorption of engines into airframes was considerably lower than the rate of production, certainly as far as Rolls-Royce was concerned, and he suggested that insufficient technical development of airframes was to blame.

> I am not very sympathetic with the people who say the machines have not been designed for production. It is all very well to say that now, but at the time the machines were designed the knowledge was not available. The aircraft designer had all he could manage to produce machines which were efficient and airworthy.

In so far as Rolls-Royce was concerned, Hives's solution to the problem was to expand the development organisation in which a reserve of skill could be developed on which the firm could draw on later if necessary. He claimed that Rolls-Royce had never kept an aircraft constructor waiting for engines and concluded by firing a heavy broadside at unspecified firms which made extravagant promises that they could not fulfil.[18] A more general conclusion merits repetition in full, in view of the accuracy of a forecast which it contained:

> I am convinced that the aircraft – and to a lesser degree the engines – which we are making today could never be maintained in the field on a war basis. The variety of types of machines, with their infinite variety of fittings and mechanism, and hydraulic, air, vacuum and electrical services, and the varieties of under-carriages, gun-turrets, instruments, etc., I view as being absolutely hopeless.

The serious problem imposed on the aircraft industry's efforts to attain a high level of output by this diversity was not realised until the great crises of 1940 and 1941. The main characteristic of the British motor industry – diversity not only of product but of its constituent components – was becoming firmly established in the aircraft industry, in which it had hitherto been of little significance owing to the very small volume of production. In a letter to Fedden written at this time Hives gave his opinion on the growth of the German aircraft industry:

> The gentlemen who went to Germany after the war and smashed up all their aircraft engines, factories, etc., and came away thinking that they had disarmed Germany, had overlooked the fact that they could do nothing to destroy German engineering skill. It was a condition that engineers dream about; that is, all the obsolete stuff wiped out and an opportunity of starting off with a clean sheet.

The letter concluded with a reference to Britain's own problems, and the increasing influence of Ministerial policy and practices may be judged from the remark that 'the other difficulty is the fact that we are governed by the Civil Service which does not encourage any initiative'. Fedden did not agree with these views in their entirety but he was so interested in Hives' report that shortly afterwards he went over to Germany to see for himself. This resulted in a further independent report which was circulated to interested persons through the Air Ministry. The liaison between the senior executives of Rolls-Royce and the heads of the Air Ministry and the various technical departments within the Ministry had always been very close, and an increasing number of important decisions were taken in joint conference from this stage onwards. A very high degree of mutual confidence was thereby established which created conditions in which a completely frank and unguarded expression of opinion was possible when the circumstances seemed to warrant it. Hives's most critical, and valuable, reports were invariably sent in their entirety to the Air Ministry and to those whom it was felt should see them in the national interest. This confidence was reciprocated in large measure by the Air Ministry. It was naturally of great value but obviously could not eliminate the conflicts which were bound to develop when official and private objectives and opinions differed.

There was at this time considerable discussion on the merits of the Shadow Factory scheme and its rate of output. A number of questions had been asked in Parliament on the frequency of design changes and the pressure in this direction eventually led to the appointment early in 1938 of Air Marshal Sir Wilfrid Freeman as Air Member for Production and Development. Freeman's acquaintance with Hives extended back some years, but their correspondence on matters of common interest started early in 1937. In one of the first of these letters, written in July 1937, Hives revealed his attitude towards the methods and aims of the expansion programme. The comments were occasioned by Fedden's report on Germany referred to above.

We have first got to recognise that we have a democratic form of government, and that even if we wished we could not adopt German methods in this country. Although Mr. Fedden's reports are intensely interesting and convincing, one misses any concrete suggestion to improve our present position applicable to conditions which exist here . . . My view is that our greatest weakness is that we have not sufficient good designers, technicians and factory engineers, and in our expansion programme there is no scheme for improving this position. We have built – which I freely admit – some very up-to-date and what should be very efficient Shadow Factories, but they have no technical organisation whatever, and they rely entirely on the parent firm for all the creative skill as regards design, materials and production methods. This means that the parent firm must be expected to carry a considerable increase in staff.

Rolls-Royce had often been criticised in official circles because of the management's opposition to the original Shadow Scheme. There was undoubtedly a commercial element in this opposition, but the real opposition stemmed from Hives' opinion that the scheme could not overcome the limiting factor of highly skilled labour and that the existing requirements, and the potential requirements as they appeared at the time, could be better fulfilled by an extensive use of the sub-contract system which Rolls-Royce in particular had developed so thoroughly. It was clearly appreciated at Derby that the existing management would have to carry a very heavy load whatever system was finally adopted. They did not, generally speaking, express this anticipation in so many words, but its accuracy was to be fully borne out by events both in Britain and the United States.[19] It was nevertheless clearly appreciated at Derby quite early in 1937 that the Shadow Scheme had caught the public and official imagination. Hives therefore suggested that although the scheme could only operate on an established design and would therefore always produce something that was out of date, it had 'come to stay' and the company should adapt itself to the idea. This was in a minute written in March 1937, but it was not until 8 October 1937 that the Air Ministry was informed that Rolls-Royce would not object to its products being shadowed.

As early as May 1937 Swift had sent a request for assistance to the chassis department which replied that of the 870 machines on chassis production, 604 were required for the production of chassis, and that 142 of the remainder were already on aero work, leaving only 44 surplus and available. Since the management did not contemplate any major extension of the plant at Derby, this almost complete absorption of existing capacity undoubtedly influenced their decision to encourage the erection of a new plant. Shortly after this Air Ministry orders were further reduced by 226 engines, and a new programme was drawn up which moved much of the production originally scheduled for 1938 forward into 1939. On 29 September Swift estimated that 500 Merlins would be delivered in 1937 (production having been held up early in the year by cylinder-blocks and Breeze ignition-harness shortages) but the actual total achieved was 692, including six civil engines. Of this total 193 were produced in December.

Compared with the year to follow, 1937 was relatively quiet. The Third Reich was consolidating its gains in Europe and it probably suited Hitler's purpose to allow the British Government and the British people to relapse into a sense of security and prosperity. There were no sudden international crises causing the Air Ministry to discover that it required several thousand engines before some hypothetical M-day and the Government felt confident that the existing rearmament measures provided adequate deterrence. The exuberance of the Coronation acted as an effective antidote to the unwelcome doubts of rumour-mongers and pessimists. This change of mood was viewed with great concern at Rolls-Royce, where the real danger of the situation was all too clearly appreciated, but the inexorable logic of events on the continent soon terminated this short-lived optimism.

A total of just over a thousand engines, of which just over two-thirds were Merlins, were produced at Derby in 1937, 400 less than the previous year. Though partly explained by the change from Kestrel to Merlin production there is no doubt that the Air Ministry shared the prevailing optimism – ostrichism would probably be a better term – and reduced the pressure of its demands on Rolls-Royce. It is none the less surprising that the Air Ministry made no clear statement of any reduction in its requirements except on the one occasion cited. Statisticians and 'planners' are inclined to argue from the mere existence of a contract to an inevitable and predictable series of events resulting in a given rate of output. The reality was much more complex. What happened at Derby was a function not only of firm orders, but of the conviction, or equivocation, which lay behind them, of the atmosphere in official circles, and the reliability of unofficial intimations of the potential capacity which the firm would be required to create in the event of a serious deterioration of international relations. Fear that undue optimism on the part of the Air Ministry's technical advisers would lead them to recommend the production of untried engines with an attractive potential performance was an important influence. Nor could the management neglect the effect of the creation of shadow capacity on the firm's future. Major factors such as these determined policy at Derby. A good many minor factors played their part and the period from the end of 1937 up to the outbreak of war throws some light on the complex interaction of all these forces.

12 Rearmament: the Pace Quickens

Towards the end of 1937 there was a considerable revival of interest in official circles which may have been caused by the increasing dissatisfaction with the progress of the rearmament drive. An enquiry from Captain Halam, then Director of Aircraft Production at the Air Ministry, elicited the reply from Hives that Rolls-Royce could produce 100 engines a week 'provided we can have complete control of our sub-contractors and augment their plant where necessary'. A discussion on the subject of foundry capacity took place between Hives, Sidgreaves and Air Vice-Marshal W. L. Welsh (then Air Member for Supply and Organisation) at which the latter was informed that Rolls-Royce had decided to go ahead independently and employ its own capital in creating this capacity. This preserved the management's complete independence of action in a sphere where unfettered and immediate action was of decisive importance. In a letter to Colonel Disney written on 20 December Hives informed him that 'this does not mean that we have lost interest; it really means that we have decided to go ahead on our own. I can promise you that in four to five months time our foundry and our technical organisation connected with it will be equal to anything else in the world.' On 15 December the board authorised the immediate expenditure of £39,000 on this project.

A series of discussions on the subject of shadowing the Rolls-Royce engines took place following a letter from Hives on 8 October in which he admitted that the firm was prepared to discuss various arrangements. As a result of these discussions two schemes, to be known as Scheme 1 and Scheme 2, were evolved. The first was supported by Rolls-Royce, the second by the Air Ministry. The first scheme involved removing, at the Air Ministry's expense, all car production from the Derby factory, which could then be turned over completely to aero production, all the necessary jigs, tools and machinery for the increased output required being purchased by the Air Ministry and rented to the company. When Scheme 1 was first suggested Hives had

174

in mind a factory at Burton which Rolls-Royce could acquire for its chassis production. There were two principal reasons for this proposal. The first of these was the serious decline in chassis demand which had taken place during the previous year. This presented a difficult labour problem and, in reply to a query received from Colonel Disney shortly after the invasion of Austria, Hives wrote that 'it would be impossible to run this factory with the Aero Division working with additional unskilled labour and the chassis division working practically short time.' The second reason was that Hives would have welcomed an opportunity of removing chassis production from Derby.

His idea was to convert the existing chassis division to the production of the Vulture, since this undeveloped engine was far beyond the technical resources of a new shadow factory. The Merlin, whose production was merely a question of 'equipment and manpower' could gradually be transferred to the shadow factory if necessary without seriously affecting its production. A sudden transfer was another matter and would have reduced total output very seriously. The Vulture was even more of a production problem. This engine was in a different position, said Hives, 'because we do not know what the engine is going to be like. To get the Vulture going is going to be a terrific job, the biggest we have ever had to tackle.'

The transfer of chassis production was considered to be the only method by which Rolls-Royce could fulfil the requirements of the Air Ministry but Hives thought that it might also be 'the salvation of our motor-car business. We can go in and start in a fresh atmosphere and not be tied to the traditions of thirty years at Derby.' It was to be nearly eight years before such an opportunity was to present itself.

When the Burton scheme was rejected almost simultaneously with the receipt of instructions to proceed with 1900 additional Merlins a further suggestion was made that the chassis division should be transferred to the repair shop at an estimated cost of some £600,000. This would have enabled Derby to achieve a production in the neighbourhood of 240 engines a week but before anything could be done along these lines approval was finally given to the Crewe scheme.

The existence of a section of the factory producing chassis was by no means the handicap to expanding engine output which the above may appear to suggest. Hives looked upon it as a real advantage in many ways. 'It is only when we come to plan a new factory', he said, 'that we realised what a tremendous advantage we have at Derby by having a large motor-car factory in the same unit. We use the motor-car division as a pool. If we are short of labour on the aero side, we transfer it from the motor-car; if there is likely to be a hold-up due to failure of a sub-contractor, or excessive scrap, we still draw on the motor-car division to help us out. At Crewe we shall not have that advantage and therefore we have got to anticipate equipment being idle due to shortage of labour and other causes, which means that we shall want relatively more room and more equipment at Crewe, compared with Derby, for doing the same job.'

The second scheme contemplated the erection of a new factory by the State which would be managed by Rolls-Royce and which would be partially dependent on a considerable extension of the sub-contract organisation which had been created from Derby. Hives had always consistently favoured the creation of capacity on the basis of sub-contracting, but the vulnerability of Derby as the only assembly centre had to be taken into consideration and this was an important factor in the location of the new factory suggested by the Air Ministry.

Both these schemes were under constant discussion during the early part of 1938, but neither had been finally agreed by the Air Ministry when the invasion of Austria took place on 11 March. On 15 March Lord Herbert Scott wrote to Hives informing him that he believed the Prime Minister intended 'to press on armaments at once' and that he might also wish chassis work to be suspended. On the 18th the Air Ministry asked for information on how many employees Rolls-Royce could employ on the basis of two shifts and overtime, and requested a forecast of deliveries up to March 1939. This date did not make sense in view of the great urgency of the situation but a reply was nevertheless sent that the firm could deliver 1385 Merlins with the present organisation, and that this could be stepped up to 1885 if chassis production was suspended.[1] Hives considered this to be unavoidable in a national emergency and he declared in a minute to Sidgreaves that 'we cannot allow ourselves to be accused of obstruction.' He also wished to substantiate the claim, made on 27 January to the Air Minister, that the energy and capacity of the firm was not fully absorbed in the production of aero-engines. Sidgreaves replied to this minute that he could not suspend the production of chassis without the full sanction of the board, but in this event this was not necessary. At this time (28 March 1938) well over half the firm's employees were engaged on aero-engine production[2] and the volume of sub-contract labour was increasing steadily.[3]

It was estimated that an increase in output of 500 Merlins would require an additional 1600 skilled, 200 semi-skilled and 200 unskilled men and that it would take at least three months for this labour to become productive.

All this information was readily provided for the Air Ministry but the indecision in official quarters generally caused considerable dissastisfaction at Derby. Definite decisions as to the quantity and types of engines required could not be obtained. When the announcement that Scheme 2 had been chosen was followed a few weeks later by the announcement that Scheme 1 was to be applied, the confusion and disillusionment at Derby can well be imagined. In a letter to Lord Herbert Scott, Hives gave vent to his irritation and disquiet:

> The manner in which the air expansion programme is being handled is terrible, and one cannot see any signs of it improving. Essentially Britain has always had to depend on private enterprise, and to encourage private enterprise they must allow firms to make a profit – even if they take most of it away by taxes – but the government-cum-private factories leave it so that no one is responsible; each can blame the other. The attitude of mind I have adopted is to make sure that we are doing our job as well as we possibly can and to fight anybody who prevents us carrying this out.

The absorption of engines into aircraft was also very unsatisfactory and a graph drawn in December 1939 revealed clearly the gross disproportion between the two rates of increase. It was not in fact until the end of 1938 that an airframe programme was drawn up at the Air Ministry, and only in January 1942 was any attempt made by the 'planners' at the Ministry of Aircraft Production (M.A.P.) to relate the engine and airframe programmes one to the other.[4]

Sidgreaves and Hives continued to discuss the Rolls-Royce shadow factory throughout the month of May. On the 16th Sidgreaves attended a meeting at which he advocated the Burton scheme, but this was not approved. On 23 May he suggested the erection of a shadow factory at a cost of £1,500,000 to supplement assembly capacity at Derby. This was finally agreed in principle, though it was considered that a capital grant of £1 million would be sufficient.

The location of this factory caused some difference of opinion between various ministries. Rolls-Royce favoured Crewe, while the Ministry of Labour favoured Liverpool on the assumption that more of the type of labour which Rolls-Royce required would be available in this district. Hives was under no such illusion and in a report on the various possible schemes argues that the mere physical supply of labour was no criterion at all.

> It is no use thinking we could place this factory anywhere to absorb existing labour. Labour of the type we require does not exist. I think there is much more likelihood of getting the right type if we have an attractive site where the men have good amenities than if we attempt to take advantage of casual labour near a big town.

He also stressed the importance of the subsidiary sub-contracting organisation which could either be designed round the capacity already existing or designed to create potential capacity. Hives favoured the latter since the whole object of the shadow scheme was the creation of potential capacity for quantity production. Here again the problem was far from simple.

> The most valuable people as regards sub-contractors are − as one would naturally expect at the present time − full up with work. People who are not full up with work are those businesses which have been badly run and are inefficient.

On 24 March Sidgreaves visited the British United Shoe Machinery Company and found them fully occupied with Admiralty orders, for which they expressed a strong preference on the grounds that 'in the case of Admiralty contracts they submitted prices about which, if the Admiralty accepted them and placed contracts, there was no enquiry and no alteration on further orders.' Sidgreaves also discovered that the best firms were not interested in orders for 500 sets of a particular component and that many of them demanded conditions and prices which the Air Ministry would not accept.

There were indeed a great many difficulties and the Derby management was acutely conscious of the fact that all would have been much easier had the orders for volume production been given eighteen months earlier. But regrets were pointless and the management was determined to make a success of the scheme. Hives thought that a shadow run directly by the parent company would be much more successful than the other types of shadow factory. Sidgreaves endorsed this opinion in a minute in which he declared: 'I feel that if we start on this scheme we must make a success of it because it is going to be in competition with the National Shadow Factories and it is to the advantage of the whole industry for us to show that a shadow scheme controlled by the parent firm is more successful and more economical than the Government controlled factories.' He added the pointed conclusion that 'we must not expect the D.A.P.[5] to be anxious for this to happen'.

The management's enthusiasm for the Crewe project was somewhat diminished by the news, received early in April, that an official secret mission was to be sent to the United States to purchase engines. Sidgreaves thought this a bad policy, not only because it would discourage British engine manufacturers, but because it revealed the inefficiency and incompetence of government. He also considered that 'the Powers that Be would have to give way on all sorts of points that they have stood out against in regard to British aircraft, i.e. they would have to accept the machines with different equipment, different sorts of tests, no A.I.D. inspection, no control of firm's profits, and additionally they would be giving financial support to the American aircraft industry.' But though he was strongly opposed to this mission, largely on the grounds that a little foresight and firmness would have made it unnecessary, he was not unduly perturbed because of the very small capacity of the American aircraft industry at the time. Hives was less equivocal. In a minute to Sidgreaves, he developed the view that there was no justification for the mission buying engines, even if they considered it necessary to buy aircraft.

> I think we ought to fight like wildcats to make sure that even if they buy American aircraft they should be installed with British engines ... I claim it would take all the heart out of our efforts if when we struggle and scheme and give the Government everything they ask for, they should then go and hand out engine business to a foreign government.

While these discussions on Crewe were still proceeding, the Air Ministry was informed that Rolls-Royce could not afford to spend any more of its own capital on rearmament. In a report written on 16 May Hives pointed out that Rolls-Royce had spent £320,000 of its own capital since January 1937 on rearmament facilities and that £750,000 of the company's own resources were tied up in this work. Shortly before this Derby had been informed by telephone that an order for a further 2000 Merlins could be expected. As the Crewe decision had not yet been finalised this prospective order, coupled with a letter received from the Air Ministry in April intimating that the increased production was to be obtained by converting the Derby factory, persuaded the management that any further expansion of capacity would have to be carried out directly by the Ministry. Detailed information on the new Daimler shadow factory erected by the Ministry was available[6] and it was realised that such a project was beyond the firm's financial capacity on the basis of its existing capitalisation. The Air Ministry did not consider this an unreasonable attitude and its adoption probably played some part in hastening the decision on Crewe. The location of the new factory at Crewe was finally approved by the Air Ministry and Ministry of Labour (which had raised strong objections to Shrewsbury) on 24 May, the principle of the scheme having received the approval of the Air Council Committee on Supply the previous day. At a joint meeting held with the firm's representatives the same day it was decided to expand some portions of the Derby factory at the same time. Documents produced at the Nuremburg trials from the German General Staff archives have revealed that Hitler ordered the preparations for the invasion of Czechoslovakia in October on 28 May. During the following months there was a considerable increase in tension over the Sudetenland. In a personal letter to Hives written a few days after this meeting Sir Wilfrid Freeman expressed an earnest desire to 'see this Shadow Factory "en train" at the earliest possible moment'.

Rolls-Royce succeeded in persuading the Air Ministry to pay the capital costs of erection and equipment and to lease the plant to them. From the accounting and costing point of view, Crewe was to be regarded as an integral part of the Rolls-Royce organisation and the output of both factories was to be treated in exactly the same way. Rolls-Royce agreed to pay the prevailing bank rate of interest as rent, and the Air Ministry agreed that all Crewe overheads should be compounded with Derby overheads at least in the initial stages. The company retained the option to terminate the tenancy at any time and to purchase the machine tools at a price to be agreed between the firm and the Ministry. It was intended from the outset to develop a sub-contracting organisation to meet Crewe's requirements and the Ministry agreed that Rolls-Royce should rent and control any machines which the Ministry installed at sub-contractors at the firm's request.

The project was supported with enthusiasm by the Crewe municipal authorities and 65 acres of ground were acquired forthwith. The L.M.S. railway works were discharging men at this stage, and the possibility of their re-employment by Rolls-Royce was obviously of great advantage to the community. A town of some 46,000 inhabitants, its 'economy' had in the past been very largely dependent on the activity of the

L.M.S. works, and in consequence Crewe looked with considerable favour upon the new enterprise.

It was decided that wherever possible, and without prejudice to the efficiency of the new factory, the accounting, payroll, secretarial and general administrative work should be handled by the existing organisation at Derby. But a separate and more modern costing system was installed and full advantage was taken of the opportunity to install the most modern machines and to introduce the latest methods. It was also decided to employ a straight bonus system of wage payment. On 14 June Rolls-Royce was informed in a letter from Sir Henry Self (now Permanent Under-Secretary to the Air Ministry) that the Ministry had sanctioned a total expenditure of £1 million, for both the erection of Crewe and the expansion at Derby. It was immediately realised at Derby that this figure would soon be exceeded but this caused no hesitation whatever in view of the continued warnings received from the Ministry that the engine requirements were likely to be increased. On 27 June the secretary of the Air Council Committee on Supply intimated that there was a strong probability of a further order for 1000 engines and requested separate estimates on the cost of expanding Crewe to half the size of the Derby factory and to equal the size of the Derby factory. On 27 July the capital allocation was increased to £1,220,000 and within two months an extension costing £732,000 was authorised. It was estimated that this extension was necessary to secure the additional output of 35 engines a week which the Ministry considered to be necessary.

The erection of Crewe was begun by a private firm of contractors almost immediately, and the first complete engine was produced in June 1939. This is a considerable achievement, particularly when compared with the period of fifteen months required by the No. 1 Shadow Group to produce its first set of components. It is nevertheless significant that the planning of production in this factory was considerably hampered by the inability of the Air Ministry to define precisely the number and types of Rolls-Royce engines required and the period within which they were to be produced. This was not of course entirely the fault of the Ministry, whose actions during 1938 were to some extent subject to the vacillation of the Prime Minister and his Cabinet on rearmament. But during this year the Ministry evidently began to feel the weight of the administrative responsibility which the co-ordination of the aircraft programme was to impose on it, while the industry suffered quite considerably from the inability of the Ministry to define and evaluate its objectives. This had an adverse effect on the confidence of the industrial executives who were expected to produce the nuts and bolts of the rearmament programme.

The original requirement for 1938 was for 2070 Merlins. This was revised to 2270 in May and shortly thereafter revised downwards to 1680 and 1470. This was soon followed by an upward revision and 2390 were in fact completed. Actual orders for which contracts were received during the year were as follows:

February	513
June/July	3578
November	1489
December	2970

On 15 October instructions to proceed (known as ITPs) had been received for 5339 engines in all. Material had been ordered for 3431 engines and 1753 had been delivered. In addition a relatively small but significant number (450) of Vulture engines (a much more complicated engine than the Merlin to produce) was ordered during the year. The output achieved in 1938 was naturally little affected by the decisions taken in 1938 and reflected the decisions taken and postponed by the Ministry during the previous two years. When the second extension of Crewe was authorised on 6 September the position of the following year was extremely confused.

Hives pointed out that the 1938 rate of expansion of Derby and Crewe (plus the sub-contract scheme) would provide an output of 350 Merlins a month by September 1939, and that the second extension would increase the output to 500 a month. He considered that there should always be at least eight months' work on order and on this basis the minimum should at this stage have been 4000. It was therefore proposed that the total number of engines on order should be increased to 12,750 by a further order for 6500 Merlins which would keep both factories running until the end of 1941. Hives was becoming increasingly concerned with absorption into airframes at this stage. 'Our concern', he said, 'is that we cannot see where the aircraft are coming from to absorb these engines.' He was equally concerned with what would happen if the orders were suddenly reduced and in view of Mr Chamberlain's 'success' at Munich in September this cautious attitude was by no means unwarranted. There was however more to it than this.

In what light did the Air Ministry regard the Crewe factory – as a plant to enable Derby to obtain the maximum immediate increase in production during 1939 and 1940 or as a plant which, while its development was intended to assist Derby to fulfil its commitments, should be developed as war potential? This question was not answered, mainly because it was not generally realised that different answers would lead to the employment of different productive techniques. Immediate capacity, ultimate capacity and the period elapsing between these two limits were all determinants of the policy most suitable to the end in view. On the answer to this question depended the employment of the available machine tools between the parent factory (Crewe) and the sub-contractors. 'If it is a question of increasing peak production', said Hives, 'we are strongly in favour of using the existing engineering facilities throughout the country, and where necessary taking the machines and tools to where the labour is rather than moving homes.' If Crewe, on the other hand, was to be looked on as a war emergency plant (rather in the sense of the original shadow factories) then Rolls-Royce would employ a different layout, installing at Crewe 'only plant which is necessary and which does not exist anywhere else in the country'. The remainder of the equipment would be used 'to enable us to get the best results out of our family of sub-contractors'.

Most of these points were raised at a meeting with the Air Ministry officials on 12 September but the only conclusion reached was that Rolls-Royce should adhere to the March 1940 programme and that Crewe should be able to duplicate all special processes carried out at Derby.[7] This programme envisaged the completion of 3139 Merlins and 50 Vultures and was based on the policy that Derby should switch generally from the manufacture of Merlins to the Vulture, the former being entirely taken over by Crewe. A somewhat vaguer 'authorisation to proceed' covered a further 4459 Merlins and 400 Vultures to be completed after this date.

There is evidence that the responsible officials at the Air Ministry failed to understand why their inability to formulate a clear policy on these matters should have restricted the management's ability to decide on the best course of action. The inevitable result was a compromise with a bias in one direction or another. On 28 September, for example, just after Chamberlain's return from the Godesberg meeting with Hitler and the day before the mobilisation of the Fleet, Colonel Disney informed Sidgreaves that he wanted Rolls-Royce to proceed 'with the maximum production of Merlin engines at the earliest possible moment'. Such instructions were virtually meaningless.[8] Even the demand for maximum production within a strictly defined period is meaningless unless it is known to what extent this is to be at the expense of production after that date. Such a decision leaves a wide latitude of interpretation which cannot be narrowed without assuming direct responsibility for the more detailed judgements which are involved.

The same problem reappeared in a slightly different form on 30 December when a Major Bulman (then Deputy Director of Engine Research and Development under Sir Wilfrid Freeman) informed Sidgreaves that the government still looked upon April as 'a possible date when we may be involved in a war' and asked how many engines Rolls-Royce could produce by April. 'I told them', said Sidgreaves in a departmental minute, 'that the question was the wrong way round and that we should have much more to work on if they would tell us what output they require by April.' The limits of any such forecast were probably not so wide as Sidgreaves imagined but they were sufficiently wide to require as a basis for its judicious interpretation a complete statement of the assumptions upon which it was based. What must frequently have been attributed in official circles to the intransigence (or stupidity) of private enterprise should in fact have been attributed to the inability of any human being or organisation to solve a problem where there are more unknowns than equations. The Ministry officials were faced with very much the same problem. Such situations can only be solved by the exercise of judgement and subordinate decisions are greatly facilitated if the main assumptions upon which the judgement is made are communicated to those responsible for their application.

Progress at Crewe was not quite as rapid as was hoped and in December the contractors were warned that Rolls-Royce might take special measures to complete the factory. There was also very little progress in the housing scheme, which was a vital part of the whole project, and these factors, coupled with the fact that only 680 of the 2390 Merlins delivered to the R.A.F. had been installed in aircraft, caused Hives considerable concern. There was a natural fear that Rolls-Royce would rapidly produce themselves out of work. As early as November Sidgreaves had commented in a minute to Swift that production appeared likely to exceed by a substantial margin the existing Air Ministry Merlin programme for 1938 (1575) and he added that 'Hives and I have been trying for two months or so to ascertain from the government whether they want us to go faster or slower than this but so far we have not been able to obtain any information.[9]

Under such circumstances it is natural that the greater flexibility in both directions of an expansion scheme based on sub-contracting should have made a strong appeal to the management. Quite apart from this the Rolls-Royce scheme was working with great success and as early as August 1938 Mr Ernest Lemon, then Director-General of Production, had asked for Hives' assistance in organising a sub-contracting scheme on a much wider scale for the whole industry. 'You at Rolls-Royce', he said, 'have developed this system of sub-contracting to a fine art, and I want to be able to make the system available to the whole of the aircraft industry apart from engines.' The scheme certainly had many advantages. It was the most satisfactory way of dealing with the labour problem and it ensured that in the event of war there was a wide dispersal of skill and component production, thus reducing the vulnerability of the air force to the destruction of the parent factories by bombing. It was the most economical method of achieving the production of a given number of engines in a limited time with a given capital outlay and it was certainly the policy which conformed best to the Cabinet directive (issued after Munich) that rearmament should proceed as fast as possible 'without disturbing the trade of the country or irritating the Germans and Italians by large-scale measures'.[10] In the sense that such a system involved provisioning the rearmament programme by pulling in the slack[11] in the whole industrial system it offered very great advantages. An extensive sub-contract programme may well be, in purely economic effects, a more efficacious anti-deflationary device than an equivalent public works programme.

The system had its disadvantages, the greatest of which was the increase in the administrative load borne by the parent company. Care had to be exercised, especially in the case of firms with no previous experience of precision engineering work, to preserve quality and interchangeability and a complete and up-to-date control of output at the various sub-contractors' plants had to be developed and maintained. It was also found that firms undertaking these orders required long runs of the components which they were asked to produce and invariably sought an assurance that they would be offered this work in the event of war breaking out. Having no overall instructions from the Air Ministry it was difficult for Rolls-Royce to fulfil these requirements adequately.

The scheme had nevertheless proved itself, and Hives was against a further rapid expansion of Crewe before the first section had been completed.

As a policy we do not want to make the Crewe factory any bigger than is essential to meet demands. My present views are that instead of going on with the second portion of Crewe we should expand our sub-contracting policy. We know that there are ample facilities round the country and if we can get it agreed (the principle has been agreed) that the additional equipment for the second portion of Crewe can be distributed round the country at our discretion at various sub-contractors we can accelerate output in a very much shorter time and with all the known advantages of the sub-contracting method . . . We estimate that we could produce at least twice as many engines by making use of the money allotted for the second portion of Crewe to extend our sub-contracting compared with the expenditure of the same amount of money in increasing the size of the Crewe factory. From the national point of view there is every advantage in this scheme, firstly because the production would not be so vulnerable, secondly because we should get a considerable expansion of engineering talent on our work.

Despite these arguments the Ministry decided to proceed with the second extension and the management was instructed to carry out this instruction as soon as possible. Events in Europe were soon to underline the wisdom of this decision.

13 Rearmament: in Full Spate

The final occupation of Bohemia and the total subjugation of Czecho-slovakia began on 14 March and in his Birmingham speech a few days later Mr Chamberlain made it clear that the years of illusion were over. But the lingering hopes for peace still prevented full-scale industrial mobilisation, and this is clearly reflected in the figures of engine production for the first few months of 1939. The December 1938 total was not again exceeded until the following October, and in April production fell as low as 145. This reflects to some extent the limited capacity of Derby as a production factory, particularly when still encumbered with chassis production. It does not take into account the very great efforts which were being made at Crewe, and which were subsequently to be made at Glasgow, to expand the potential of the group. Sub-contract work also increased steadily in volume.

At the beginning of 1939 the management had good reason to regard its achievement with some satisfaction. The delivery of engines was still well ahead of absorption in airframes though the Air Ministry programme current in January contemplated a production figure nearly 600 greater than that of the firm's own programme. At this stage the Air Ministry was budgeting for a production of 3422 Merlins and 1369 Vultures as the main items in the 1940 programme. A great deal was to happen to upset the Vulture forecast, but the 1939 production was not seriously affected one way or the other by the eventual outbreak of war.

The subjugation of Czechoslovakia was all the proof which the Air Ministry needed that the actual outbreak of war could not be long delayed and engine requirements were drastically revised in this light. Although the Crewe factory was not yet complete, the training of employees and the production of parts began as soon as physically possible. Portable boilers were installed in the factory to provide heat so that the new employees would not have to wait for the completion of the whole factory to acquire experience on a type of work which was new to most of them. But despite this progress the only visible output of complete engines was that at Derby. The Ministry was not satisfied that the potential production of these two factories[1] would meet its requirements in the event of war, and the erection of a third shadow factory now became an urgent topic of discussion.

On 10 March Sir Wilfrid Freeman (Air Member for Development and Production) informed Hives that he would like Rolls-Royce to plan an output of '900 engines per month on a one-shift basis'. On 23 March a letter from Sir Henry Self authorised the production of a further 2970 Merlins and 440 Peregrines[2] and informed the management that the Air Council wished them to take all necessary action for a further pro-gramme of 1420 Merlins, 1960 Peregrines, 1560 Vultures and 275 Exe engines. The Exe engine was still in the experimental stage but a considerable amount of effort had been put into it as the engine seemed particularly suitable for Fleet Air Arm aircraft.

It is hardly surprising that this series of orders should display all the signs of a last-minute decision made under the stress of an emergency.

19.   Merlins under construction at Derby

The first production Vulture was not dispatched until April 1940, the first production Peregrine until February 1940. Both were unproved experimental engines at this time and on neither engine had the firm had any production experience whatsoever. To this extent the orders were largely meaningless but they did serve the very useful purpose of convincing the management that the volume of orders would no longer be a matter of any great concern. Once again, as in 1917/18, the purely physical and technical problems of production were to absorb their entire attention over a period of several years. A programme received from the Air Ministry in the same month envisaged a production of 15,000 engines from the Rolls-Royce group between November 1939 and April 1941.

On 15 March 1939, Hives completed a report in which he endeavoured to set all these facts in their proper perspective. He considered that most of the Peregrines would have to be made at Crewe, and that a further new factory capable of producing 400 engines a month would have to be erected. Sub-contracting would provide no less than 20 per cent of its requirements if this was properly organised and the new factory located in a suitable area. There followed a lucid summary of the relationship between the old and new factories.

The Rolls-Royce factory at Derby has been built and developed around the problem of producing high-class engineering in relatively small quantities with the capacity to change or modify the product quickly. In other words, I should describe the Derby factory as a huge development factory rather than a manufacturing plant. The very structure of the organisation necessitates a large proportion of skilled men who fortunately are available.

As a super aircraft engine development factory there is nothing like it in the world, and therefore in planning for the very big production we want to make sure that Derby is used to the very best advantage. In any big scheme we consider that Derby should be expected to carry all the development work; it should also carry the prototype production over the first two or three hundred engines until all the engineering 'bugs' in the new type of engine have been cleared. It would also have to be responsible for all the inevitable jobs which it is impossible to avoid such as odd spares, changeovers and modifications. *This class of work can be done at Derby but upsets the whole scheme of things in a true manufacturing plant.*[3] There is quite a programme of work ahead for Derby if run on these lines. We have the Vulture, the Peregrine, the air-cooled Exe, the new 37-litre, which will have to be tackled in this order, apart from such odd jobs as the compression-ignited engine, propellor development, and armament work.

The production at Crewe has been planned on very different lines to Derby. We are making use of very much more unskilled and semi-skilled labour. There is not doubt we could go further, but we do not wish to have any trouble with labour. Crewe cannot absorb modifications and alterations like the Derby plant. It would be very much more expensive in both tools and delays.

There is no mystery or fundamental difficulty in producing Rolls-Royce engines with unskilled labour. It means a longer time in planning the production, more expense on jigs, tools and fixtures, the co-operation of the machine tool makers, freedom from alterations, and a longer time before production can commence. We could never hope to obtain sufficient skilled men at Crewe if we were using the same ratio as we are at Derby.

It must be appreciated that the Crewe factory was planned to make more use of sub-contractors than we do at Derby. For instance, it has no pattern shop or foundry and no drop forge; it does not produce crankshafts, cam shafts, cylinder liners, pistons or gears. We were able to sub-contract these parts successfully to look after the first portion of Crewe but now we have started on the second portion we find that we shall have to produce in that unit a number of parts which were not originally planned for because we have failed to get the necessary numbers from sub-contractors.

If it is decided to go ahead with another factory we recommend that it be located in Scotland, preferably near Glasgow. We have had one of our men up there who has located a suitable site . . . The chief advantage in going to Glasgow is that labour should be available. It should also be available for whatever size it is decided to make the factory. We have definitely decided against recommending any further extensions at Crewe because there is insufficient labour to draw upon, and, so far, insufficient houses . . .

Another advantage of Glasgow is that we are now planning to obtain supplies of steel and forgings from Scottish firms and we feel confident that they will prove satisfactory.

The report concluded with a recommendation that the factory should be planned so that the whole of the engine could be produced in

Scotland. It was estimated that on the basis of 20 per cent of the work being sub-contracted the new factory would cost £6.3 million, its size being approximately five times the size of the first portion of Crewe. The final remark of this section of the report – 'it can be assumed that a factory to produce 200 engines a month would cost half the price' – indicated how little attention is paid to the factor of economies of scale when the decisions involved are of this order of magnitude.[4]

This report reveals how clearly Hives appreciated the exact nature of the problems facing the organisation, in particular the competing and contrasting claims and methods of development and production. The comments on the absence of skilled labour and the importance of employee attitudes (particularly towards dilution and the acquisition of new skills) are particularly significant. The next decade of British industrial history was to reveal the full extent of productivity variations which could exist in a group of plants with a similar degree of mechanisation and production techniques. The firm's experience at both Crewe and Glasgow also emphasised the overriding importance of housing, the supply of which in both areas was very slow to respond to the needs of the employee force eventually required by these two factories. This experience suggests that when the requirements of a firm or industry extend beyond a certain scale mobility of labour becomes a completely meaningless term. The provision of housing at Crewe in itself would have been quite insufficient to attract to that town the number of employees eventually employed at Glasgow and the payment of the most exceptional wages would certainly not have solved the problem. Within a fairly stable industrial system the term can mean little more than the movement of very small numbers in response to a number of stimuli. It also seems probable that geographical mobility is of far less importance in an industrial society than occupational mobility. The flexibility of an industrial system is probably far more dependent on the latter than the former. An industrial system which succeeds in maximising its occupational mobility may well be able to afford the social indulgence of geographical immobility.

The efficiency of a sub-contract system depends primarily on occupational mobility, whereas a shadow factory scheme, unless the factory is erected in an area where there is considerable unemployment, depends primarily on geographical mobility. In the case of both Glasgow and Crewe, however, the management had to tackle both these factors. The labour had to be obtained and trained. The extent to which retraining is necessary naturally depends on the degree of similarity between the new and the old techniques and the extent to which the new techniques require genuine judgement, skill and ability (i.e. the extent to which they are genuinely skilled trades as opposed to the generally accepted meaning of this term to define a wage-status). As Hives frequently had occasion to point out in the earlier years of the war, the volume of genuinely skilled labour, by whatever name it was called, could not be rapidly or easily increased. To a very considerable extent the requirements of Crewe and Glasgow were met by drawing on the reserves of Derby. But in both these centres a large number of employees had to be trained in operations of average skill with which they were largely (and in the case of the high proportion of women totally) unfamiliar.

Faced with these new demands on the firm's capacity management no longer contested the need for yet another factory. They were equally adamant that the firm itself could not contemplate any further capital investment in this direction. In a letter to the Supply Committee of the Air Council written on 21 March Sidgreaves pointed out that the Board 'cannot sanction any further financial commitments of this nature'. The firm was nevertheless quite willing to place its technical and administrative experience at the disposal of the Air Ministry. When shortly after the outbreak of war it was suggested that Rolls-Royce should 'parent' yet another shadow factory the management realised that the existing organisation had already strained its capacity and resources to the limit and that if this limit was exceeded the efficiency of the entire group would be seriously imperilled.

The letter also pointed out that the firm had put £750,000 of its own working capital into the Crewe factory which was of course rented as a complete unit from the Air Ministry and treated as an integral part of the Rolls-Royce organisation. This was not possible in the case of the Hillington factory at Glasgow which, although it bore the Rolls-Royce name and was managed by the Rolls-Royce Company, was erected, owned and completely financed by the Government. Rolls-Royce agreed to undertake the work on two important conditions. The first of these was that the firm should have a completely free hand for the first six months, as at Crewe, and the second was that the impact of any possible reduction in aero-engine output should fall first on Glasgow. The management also insisted on the unfettered right to decide at all times which mark and type of engine would be produced in each of the factories under its control.

In return for its managerial services Rolls-Royce would receive a management fee and a royalty, to be calculated on the following basis:

Management Fee

15.5.39–30.6.40	£50,000 in 13 instalments
1.7.40–30.6.41	15,000
1.7.41–30.6.42	30,000

Royalty

First	1500 engines	£70 per engine
Next	500 engines	£60 per engine
Next	2000 engines	£50 per engine
All over	4000 engines	£40 per engine

At a meeting presided over by Sir Henry Self these details were discussed in some detail and it was decided to proceed with the construction of the factory immediately. It was agreed that the essence of the problem was speed and that the construction of the factory should proceed while production planning took place. Prices of materials were kept as near as possible to the schedule of prices obtained in the construction of the Castle Bromwich Spitfire Factory.

Agreement was not reached immediately on two questions – the initial allocation of all orders through Derby and the right of Rolls-Royce to close the Glasgow factory first. The management was acutely aware of the great danger of erecting, equipping, designing and launching a large modern aero-engine factory whose employees had been made familiar with Rolls-Royce technique and methods and handing the direct control of this factory over to its best customer, the State. Clearly a management fee of some £75,000 per annum would be paltry compensation in the event of the Air Ministry deciding to supply its own needs directly through the medium of such a factory. The danger was of course exaggerated for reasons which Hives has himself pointed out. Both Crewe and Glasgow were production and not development factories. The former can be created in a couple of years. The latter require the formulation and application of a great tradition of technical originality and engineering skill. These things cannot be created in two years, and some organisations do not succeed in creating them in twenty. But the management's fears were not groundless. The costs of development were recovered, with the exception of special development contracts which generally covered only a fraction of the overheads of the development organisation, through production contracts on engines which had become relatively stablised technically.

Had the Air Ministry's production orders been removed entirely from the control of the parent organisation this would undoubtedly have prejudiced its financial stability.

On this score Hives was quite frank. He pointed out that Rolls-Royce was in a very weak position since the Air Ministry was the firm's best customer. The position was clearly stated in a letter to the Air Ministry:

> We have sacrificed the balance of the factory at Derby in order to obtain the maximum effort; that is, we have stopped producing parts at Derby which we can get produced by sub-contractors, and have increased our capacity on the difficult pieces which we cannot get made elsewhere. This also applies to Crewe.

Sir Henry Self realised as much as anyone at the Air Ministry at this time how vital the complete goodwill of the senior Rolls-Royce executives had become to the success of the engine programme and summed up the attitude of the Air Ministry as follows: 'We cannot allow the situation to arise in which Rolls-Royce are placed in a dog in the manger position, both entitled to prevent us resuming control of Glasgow and entitled to prevent us putting work into Glasgow. But', he added, 'I should record first that the Air Ministry is fully prepared to give Rolls-Royce an undertaking enforceable at law that orders should not be allocated to Glasgow so as to deprive Derby of normal full employment.'

The definition of 'full employment' alone would have taxed any court of law, however precise the drafting, but what the proper context of the term 'normal' would have been, with Rolls-Royce arguing that one decade in three had been spent at war, leaves much to the imagination of the lawyers who might have been involved. Sir Henry elaborated his point of view extensively:

> The Air Ministry cannot burke that issue by adopting your suggestion that Rolls-Royce should be free to allocate orders between the three factories and to give an undefined preference to Derby. For the Air Ministry to do this would be formally to abrogate the functions of government to a firm which, however trusted, must be expected to concern itself with its shareholders rather than with the public interest. The Air Ministry is responsible to Parliament and cannot enter into an agreement which would debar Parliament from exercising its right to allocate defence orders in the best interests of defence. Nor can the Air Ministry undertake to regard as full normal employ-

ment for Derby the turnover which, under extreme pressure, is at present being reached there. The turnover of Rolls-Royce from Air Ministry orders was about a quarter of a million pounds in 1926, it was £4½ millions in 1938, and is estimated for 1939, with Crewe only partially operative, at £8½ millions. We do not think that you would wish this to be regarded as a permanent and normal arrangement.

Following a suggestion which Sidgreaves made to Sir Wilfrid Freeman, Self suggested that a clause along the following lines should be incorporated in the agreement:

The Air Ministry cannot now abandon its duty to allocate work in the best interests of defence, but it is willing, in the circumstances of the three initial years of this factory, to agree that Rolls-Royce should be free to allocate work between Derby, Glasgow and Crewe on the understanding that Glasgow when completed will be allocated sufficient employment to try out equipment, to train labour and to attain such degree of efficiency as would allow of increase to full planned war capacity within six months of war breaking out.

This controversy illustrates the dangers of a false antithesis, produced by the attempt to find a plausible, simple explanation of a certain situation or type of behaviour whose complexities, if understood and admitted, inhibit the formulation of a solution sufficiently positive or negative to provide support for administrative or political decision. In this case, the antithesis is clearly implied in the phrase 'concern itself with its shareholders *rather than* with the public interest'. It should by now be sufficiently obvious that no firm in the position of Rolls-Royce could possibly benefit the long-run interests of its shareholders by causing grave offence to the public interest. Indeed, the obverse of this proposition is much more likely to be true. This fact, at first intuitively and later quite consciously appreciated by the management, has influenced many significant policy decisions and in several cases the management has shown itself a better judge of the 'public interest' than either its official or its self-appointed guardians. In view of the controversy which arose over the future of the Hillington factory at the end of the war and the course of action finally followed by Rolls-Royce over this factory, these arguments are of considerable interest. They illustrate a conflict of attitudes which is probably unavoidable when the State becomes the principal customer of a large private concern. Neither the 'public' character of officials nor the 'private' character of managers guarantees that the judgement of the former is invariably right or that of the latter invariably wrong.

Sir Henry Self in all probability imagined a situation in which Rolls-Royce would have immediately transferred all work from Glasgow to Derby if a large order was suddenly cancelled. Such a cancellation is only likely to have taken place in the event of the almost complete removal of any immediate threat of war. In such a case the firm is likely to have acted as he suggested but it is a very debatable proposition whether or not it would have been in the public interest to divide the production of a considerably reduced number of engines between three widely-separated factories thereby greatly increasing the cost of their production. If put forward on the grounds of national security it could be countered that this would be more seriously imperilled by a reduction of development work than it would by a precipitate reduction in the actual production of a standardised engine such as Glasgow was designed to produce. But this would itself be a false antithesis since national security depends on the balance between quantity and quality – the capacity to produce something which is worth producing. Had it been desired to continue the production of a limited volume of engines of a given type, or of a given percentage of the orders annually given to Derby, the cost of such a project (and it is almost entirely a national cost from whatever angle it is viewed) could have been clearly ascertained and provided for in any contractual agreement between the firm and the State. Some such agreement would undoubtedly have been reached and the extent to which the public interest was served would have depended on whether the emphasis given to cost of production or that given to national security proved in the event to be the more far-sighted and beneficial. If the policy of any form of enterprise, whether private or public, is to be judged by the criterion of public interest it is essential first to define the criteria by which that interest is itself to be judged. That is an assignment from which philosophers and politicians alike are inclined to shrink.

The opportunities open to the managements of independent concerns to contravene the public interest for any length of time to their own advantage – even if they should wish to do so – are far fewer than some critics of the free enterprise system would find convenient to admit. The proportion of policy decisions which are of sufficient importance to warrant their assessment primarily by this criterion is, in any case, small and the number of decisions contrary to the public interest which are reached after a careful contrast of private and public advantage is almost negligible. It may be argued with some point that this evidence is exceptional and that Rolls-Royce has been fortunate in its choice of executives, but the argument implies two assumptions which it is difficult to support. The first is that the average business executive is anti-social and that he will naturally, if the temptation is sufficiently great, pursue the anti-social course of action if, by so doing, he will increase his profits. The second assumption is that the occasions on which it is profitable for him to do so are very numerous. There is little *a priori* evidence for either of these assumptions. Even in this era of comparatively unbridled capitalism responsible executives in organisations such as Rolls-Royce took a fairly broad and enlightened view of their responsibilities.

Though important because of the light which it throws on some of the attitudes which affect the relationship between industry and the State, this controversy did not seriously impede the construction of the Glasgow factory, which was begun in June. The first building was occupied in November, one month after the outbreak of war.

In the planning and erection of the Glasgow factory the experience already gained at Crewe proved a great advantage though the planned output for Glasgow was greatly in excess of the output originally planned for Crewe. In consequence, though the Crewe experience was useful in determining machine tool requirements, machining area, labour requirements and overall cost, the Glasgow factory was designed specifically to ensure a smooth flow of production. Machine tools were arranged and set for single-purpose operations and line production to a far greater extent than at Crewe. Glasgow was designed from its foundations as a production factory. In the design, erection and planning of both these factories the management leaned very heavily on the experience of a firm of industrial consultants whose services had been retained for the first time during the early part of 1938. These engineers were successful in persuading the management to adopt numerous methods and techniques which had hitherto been viewed with some suspicion at Derby, where conservative traditions die hard. Possessing the great advantage of complete independence of judgement and having a wide experience of production methods in other industries where both quantity and cost were of far greater significance than the rate of technical development, the staff of Production-Engineering Limited were able to contribute valuable advice and information and to remove a considerable burden from the shoulders of the management at Derby. An investigation carried out at Derby itself revealed serious deficiencies in the control systems and administrative techniques employed and most of the more serious faults were remedied before the outbreak of war. Control over productive efficiency at Derby had in the past depended very largely on the analysis of past costs. This information, though valuable, was insufficiently detailed, inadequately analysed, and frequently received too late to be of any significant use. The Production-Engineering staff were able to install a system which gave the management a far more direct and immediate control over productive efficiency.

The employment of a firm of outside consultants whose work was very largely in parallel with that of the existing management led inevitably to some criticism of their methods and objectives. It was felt, quite naturally, that their employment in itself implied some criticism on the part of the board and its immediate executive officers of the administrative staff of the firm. This could not altogether be denied but in retaining their services the board acted in the belief that it was far easier for an outside firm of management consultants to recommend and introduce administrative reforms and new control systems. The firm's own executives may well have appreciated the need for such changes but they could not introduce them without upsetting the informal organisation and affording grounds for complaint that the changes had been dictated by the arbitrary pressure of personal bias rather than the claims of productive efficiency. There can, however, be no doubt of the contribution made by this team of consultants even though the Air Ministry later questioned the expenditure which was involved.

An important distinction between Glasgow and Crewe is the fact that the former was designed to be almost completely independent of sub-contract capacity. That this objective was achieved is indicated by the fact that in 1941 Glasgow machined 98 per cent of its production[5] compared with 51 per cent at Derby and 57 per cent at Crewe.[6] It was also decided at the outset that the factory would have to manufacture its own castings, and for this purpose the most modern and complete light-alloy foundry in the country was erected as an integral part of the factory. This comprised fourteen standard-sized blocks, each measuring 420×320 feet, which were specially designed to facilitate the mass production of a modern aero-engine. This design enabled production, supply and inspection departments to be physically separated in a manner unknown at either Derby or Crewe. Designed to employ some 16,000 employees, the factory became, on its completion, one of the largest industrial undertakings in Scotland. By April 1940 seven of the main shops were occupied and in production and the whole factory was occupied by September.

The Hillington factory was an undertaking of no small magnitude from any point of view. Labour presented one of the most difficult problems and this problem was energetically tackled from the outset. Arrangements were made for the Stow Technical College to train apprentices, a toolroom was established near the site for the training of fitters and eight standard factory units were rented from the Hillington industrial estate to provide a factory in which machines could be put into operation both for training and production as soon as possible. The foundry presented by far the biggest labour problem. This type of work was completely unknown in Scotland and experienced coremakers and dressers were unobtainable elsewhere in the country. It was therefore decided to make the maximum possible use of specially trained female labour and to minimise the demand for highly-skilled labour by employing the most modern mechanised methods of foundry production. Wherever possible all materials were handled mechanically. This in itself necessitated the development of all-metal pattern equipment which was unknown to the pattern-making industry in Scotland. To make this possible local pattern-makers were sent to acquire the techniques employed at Coventry and specially selected men were given a course of training in foundry work at Derby, where the metallurgical and foundry techniques had been developed to an exceptionally high standard.

In this and many other ways the management implemented its promise to the Air Ministry to place the skill and resources of Rolls-Royce at the disposal of the nation. This was done despite the fact that final agreement on the various conditions of the management contract was not reached until the latter part of 1941.

14 The Inter-war Years: Summary and Conclusions

The salient features of the history of a great industrial company are most readily brought within focus by a study of the evolution of its managerial policy. The preceding chapters have shown that even in the case of a firm like Rolls-Royce the polished phrases of the published balance sheet often conceal long periods of struggle and crisis. The consistent declaration of an almost uniform dividend is no easy achievement and those who are most critical of the management of such enterprises have usually had little experience of the heavy responsibility and strain of industrial administration. The success of Rolls-Royce as a manufacturing concern in the inter-war years – for by any standards of comparison no other word but success will suffice – was none the less a success on balance. The achievements heavily outweighed the failures, although there was both achievement and failure in all spheres – design, development, production and administration. But the company succeeded in maintaining the exacting reputation of its products, in the case of the aero-engine by a handsome, in that of the motor-car by a rather narrow, margin. The discussion of chassis costs has shown that this margin was never entirely within the control of the firm and that it was being narrowed by the external circumstances of technical and industrial evolution rather than by any failure in an absolute sense upon the part of the firm's technicians and executives, who were probably amongst the first in the British engineering industry to realise the extent to which British industry was already, between the wars, living on its reserves of skill, enterprise and investment.

Rolls-Royce was not infrequently looked upon in industrial and financial circles as being virtually exempt from the stress and strain of industrial battle. It has been regarded as possessing a near monopoly of the most highly skilled technicians and craftsmen in the British Isles, a tradition and experience which few organisations can match and resources which are believed to confer an immense advantage over other less fortunate organisations. The name has become a talisman throughout the industrial world. Discussions of the British motor industry have thus often been prefaced with some such remark as 'leaving on one side companies like Rolls-Royce' or 'with few exceptions such as the Rolls-Royce Company which cares nothing for foreign competition'.[1] It is hardly surprising that the publicised history of the company – the history of its achievements – should have created such a myth of virtual immunity to the problems which beset the industry as a whole. Other firms in other industries have achieved, and succeeded in maintaining, comparable reputations for their products, but in its own engineering fields Rolls-Royce attempted to maintain unique standards of excellence. Such objectives were not easily achieved.

Economic forces, which are generally national in character, are not usually discriminate in their incidence. Rolls-Royce was usually amongst the first firms in the industry to feel their impact, even if it was not the first to appreciate their significance or evolve a solution. These efforts were often misdirected, but the very term history implies error and misdirection. They have involved a continual struggle on the part of the management to mould and recast conservative internal policies and methods in an endeavour to keep 'competition', in the normally accepted sense of this term, at arm's length. These two aspects of the struggle are of course the obverse and reverse of the same coin in the same way that the history of the development of Rolls-Royce policy is to a very considerable extent the other face of the as yet unwritten history of the whole industry.

In the twenties, the decline in the relative strength of the British motor-car industry was not really accepted or understood except by a few largely disinterested spectators such as *The Economist*, which, though it paid the industry little enough attention, remarked as early as 1925 that few industries in the country presented 'such a deplorable picture of wasted capital'. The British economy as a whole still had sufficient strength, despite the ravages of the First World War, to enable the country to permit, without serious question, a slow evolution of the industry on the basis of a structure which was vulnerable, extravagent, and conducive to the growth of self-perpetuating vices. Since the majority of firms survived despite continual loss and reorganisation and the home market seemed prepared to foot the bill, there were few inducements internal to the industry which might have led to the voluntary adoption of measures to achieve a more economic structure. The industry as a whole conceived its main objective – the supply of the British home Market – to be a perfectly legitimate justification of the policy of catering for the English love of variety and distinction. The export market was treated as a marginal market, to be supplied after home market wherever possible with vehicles designed primarily for home conditions. The world was invited to 'take it or leave it' and the world, for the most part, left it.

Against the threat of the continuous advance in production technique in the United States there stood always the two-fold guarantee of political protection of the home market (on the grounds of employment, defence and the prosperity of the industry) and, what was possibly even more important, the natural loyalty of the average Englishmen to the products of British industry. Their undoubted suitability to English tastes and conditions (especially in view of the taxation of cubic capacity) combined with the ready-made and generally accepted rationalisations of the price differences gave the industry a sense of security which it might not otherwise have possessed. The graduated horsepower tax, which was the height of economic folly from the national point of view, perpetuated and encouraged the costly and contagious policy of producing several sizes of practically every make of car. In serving the dubious interest of fiscal convenience it effectively prevented necessary structural changes which the industry might otherwise have introduced.

In the thirties the position was masked for most firms by the artificial prosperity of the home and export markets which had been brought about by rearmament. Even those firms which did not, unlike Rolls-Royce, participate directly in the rearmament expansion, found that their prospects had improved. The decline, relative to the United States, in the technical and competitive efficiency of the industry as a whole was camouflaged by the alternating prosperity of individual firms, although this did not apply with quite such force to firms such as Rolls-Royce. Whatever the technical merit of their products (and this was not as uniformly high or in proportion to their price as the specialist producers would have liked the public to believe) these were produced on a scale which could not possibly permit full advantage to be taken of mass-production techniques and facilities. Considering the heavy burden of indirect costs brought about by a distributive system which no manufacturer could alter, it is not surprising that many of these firms did not survive.

The entire industry operated under many handicaps, largely the product of restrictionism and conservatism which were by no means confined to the motor industry, but the small-quantity producers exemplified the vulnerability of the whole industry and were the first to experience the serious and increasing difficulties which the industry had to face at the end of the Second World War. These problems were tackled with great energy and persistence at Derby, but their solution was beyond the powers of any individual management acting alone. The only real victory won in the battle of costs at Derby was a victory over symptoms, and although this was in itself constructive, it simply indicated that the removal of the underlying conditions of industrial malaise required a complete change of policy which it was very difficult for the firm itself to effect single-handed. Such a strategy would obviously have involved great risk for any individual concern and the refusal of the management to adopt it simply reflected the cautious and costly conservatism which pervaded most of this section of the industry. It is always pointless to suggest that men should have surmounted their own fears and prejudices, especially when an adequate logical analysis carried out at the time did not provide them with the necessary impetus. An industrial system, like a religion, has its myths, its folklore, its ritual and its magical incantations. Its witch-doctors are, if anything, more powerful since they rattle the conclusions of statistics and logic instead of the less intellectual – if no less effective – paraphernalia of their predecessors. Their hold over the industrial mind is equally tenacious and their authority is proof against the weightiest of arguments. As Henri Bergson once remarked, the inertia of humanity has never yielded save under the impulsion of genius. The effort which science demands is always two-fold – 'that of a few men to find some new thing and that of all others to adopt it and adapt themselves to it'. The adoption and adaptation is often a far lengthier process than the discovery.

It is easy for the historian, however, to underestimate the preoccupation of any administration with the present. When circumstances become particularly difficult it is usually a symptom of the general deficiency of overall policy,[2] but it is precisely at such a time that an administration has least opportunity to consider such apparently vague and postponable matters. The solution of the short-term problems may well be unattainable unless the long-term policy is changed, but their urgency and immediacy – the urgency and immediacy of survival – blunts the critical edge of precise analysis and blurs the perspective.

'Life is fired at us point blank', as Ortega y Gasset once remarked, and only the most exceptional men are capable of breaking the stranglehold of the present on the mind. The moral is as obvious as it is old. The longer the solution of a problem is postponed, the more fully an industry is insulated from irreversible changes in its commercial or technical environment, the more difficult and costly does the final solution become. In many cases the opportunity does not present itself twice, either to the firm or to the industry of which it forms a part.

The history of Rolls-Royce in the inter-war years also reveals the strong influence of specialisation which brought about an administrative, technical and, finally, physical separation of the production of chassis and aero-engines. The growing complexity of the latter is shown in the steadily increasing appropriations for development work and in the construction of costly and elaborate facilities which these funds made possible. The organisation which was built up at Hucknall, Sinfin and elsewhere through the foresight of the management in the late thirties was to prove a national asset of inestimable value during the war and is a most conspicuous example of the intelligent reinvestment of profits.

As an aero-engine manufacturing firm, the history of the company in the inter-war years presents a somewhat different picture. There was no 'industry' on the scale of the automobile industry, nor were the few firms producing the few hundred engines which comprised the total national output in the twenties and early thirties conscious of being an industry distinct and separate from the motor industry in which most of them had their origins. Amongst the 'big four', Rolls-Royce shared with Bristols a pre-eminence which could only be guaranteed by perpetual effort. Moreover, in the interwar years the technical merit of an aero-engine was always immensely more important than its cost, and the quantity demanded was never sufficiently large to warrant much attention being paid to ease of production. This demand was to come later under very different circumstances. The aero-engine industry in the United States was in an exactly comparable position in relation to the automobile industry of that country, and though if anything the famous American firms were ahead on the air-cooled radial, for which there was a substantial and growing demand from civil airlines in the thirties, they were well behind on the liquid-cooled in-line engine in whose ultimate potentialities Sir Henry Royce had bequeathed such a strong faith to his successors.

In this field European technical competition, German, French and

Italian, was a much more serious consideration than American productive efficiency. But it was a field in which British technicians and craftsmen had always excelled, and whenever it came to the test, as it did in the Schneider Trophy contest, the name of Rolls-Royce invariably emerged with added prestige. The tradition and organisation which Royce had developed, first for the car and then for aero-engines in the First World War, was peculiarly suited to this sort of work and it was not until the Second World War that the firm revealed certain deficiencies as a production unit of the same type that had been discovered to exist in the chassis division in the late thirties. The outstanding performance of the firm during the Second World War was skewed in the direction of development rather than production though, as will be seen, it was from many points of view most fortunate that this bias in performance existed.

From the economic point of view, however, there is little doubt that aero-engine manufacture – undoubtedly one of the riskiest types of manufacture in the entire engineering industry, even for those firms which had managed to shelter in the penumbra of state patronage – gradually became the mainstay of the firm. In the early twenties, aero-engines were developed at great risk, without much enthusiasm and with comparatively little support from the Air Ministry, which had no funds to disburse. In these years the main preoccupation of the policy-makers was with economic rather than technical matters. The decision to continue manufacture and development depended on a careful assessment of many factors, military, civil and political, as well as on confidence in the future of chassis production. The manufacture of aero-engines could have been abandoned, and though this was never seriously considered, the possibility existed. In the thirties, however, the focus shifted completely. There was now no doubt about the future of the market for aero-engine production. The problem assumed much more of a logistic character – what volume of production per unit of time to plan for, and the extent to which the resources of the organisation should be expanded to meet this demand or diverted from the periodically unprofitable production of chassis.

On the whole, however, the position of the firm as an aero-engine manufacturer was much stronger than its position as an automobile manufacturer. Not only did the aero-engine firms have a partially guaranteed market, their products also required a level of engineering skill which was not found outside a few important firms in the most advanced industrial countries of the world. The British aero-engine industry catered more for military than civil aviation requirements, since it was Europe's misfortune to be more concerned with war than with peace, and in the equipment of military aircraft performance rather than cost is the main criterion. The industry's attitude towards the export market was only a little less cavalier than that of the motor industry, but the world in this case for the most part took what was offered.

The history of the firm during these years, regarded primarily as a manufacturing concern, reveals the extraordinary complexity of managerial decisions. Such decisions have to be made under any system of production and ownership whatever, and they would not be greatly facilitated even by the most fundamental changes in the structure of the system. They bear striking witness to the innumerable occasions on which managers have to exercise judgement upon the basis of incomplete and inadequate information. The development of administration as a science lies in the progressive reduction to a precise routine of as large an area of decision as possible, but in any rapidly changing industrial system, management will always be an art rather than a science. The genius of the successful administrator or executive will always lie in his capacity for 'masterly administration of the unforeseen'.

The area of the unforeseen is so vast compared with the predictable that it is dangerous to neglect any opportunity of widening the bounds of the latter. It seems reasonable to conclude that the introduction at a much earlier stage of a more precise and analytical system of control – intelligently conceived statistics of production and cost amenable to straightforward interpretation and rapid application – would have made it possible for management to become much more quickly aware of underlying trends and the need for progressive adjustments rather than more radical and damaging changes in policy. It should not have taken management so long to discover the real situation in the chassis division during the thirties.

The conclusion may equally be applied to the industry as a whole. An exaggerated sense of the importance of keeping production and cost information secret was responsible for the complete lack of any industry-wide cost or production statistics. In this, of course, the motor industry does not by any means stand alone in its failure to appreciate the tremendous advantages which would accrue to the industry – efficient and inefficient alike– from such an interchange of information.[3] An acute poverty of strictly comparable industrial statistics characterises the whole era and the cost to the entire industry in productive efficiency must far exceed the cost which the preparation, collection and distribution of such information might have entailed.

Knowledge of comparative manufacturing efficiency should not be dependent on such fortuitous circumstances as personal friendship between senior executives in two companies or on sub-contracting information becoming available as the result of rearmament. The formulation and collection of such information may be laborious and comparisons of relative costs may not always be very rewarding. Still less will they suggest answers to problems in those areas in which statistical comparisons may be of limited value or even positively misleading. But these will at least enable executives to ask more significant questions, and to ask them sooner. This argument would seem to apply as much to firms employing similar processes in different industries as to firms employing different processes in the same industry. As far as can be judged from the published material relating either to the motor or aircraft industries, and from the internal records of one of the most important constituent units of both, there was during this period an almost complete lack of intelligently conceived or relevant statistical information. Its collections, preparation and distribution should be the prime function of any institution claiming to serve, and to represent the interests of, the entire industry. Such information as was published in the motor and aero-engine industries seemed designed to conceal rather than to reveal the true facts of the situation.

The value of such information does not necessarily depend on it being strictly contemporary, nor need it be released outside an industry until after the lapse of a considerable period. But where an industry comprising many independent units is under an obligation to make the most intelligent use of its resources, not only in the interests of the consumer on the home market, but also to enable it to compete in the export market with other producers who possess great advantages, it will do so with greater success if the managements of individual firms can assess the relative efficiency of different processes, operations and methods and compare the distribution and intensity of effort. Mutual assistance of this nature would be far more constructive than many other types devised during the inter-war years. The failure to make full use of such comparative information as was exchanged between Springfield and Derby (due mainly to a lack of comparable records at Derby) nevertheless indicates that if such information is to be of any value there must exist the will as well as the capacity to make full use of it.

It might well be argued that in a highly competitive industry individual firms could never be persuaded to exchange information of this character since it would be too revealing and might make it difficult if not impossible to maintain a position of competitive advantage which was the result of a quite genuine difference in effort or ability. It will be argued that if A's costs over a series of comparable processes are known to be considerably lower than B's, A will be bound to advertise the fact and in due course the information will reach the public to the grave detriment of B's market. Overt publicity of this nature could of course be ruled out without much difficulty, but the latter argument indicates a somewhat naive oversimplification of the nature of competition in the field of durable consumer goods or high-quality technical products such as an aero-engine. It certainly ignores the influence which the achievement of a full employment economy (though we may not yet have discovered how to guarantee an economy against under-employment) must exert on this problem. If the whole industry is prosperous and efficient and if there is no reason to expect this state of affairs to change, then the relative position of different firms within the industry should vary little and be of small importance. The security of the parts cannot in the long run be greater than the security of the whole and, though the latter can never be completely guaranteed, a properly regulated but relatively unimpeded circulation of knowledge and technique within the industry will provide a greater degree of security than can be obtained by other means. Those that have little to contribute will gain much. Those that have much to contribute will not thereby cease to be able to do so, or to reap the more immediate and legitimate rewards of their effort or ingenuity. All will become more aware of their relative proficiencies and weaknesses and will be under a much stronger inducement to strengthen the former and eliminate the latter than that provided by the indirect and long-delayed spur of declining sales – a symptom whose causes have always been open to much misinterpretation.

Though a full-employment economy perpetuates many of the conditions which made it possible in wartime for businessmen to overcome their traditional misgivings on this subject, a controlled interchange of technical and manufacturing information does not find its sole justification or support under these conditions. Under any circumstances any measures which tend to increase the all-round efficiency of an industry are justifiable. If the level of demand for a whole industry is declining, as may well happen even under conditions of full employment, and if this decline is attributable mainly to high costs and high prices, then a policy of *sauve-qui-peut* seems, to each individual firm, natural and unavoidable. The inefficient must go to the wall. But if the latter can become aware, in good time, of the trends of the various indices of efficiency, they will be able to take energetic measures to remedy the situation. And if conditions are such that there is no possibility of avoiding a general reduction in the capacity of the industry, then the industry as a whole will at least have the information from which to judge more intelligently what needs to be done, individually and collectively.

The efficacy, desirability and feasibility of such arrangements in the event of a decline in demand due to a change in tastes (in the direction of other products) is not in any way altered, since it is still in the interests of those units of the industry which continue in production that the average level of efficiency should be as high as possible. The problem of reducing capacity arises in this case, but this is a very different and probably insoluble problem.

Where the level of demand for the whole industry remains unaltered but there is a redistribution of demand within the industry, this may be attributable either to a change in preferences or a variation in prices. If it is the latter, then it will be argued that those firms which have reduced their costs through the evolution and application of more efficient methods will not readily be persuaded to broadcast their knowledge and technique. This may well be so, but no harm will be caused to the firm concerned if the rest of the industry is made aware that an increase in efficiency has been achieved. The *knowledge* of differences in efficiency can be separated from, and is independently useful without, a knowledge of the *causes* of these differences. Its value is that of an arithmetic book without the answers at the back. No process or method is ever quite the final last word, and there are well-established and secure methods of preserving any legitimate relative advantages between individual firms. Moreover every process has its price. The length of time for which such relative advantages should be preserved, mainly as an incentive to continued progress, is another problem for which there is no general solution out of the context of the specific instance, but though there may be very strong arguments for limiting, in the initial stages, the use of a process to the organisation which developed it, there is no argument whatever for limiting the knowledge of its existence or the effect which it has on final costs.

Where a completely new process or method has been developed the problem naturally comes within the scope of patent law, but overall differences in efficiency between firms and industries are more usually attributable to varying proficiency in the application of existing processes or methods, and here it would seem that the mere knowledge of comparative efficiency would do much to stimulate a reduction in the gap between the average and the most efficient. Although skill in the application of a method amounts virtually to a new method and may be the result of strenuous and costly experiment over a long period, it is precisely in this gap between what is patentable and what is not necessarily patentable, but nevertheless important, that the greatest difficulty arises. But here again the mere knowledge of the efficiency with which a particular firm is applying a standardised method of production does not necessarily involve knowledge of the details. The main argument here is that the former alone has an important contribution to make. It was not made in the inter-war years and was not being made in the years immediately following the Second World War in the British motor industry. Where an industry's survival is vital to the economy of the country, this indulgence in the dubious virtue of secrecy seems to be a particularly costly and dangerous folly.

Where an alteration in the pattern of demand takes place within an industry due to a change in preferences, those firms for whose products demand is declining have no alternative but to seek new markets with new products. Such an alteration in preferences might, in the motor-car industry for example, take the form either of a redistribution within the different price classes or a redistribution between the different price classes. Both trends may occur simultaneously and be indistinguishable, but in the first case the argument is not affected since all-round efficiency in production is still desirable and the change in demand is due, generally, to changes in the superficial aspects of the product. It is usually therefore temporary in nature – the firm which has brought out a new body style will increase its sales in that year only – and should not affect the relative position of the firms in the class over a period of years.

In the second case a more fundamental change in the character of demand resulting usually, but not necessarily, from a change in the distribution of incomes, has taken place. In an increasingly egalitarian society this will probably result in a decline in the demand for high-quality articles such as expensive cars, and this decline is likely to be the more severe the greater the disproportion between the difference in price and the difference in quality of the average and the best. Myths are powerful while they last, but once exploded they leave not a wrack behind. In this case, a firm's share of the turnover of an industry can be retained only by changing its products to conform to the new trends. Such a firm would obviously benefit from a knowledge of comparative costs and would be able to restructure its output in a much more rational manner. The remaining firms in the industry could not well object to imparting information which would facilitate a more constructive and possibly a more gradual transition, since they already possess the immense advantage of experience, and there is no likelihood of their share of the turnover of the industry being diminished.

Differences in efficiency between departments, firms or industries are more frequently than is generally realised the result of differences in organisation rather than in method or technology.[4] The advantages of a new method or system of organisation can be completely nullified by failure to consider its effects on the human beings who are involved in the change. In some cases this is all important and if two firms employ identical machines and techniques and obtain vastly different results, the knowledge of these differences is likely to bring about a much more intelligent investigation of their causes.

This leads on inevitably to a discussion of the meaning of the term 'competition' in an industry such as the motor or aero-engine industry. Competition is a term which is variously used to describe many different things. To some it immediately conjures up a picture of the apparent waste of competitive advertising, to others it describes a system of production by independent firms which they consider to be essential to the efficient use of resources in a free-enterprise system. In the most general sense it may be thought of as an attitude of mind which is essential to the continual improvement in quality or reduction in cost of either consumers' or producers' goods, under whatever system or production or ownership this operates. If the desire to produce something of better quality, more cheaply, or altogether new is a competitive desire, whatever the consequences of success, then undoubtedly most of the 'progress' of Western civilisation has been the result of the competitive endeavours of various individuals motivated by the whole complex of forces which the private enterprise system has aligned in a way so satisfying to its advocates and exasperating to its critics.

But though its economic achievements have been demonstrably more impressive than any other system in any other age, this alignment has not always been uniformly constructive. The institutional structure which Western industrial civilisation has developed ostensibly to nurture or restrain the competitive spirit has often succeeded in cramping or destroying it. The preservation of the forms of competition has been confused with the preservation of the substance and elaborate means of reducing the stress and impact of competitive endeavour have often delayed the speed and spread of technical advance, with little to show in return. It has consequently laid itself wide open to attack. The failings of the system have been magnified out of all proportion to its achievements, and in seeking to introduce reforms designed to eliminate competitive waste, the essential nature and mode of operation of purposeful and constructive competitive activity has frequently been overlooked or discharged. A preoccupation with the more serious and damaging aberrations of[5] competitive behaviour has often been responsible for reforms which ignore the essential purpose of the institution and the ways in which this can be achieved. The failure to define such purposes clearly and to accept the limitations which such a definition usually creates, is responsible for politically attractive reforms which end up as 'out of the frying pan into the fire' panaceas.

The trend from competition in essentials to competition in superfluities is almost inevitable as the rate of technical advance in an industry slows down. The former is desirable, the latter is a pure waste of resources. But the history of most industries shows that competitive effort has never been entirely confined either to the essential or the superfluous. The more equal the achievement of competitors, irrespective of the actual rate of advance, the large is the expenditure of resources on the superfluous likely to be. This is probably the strongest argument against a distribution of information which would enable firms to direct their resources more rationally and thus make for a more even rate of advance throughout the industry. But if this is not really an argument in favour of secrecy, it may be an argument in favour of a more intelligent industry-wide approach to the problem of eliminating another costly and largely unnecessary feature of the existing system, the burden of which is borne by every firm and finally by every consumer.

The 'overhead' problem of all three companies which have been discussed in the foregoing pages – all three of which in fact failed though only two were forced to discontinue operations[6] – is very largely the result of this competition in superfluities, especially exemplified by frequent changes in body style which are not necessitated by any technical advance. This is even more the case in the United States then in Great Britain. The problem posed by competitive advertising is not dissimilar to that posed by armaments. If everyone gave them up everyone would be better off and no one would need them again. But to act alone is to invite disaster, and mutual suspicion and hostility always seems too great ever to allow everyone to act together. In the international sphere, however, there is no one to enforce the agreed rules, to impose penalties or to dismiss or punish offenders. There the analogy fails, for, if the agreement in an industry can once be formulated, there exist many sanctions, legal and otherwise, from which a constructive measure could derive strong support.

The cost of luxurious distributive facilities, though beyond the direct control of any individual company, falls into much the same category of wasteful and largely unnecessary expenditure. All of it must ultimately be borne by the consumer and its main effect is to limit the market (through higher prices) and make it all the more difficult for each firm to operate profitably and for the industry as a whole to compete in the export markets of the world. It is indeed fortunate that the British motor industry is by no means alone in having to support the burden of its own folly. In the United States the annual cost to the industry (and thus ultimately to the consumer) of these various forms of expenditure must be very great indeed. The volume of production is so large, however, that the addition to the cost per vehicle cannot be more than a small fraction of its British counterpart. The cost to the consumer of his own susceptibility must be a somewhat startling figure. If an analysis could be made of the jig and tool costs and development expenses of the whole industry it would be surprising if the amount spent on the pursuit of what was thought at the time to be genuine technical advance was greater than the amount spent on features designed to give the appearance of novelty and change. The exactions levied on the consumer by the distributive system are much greater, and less excusable, than the toll levied on commerce by feudal privilege in those centuries in which the public interest was an orphan concept of most uncertain parentage without any pretensions to an ideological pedigree. On such a problem, however, unanimity of opinion provides little more than a blueprint for unanimity of action. Either the catalyst of stress or the compulsion of law may be necessary to ensure that effective action is finally taken.

On this subject the difference in the nature of the automobile and aero-engine market is significant. The aero-engine is bought and sold by experts. It is delivered direct from the factory to the customer and is to a very large extent self-advertising. The principal indirect costs in aero-engine production are development expenses which must cover the cost of developing those designs which finally prove, after considerable development, to be failures. Any sort of guarantee is likely to prove a costly undertaking which has to be recovered in the final price. In the aero-engine field price competition as such is comparatively unimportant.[7] In the motor industry, it is all-important. If an aero-engine has the requisite technical merit and fulfils the all-round conditions of operation demanded by the customers, it will usually sell irrespective of price, especially within a protected military aviation market. Differences in initial capital cost are small compared with the differences in operating cost, even where two engines appear to be in much the same class as regards power output. In the motor industry, on the other hand, practically every car made has the necessary minimum of technical merit and since many cars produced in all price classes are almost identical in all but appearance, price competition is of great importance. The fundamental difference between the two products is that the one is a relatively stablised design produced on a large scale and sold to a relatively inexpert and fashion-conscious public, whereas the other is in a relatively fluid technical state, produced, except in time of war, on a small scale and always sold to an expert and discriminating consumer.

There is thus a profound difference in the nature of competition between two firms in the aero-engine and two firms in the motor industry. In the one case the efficiency of the product is almost all-important, in the other case the efficiency of the product is so much taken for granted that the efficiency of production has almost become the main preoccupation of the management. It is thus difficult to assess the nature or extent of competitive advantage in the engineering industry, particularly where several firms are engaged simultaneously in several fields and when some if not all of the products are undergoing continuous technical development.

Throughout the aero-engine industry the achievement of technical superiority in some direction is the major aim of policy. Oddly enough in this case the basis of economic success – the technical merit of the product – is well known; Its details are published in a specialised technical press and they provide the main spur to competitive endeavour. In the motor industry the basis of economic success – a composite of technical merit and efficient production with most emphasis on the latter – is known only in the most indirect manner. Thus within the same institutional framework the stimulus to constructive competitive endeavour is far weaker for motor cars than for aero-engines. The knowledge of difference in manufacturing methods and efficiency is so limited in the former case and obtained in such an indirect manner that most firms direct their energies towards preserving their markets by neutralising the expenditure of their rivals. There is little doubt that here an abuse, in Ortega y Gasset's terminology, has developed into a usage which can only be eliminated by an agreed and concerted change of policy by the whole industry, in the interests not only of the industry but of the whole country.

The achievements, failures and policies of an institution, like those of an individual, cannot be judged in isolation from the framework of the society of which it forms a part. It is inevitable that a study of an organisation of this nature should reveal the operation not of one, but of several sectional interests, all of which at times make special claims upon resources and policy. All these interests – labour, capital, the solidity of the informal social structure, the social and economic security of individual groups – are liable to some into conflict with the interests of the whole and even with the public interest. Where they are strong and articulate they will endeavour to secure and will often succeed in securing for themselves exceptional advantages which become embedded in the institutional structure and quite soon come to be regarded as the natural ordering of affairs. The extent to which such an institutional structure conflicts with the public interest is always likely to be exaggerated since deficiencies are more conspicuous than merits and provide the substance of political controversy. But in an imperfect society, whether it be agrarian or industrial, capitalist or communist, this conflict cannot be eliminated unless progress is to cease or unless there are basic changes in human behaviour. The conflict with the public interest, which is generally marginal in character – a deduction from a total positive contribution rather than a negative exaction – is the main problem to be solved by any ordering of society. Every generation is left with the inadequate solution of its predecessor and the intractability of the problem is particularly distressing to Utopians who see wilful and malicious obstructionism behind every institutional imperfection. Blind to the nature and cost of change and progress, the immutability of human nature, the complexity of justice and the often indefinable nature of the public interest, they are perpetually outraged by the gross disproportion between the intensity of their moral indignation, the logical coherence and practicability of their proposals, and the executive power at their command.

The important point is that the contribution of individuals and organisations to the public interest can be maximised only by institutional arrangements which permit and encourage, within certain limits that must continually be tested and modified, the service of sectional interests. The latter provision seems to bring forth, under circumstances which are never constant, an energy, enterprise and initiative which so far it has not been found possible to produce on a significant or sufficient scale in any other way. This is an argument in favour, not of public or private enterprise, but of enterprise, since provided the institutional structure offers it sufficient scope and provides the necessary incentives, the private or public character will be of negligible importance. If the history of Rolls-Royce in these years has revealed nothing else, it has revealed that the problem of maintaining the conditions under which enterprise can flourish is one of peculiar complexity and difficulty, that it is a problem common to all forms of organisation at all times, and that its complexity is but a reflection of the subtlety of human nature itself. Enterprise is inescapably human in character – the product of will, of circumstance and of personality. It is a response to a situation whose intensity and frequency shows no uniform correlation with any single motivation of human endeavour or effort.

The solution of this problem lies within the joint province of economics, politics and sociology, but the techniques which practice and theory evolve will serve the ideals whose proclamation is so often considered to be an adequate substitute for their achievement if more attention is paid to the characteristics of *homo industrialis*, the legitimate successor if not the proud superior of *homo sapiens*.

'Why', asked *The Economist* in 1929, 'do so many British motor companies find it, apparently, so much simpler a matter to make cars than to make profits?' The answer to this question is not difficult to find in the preceding pages. The general problems of the industry, as illustrated by the history of the three companies discussed in this study, arise very largely from the simple fact that there are too many firms producing too many cars of too many types. The limited evidence available suggests that the industry would obtain substantial economies from a relatively small reduction in the number of producing units. The average cost-steps decline fairly steeply over a fairly short range of output, and, provided that the most modern methods are employed, the cost per unit of producing 10,000 cars per annum should not greatly exceed that of producing 50,000. In the British motor industry a very large number of firms produce considerably less than 10,000 cars per annum and thus must operate under the most disadvantageous cost conditions. For all these firms unit selling prices are raised even higher by the cost of trade practices which could be greatly reduced by intelligent co-operation.

There would thus appear to be five directions from which the problem of cost in the British motor *industry* as a whole might be attacked:

(1) A reduction in the number of specialist firms producing less than 10,000 chassis per annum.
(2) A reduction in the number of types produced by all firms resulting in a concentration of each firm on one basic chassis.
(3) The collection and distribution of comprehensive and significant statistics on an industry-wide basis.
(4) A thoroughgoing rationalisation of the distributive system.
(5) The elimination or reduction by agreement of some of the more wasteful features of competition.

These are far-reaching proposals and it would be foolish to underrate the magnitude of the first two especially. All five would undoubtedly meet with considerable opposition. But it would be both culpable and absurd to attempt to mitigate in any way the conclusion that there is no hope of conserving, still less of increasing, the economic strength of the industry, and particularly that of the high-quality producers within it, by any less drastic measures.

Only the third of these recommendations applies with any force to the aero-engine industry at the present time. The industry is young and vigorous and has benefited from many of the mistakes of its parent industry. It is well adapted to the market which it serves. Essentially a development rather than a production industry, its problems are basically technical rather than economic in character. The achievement of a wise distribution of resources within the industry cannot be solved by any economic criteria and must depend on the experience and judgement of those intimately connected with the problems of this highly complex and fluid type of manufacture. The conservatism is much less marked and the continuing rate of technical development gives it little opportunity of becoming established. There are still far too many energetic and plausible heresies, both in design and production, to permit the ascent of an established orthodoxy.

The character of British society is conservative, in industry, in art, in social life and in politics. Conservatism in art, politics and social life is a necessary and sometimes constructive indulgence, but the same cannot always be said of industry. The Cotton Manufacturing Commission has shown how great the cost of past and present conservatism in the cotton industry is likely to be.[8] The motor industry cannot make great claims by comparison. Its conservatism shows itself more in rigidities of structure than in any reluctance to develop or apply new techniques as such. In the motor industry industrial evolution has failed to keep pace with technical evolution and whether or not the latter has taken place at home or abroad has made little difference.

Before the Second World War the conservatism of British industry was financed, indirectly, by the savings of the nineteenth century. The savings are gone but the conservatism remains, and the possibility of national solvency is being brought within reach only by the most herculean efforts to make the existing system work. There is in consequence an enormous diversion and dissipation of effort in counteracting the political and social friction which is generated when the system is speeded up beyond a certain point.

An industrial society cannot escape the consequences of living in an age of technical and economic evolution, especially when these trends are accelerated and reserves are exhausted by periodical wars. It cannot expect to absorb all technical and economic changes within an unchanging institutional structure, nor can it for long evade the choice between reforms which will inevitably impinge on vested interests and which will require far-reaching and sometimes distressing alterations in industrial and social institutions. These often require an alacrity which simply will not permit a scrupulously exact consideration and assessment of social and economic justice. However desirable such a process may be, it is in great danger of becoming regarded as a right which overrides the right of the society to live. These reforms will naturally cause the most viciferous opposition from groups whose members naturally cannot be expected to admit that under certain conditions the survival of the whole demands a radical readjustment of the contributions demanded from and the rewards given to the parts.

When the most strenuous measures fail to restore the solvency of a national economy this is usually a sign that there is an inherent imbalance between the measures required to maintain the security of the whole and those which have been developed to maintain the often legitimate and desirable security of the parts. There is an irreducible antagonism between economic security and economic flexibility. Life cannot be guaranteed. It is the opportunity and obligation of statesmanship, at all levels of society, to mitigate the consequences of this antagonism. But there is an even more serious obligation which demands that the fundamental nature of the choice should always be made plain. To order a society on the basis of the comfortable pretence that the antagonism does not exist is a sure road to disaster.

Appendixes

I TABLE OF CAR PRICES CONSIDERED BY MANAGEMENT IN FIXING THE SILVER
   GHOST CHASSIS PRICE IN 1919

Make	Cylinders	h.p.	pre-war price	post-war price	% Increase
			£	£	
Daimler	6	45	925	1300	40
		30	690	1060	54
		30	690	1000	45
Sunbeam	4	16	350	655	85
	6	24	585	965	65
Crossley	4	25/30	475	850	79
Vulcan	4	15/20	325	445	37
Humber	4	10	250	425	70
	4	15	395	600	52
Talbot	4	12	350	610	52
	4	25	425	850	100
	6	36	565	900	59
Wolseley	4	16/20	475	675	42
	6	24/30	695	875	26
	6	30/40	945	1075	14
Swift	4	12	285	450	58
Vauxhall	–	25	480	875	82
Rolls-Royce	6	40/50	985	1450	47

The unweighted average increase was thus 57 per cent.

II   CALCULATIONS MADE ON 1 OCTOBER 1920 OF CASH OUTGOINGS AND REQUIREMENTS AT THE SPRINGFIELD PLANT

Heading of expenditure	Original estimate	Paid out to 1 Oct. 1920	Estimated cash still required	Total required
	£	£	£	£
Land and buildings	410,000	408,313	25,000	433,313
Equipment, machine tools and plant	633,100	529,362	74,000	603,362
Drawings, patterns, special tools, dies, etc.	300,000	518,471	329,999	848,470
Administrative, general manufact., selling and advert.	1,221,972	345,077	537,112	882,189
Material: 250 cars	582,850	196,377	669,999	866,376
1921 – 250 cars	440,450	—	150,000	150,000
Direct labour	615,796	14,647	443,500	458,147
Chassis and body trading a/c	None	168,910	60,000	228,910
Cash advances and loans	None	21,922	—	21,922
Long Island Service Station	None	—	81,050	81,050
New York Sales Office	None	239,055	—	239,055
Special experimental work	None	4,387	15,000	19,387
	4,204,168	2,446,521	2,385,660	4,832,181
Estimated receipts from 106 chassis	986,330	Estimated receipts from 58 chassis		681,500
	3,217,838			4,150,681
		Cash provided up to 30 April 1921		2,721,250
		Shortfall		1,429,431

III CALCULATIONS OF THE CHARGES LEVIED ON ROLLS-ROYCE CHASSIS
IMPORTED INTO THE U.S.A. IN 1929

       A = Figures given by Springfield

       B = The same with a discount of 33%

       C = Springfield figures with the maximum duty

       D = (B) with the maximum duty

	A	*B*	*C*	*D*
	£	£	£	£
Chassis price £1900 less discount:	1473	1267	1473	1267
Duty	491	422	538	538
Packing, freight	100	100	100	100
Miscellaneous expenses	100	100	100	100
Body	970	970	970	970
Landed cost	3134	2859	3181	2975
Selling expenses including trade allowance and used car allowance	941	941	941	941
	4075	3800	4122	3916
10% profit	407	380	412	392
	4482	4180	4534	4308

These figures indicate that the minimum price at which the car could be sold in the
United States was $16,800.

IV   TURNOVER, DISCOUNTS AND SELLING EXPENSES, ROLLS-ROYCE INC.,
     1927–33 ($)

Year	(A) Turnover (realised prices)	(B) Discounts and trade-in allowances	(C) Selling expenses	Total Expenses (C+B) as a % of (A)
1927	5,676,121	471,981	1,086,823	27.4
1928	6,395,562	821,720	994,308	28.4
1929	8,355,944	977,153	1,151,040	13.6
1930	5,672,030	1,030,912	859,410	33.3
1931	2,668,092	618,606	546,217	43.7
1932	1,276,613	—	267,508	—
1933	1,413,763	487,736	214,940	49.7

V BRANCH TURNOVER AND SELLING EXPENDITURE, ROLLS-ROYCE INC., 1928–30

Branch	1928		1929		1930		Ratio of turnover to selling cost			
	Turnover (Chassis only)	Selling Exp.	Turnover	Selling Exp.	Turnover	Selling Exp.	1928	1929	1930	Average
	$	$	$	$	$	$				
Springfield	325,313	66,741	373,376	75,399	346,234	93,306	4.87	4.97	3.72	4.52
Dealers	152,102	167,571	259,722	116,004	101,738	116,329	0.90	2.23	0.87	1.30
New York	2,029,470	278,565	2,423,278	313,580	1,711,748	397,708	7.28	7.74	4.30	6.74
Boston	498,291	93,172	649,093	99,143	410,043	114,096	5.35	6.55	3.59	5.16
Chicago	393,093	74,598	514,181	88,626	353,644	130,217	5.31	5.82	2.71	4.61
Cleveland	99,596	37,695	139,159	37,643	162,901	44,565	2.67	3.75	3.68	3.33
San Francisco	93,430	50,864	250,354	54,049	151,480	59,658	1.86	4.63	2.55	3.01
Los Angeles	486,773	92,961	381,970	109,705	430,088	116,057	5.28	3.49	3.70	4.15
Pittsburgh	259,252	33,265	202,281	51,680	108,725	31,480	7.84	3.96	3.48	5.09
Cincinnati	115,346	31,537	174,858	33,722	145,757	44,343	3.71	5.27	3.29	4.09
S. Eastern St	53,961	26,732	66,596	23,423	—	—	2.03	2.87	—	2.45
C. Western St	263,814	76,485	229,191	68,417	—	—	3.46	3.36	—	2.37
Columbia	125,151	19,947	35,724	32,121	—	—	6.57	1.10	—	2.55
Philadelphia	389,002	72,669	292,793	64,740	166,915	43,942	5.40	4.56	3.86	4.60
	5,284,594	1,122,802	5,992,576	1,168,252	4,089,273	1,191,701				

VI   ROLLS-ROYCE INC.: FINANCIAL 1927–33

	1927	1928	1929	1930	1931	1932
Sales (chassis and maintenance)	5,676,121	6,395,562	7,151,067	5,672,030	2,668,092	1,276,613
less used car loss concessions etc.	471,981	821,720	977,153	1,130,912	618,606	—
Net sales	5,204,140	5,573,842	6,173,913	4,541,118	2,049,486	—
Cost of sales	3,644,430	4,082,879	4,480,579	4,244,597	2,058,054	1,252,744
Gross profit	1,539,709	1,490,962	1,693,334	296,520	−8,567	23,869
Selling and advertising cost	1,086,823	994,308	1,113,629	859,410	546,217	267,508
	452,886	496,653	579,705	−562,889	−554,784	−243,639
Other income	48,337	30,555	57,340	89,990	41,868	7,418
Other deductions	(A)501,223	527,209	637,046	−472,889	−512,916	−236,220
Interest and discount	174,619	150,032	152,448	241,353	205,445	173,910
Renting Co. loss	18,718	54	7,032	—	—	21,395
Inventory adjustments	187,238	—	326,145	—	—	—
B (total last 3)	380,557	150,087	485,626	241,353	—	−431,526
A − B	120,646	377,121	151,420	−714,253	—	—
Income tax	16,287	46,000	—	—	—	—
Net Profit	104,359	331,121	134,763	−714,253	−718,361	−431,526

Operations in 1933 were on a considerably modified scale, and a net loss of 267,000 dollars was incurred.

VII ROLLS-ROYCE (U.K.): MARKET STRUCTURE, 1914, 1922 AND 1928

	1914		1922		1928	
	No.	%	No.	%	No.	%
Export sales	248	33.4	95	22.1	128	15.0
U.K. sales	494	66.6	335	87.9	723	85.0
Total	742	100.0	430	100.0	851	100.0
Sales of chassis (U.K.)	348	70.8	259	77.8	621	85.8
to trade retail	146	29.2	76	22.2	102	14.2
% U.K. trade sales of total output	348	47	259	60.3	621	72.9

VIII ANALYSIS OF TURNOVER, ROLLS-ROYCE (U.K.), 1924–34

Year	1 Total volume of turnover	2 Net sales (chassis)	% of (1)	3 Net sales (aero)	% of (1)	4 Gross profit (chassis)	% of Total	5 Gross profit (aero)	% of Total	6 Total gross profit[1]
	£	£		£		£		£		£
1924	1,890,542	1,456,167	76.9	326,468	17.2	280,512	70.0	120,208	30.0	400,720
1925	2,175,544	1,368,926	62.8	672,068	30.9	234,303	50.3	230,891	49.7	465,191
1926	2,311,007	1,753,993	75.8	438,964	18.9	201,278	61.8	123,911	38.2	325,189
1927	2,070,466	1,463,810	70.6	510,482	24.6	221,843	54.7	182,722	45.3	404,565
1928	2,006,808	1,544,635	76.9	371,407	18.4	278,700	67.8	132,037	32.2	410,737
1929[2]	2,217,066	1,672,965	75.4	146,600	11.4	290,232	77.1	86,414	22.8	376,646
1930	1,877,174	1,251,036	66.7	406,560	21.7	258,374	59.3	176,840	40.7	435,214
1931	1,709,846	688,209	40.3	808,195	47.3	90,278	21.2	333,929	78.8	424,207
1932	1,860,261	780,707	41.9	878,261	47.2	96,744	19.7	395,444	80.3	492,188
1933	2,457,633	1,242,843	50.6	1,011,758	41.2	273,142	37.2	460,544	62.3	733,956
1934	3,096,262	1,746,248	56.4	1,145,662	37.0	388,018	39.4	597,413	60.6	985,431

1. Does not include gross profit on miscellaneous items which are included in col. (1).

2. 11 months.

In this table the totals under columns (2) and (3) do not equal the total under column (1) since the latter includes various miscellaneous receipts not included under the heading chassis or aero engines, such as bodies, spares and repairs.

IX ANALYSIS OF INDIRECT EXPENDITURE FROM MANUFACTURING ACCOUNTS OF BENTLEY MOTORS FOR PERIOD 1924–31

	Total Indirect Expend.	% of Total Direct	(1) Exper. Work £	(2) Sales and Racing[2] £	(3) Admin. Expend. £	(4) Interest on Loans £	(5) Loss on Service Dept. £	(6) Balance £	As % of total indirect expenditure						
									(1)	(2)	(3)	(4)	(5)	(6)	Total
1924	77,968	33.4	15,284	9,553	11,517	5,379	9,687	26,548	19.8	12.4	14.9	6.9	12.5	35.7	100
1925	—[2]	—	6,009						—	—	—	—	—	—	—
1926	55,359	27.9	8,130	7,361	16,657	7,861	8,557	6,787	14.7	13.3	30.2	14.3	15.5	12.3	100
1927	64,724	25.1	11,026	22,768	15,321	3,862	11,746	—	17.2	35.5	23.9	6.0	18.1	—	100
1928	77,212	32.4	10,727	24,938	15,960	4,564	14,642	6,381	13.9	32.3	20.7	5.9	19.0	8.2	100
1929	78,667	25.1	13,600	28,541	16,110	4,622	11,091	2,703	20.0	36.5	20.6	5.9	14.2	3.4	100
1930	88,253	35.4	23,356	30,979	17,096	5,150	9,030	2,642	26.5	35.2	19.4	5.8	10.2	3.0	100
1931	85,071[1]	63.6	17,505	22,080	20,137	10,586	9,215	5,548	19.0	25.9	23.6	13.6	10.8	6.5	100
Average %		34.7							18.7	27.3	21.9	8.3	14.3	9.8	100

1. After deducting a manufacturing loss of £9,291 and a loss on machine shop of £7,304.

2. Detailed figures for the year 1925 are not available.

3. Racing formed a relatively small proportion of this total, contrary to the popular belief that it was the racing activities of the company which forced it to go insolvent.

X FINANCIAL DATA FROM ACCOUNTS OF BENTLEY MOTORS, 1919-31

Year	Number of chassis	Value of chassis sold	Discount allowed to trade	Discount as % of turnover	Cost of chassis	Gross manufact. profit	Net final profit	Expend. on exp. work	% of turnover	Sales expend.	% of turnover	Wages and salaries	% of turnover	Depreciation	% of turnover
		£	£		£	£	£	£		£		£		£	
1919	*	Nil	Nil		*	*	(5,933)	7,791		348		2,425		78	
1920	*	Nil	Nil		*	*	(10,268)	8,436		43		7,197		137	
1921	*	26,759	*		*	*	(7,405)	8,000	30.7	501	1.9	13,310	51.1	265	0.1
1922	*	*	*		*	*	*	*		*		*		*	
1923	*	*	*		*	*	*	*		*		*		*	
1924	322	290,000	42,647	14.8	233,824	13,529	(56,700)	15,284	5.1	6,806	2.1	49,315	17.0	1,098	0.3
1925	*	*	*		*	56,484	19,037	6,009		5,188		*		*	
1926	306	280,076	48,299	17.1	198,744	33,033	(19,249)	8,130	2.8	4,949	1.7	63,566	22.6	2,190	0.7
1927	330	380,380	64,534	17.1	258,285	57,561	(2,219)	11,026	2.9	19,399	5.0	72,592	19.1	2,367	0.6
1928	337	393,275	67,803	17.3	238,084	87,388	1,201	10,727	2.8	22,322	5.5	84,315	21.4	2,580	0.6
1929	414	498,875	86,315	17.2	312,414	100,146	28,467	15,600	3.0	26,054	5.2	91,542	18.3	3,170	0.6
1930	301	407,365	73,378	17.9	249,900	84,087	1,023	23,356	5.6	27,609	6.7	98,337	21.4	3,540	0.8
1931	147	198,850	35,640	18.0	145,949	17,261	(84,174)	17,505	8.7	21,526	10.8	96,539	48.2	8,199	4.2

1. Spaces marked with an asterisk = figures not available.
2. The company commenced operations in 1919, in which year the total expenditure was only £11,800. There were no trading operations in 1919 and 1920, during which years the Bentley chassis was being designed.
3. The figure for chassis turnover excludes turnover arising from the sale of spares and repairs. They are thus not strictly comparable with Rolls-Royce figures in Appendix VIII, but the difference in the case of the Bentley Company is not significant.
4. The company was reorganised in 1925.
5. Net profit figures in brackets denote losses.

XI ANALYSIS OF ROLLS-ROYCE (U.K.) TURNOVER, 1935-45

Year	Gross turnover aero and car	Net chassis sales	% of col. 1	Net aero sales	% of col. 1	Gross profit (chassis)	% of Total	Gross profit (aero)	% of Total	Total gross manuf. profit
	£	£		£		£		£		£
1935	3,767,064	1,577,481	41.9	1,999,228	53.1	320,268	27.2	856,745	72.8	1,177,013
1936	4,537,380	1,486,790	32.8	2,641,526	58.2	213,353	18.1	964,010	81.9	1,177,363
1937	4,728,698	1,693,724	35.8	2,525,497	53.4	149,936	17.2	723,559	82.8	873,495
1938	6,245,779	737,279	11.8	4,693,759	75.1	64,365	4.6	1,330,378	95.4	1,394,373
1939	9,493,248	607,158	6.4	7,236,552	76.2	67,307	5.3	1,208,897	94.7	1,276,204
1940	19,147,040			18,767,557	100					2,286,157
1941	27,116,541			27,116,541	100					2,632,349
1942	34,804,314	Nil*		34,804,314	100					2,867,859
1943	38,658,409			38,658,049	100					2,413,729
1944	44,446,337			44,446,337	100					3,280,133
1945	33,942,123			33,942,123	100					3,665,478

* The aero turnover figures from 1939 onwards include chassis items amounting to a few thousand pounds. They do not include the turnover of the Glasgow Shadow Factory, whose accounts were kept quite separate from the Rolls-Royce Group.

XII   AERO-ENGINE PRODUCTION TABLES, 1915–45

DELIVERIES 1915–19

Year	RAF	Renault	Eagle	Falcon	Hawk	Total
1915	28	143	8			179
1916	72	77	386	40	65	640
1917			931	631	140	1702
1918			1797	966		2763
1919			960	346		1306

Total engines delivered 1915–19   6589
Highest monthly rate of production   336 (Oct 1918)
Highest annual rate   2763 (1918)

ANNUAL PRODUCTION 1928–36

Year	Eagle IX	Con-dor	Kes-trel	Buz-zard	R	Gos-hawk	Grif-fon	Merlin	Un-classi-fied	Total
						Total engine output for U.K.				
1928	2	16	43	4					539	67
1929			24	7	4				721	35
1930			116	4	2				726	122
1931			287	22	6				637	315
1932			285	30					638	315
1933			508	23		12	2		730	545
1934			585							585
1935			1175			3		2	2	1182
1936			1411					25		1436

Total engines produced   4602 ⎫
Average annual production   511 ⎬ All types military and civil
Average monthly production   42 ⎭

DELIVERIES, 1920–7

Year	Eagle	Falcon	Condor	Total
1920	97	177	45	319
1921	114	11	61	186
1922	59	1	1	61
1923	65		2	67
1924	117	2	29	147
1925				187
1926				116
1927				74

Total engines, 1920–7 inclusive	1157
Highest monthly prod. (Mar. 21)	52
Average monthly prod. 20–27	12
Average annual prod.	144

ANNUAL PRODUCTION 1937–9 (CIVIL AND MILITARY)

Year	Kestrel	Merlin	Civil	Air Min.	Vulture	Exc.	Pere-grine	Total (1+2)
1937	326	694	101	919				1020
1938	18	1710	34	1694	7	1	8	1728

Total engines produced, 1933–38	6512
Average annual production	1085
Average monthly production	90
Total engines produced, 1935–9	7968
Average annual production	1593
Average monthly production	132
Highest monthly production (Dec 39)	316

ANNUAL PRODUCTION BY FACTORY, 1939–45

Year	Derby	Crewe	Glasgow	Fords	Total
1939	2,230	256			2,486
1940	3,956	3,158	9		7,123
1941	5,092	5,011	1,931	193	12,227
1942	5,908	5,784	5,750	3,885	21,327
1943	6,148	6,116	6,576	6,982	25,822
1944	5,705	5,869	6,556	10,164	28,294
1945	3,200	2,294	2,986	8,021	16,501

Notes

CHAPTER 1

1. See *The Growth of a Firm*, Chapter 2. West Wittering, in Sussex, and Le Canadel, in the South of France, were used by Henry Royce as both homes and design offices after ill-health had forced him to leave Derby, shortly before the First World War.
2. Quotations in this section are either directly from the minutes of the meetings or from Johnson's own accounts of what took place.
3. These were: Arrol-Johnson, Austins, Clement Talbots, Crossley, Daimlers, Lanchester, Napier, Rolls-Royce, Rovers, Siddeley-Deasy, Sunbeams, Thorneycroft and Vauxhalls.
4. These were the Belsize, Singer, Standard and Vulcan companies.

CHAPTER 2

1. A series of booklets was produced in which the many exploits of both are recounted. The publicity was of great value.
2. See Appendix I.
3. R. Schlaifer and S. D. Heron, *The Development of Aircraft Engines and Fuels* (Bailey Bros, 1952) p. 9.
4. One of the main reasons for the failure of these negotiations was that Royce set too high a value on the specialised knowledge of spring metallurgy which he considered he would be able to impart to Firths.
5. Economists have tended to criticise the terms 'productive' and 'unproductive' for which they have substituted direct and indirect labour. This rightly draws attention to the inaccuracy of a broad classification of factory and office workers on this basis, especially for purposes of theoretical analysis. But the former terms do carry an implication which is not as unwarranted as it may seem. It is far easier to measure the productivity of direct labour, but the productivity of indirect labour is of very great importance for the simple reason that it can fluctuate with far greater amplitude and rapidity. The change is much more difficult to detect in the short run. A point is reached where any further increase in numbers, or the

maintenance of existing numbers under changing circumstances, or an absolute or relative decline in the quality of the indirect labour, can result in the overhead organisation becoming a very heavy burden on the direct costs of production. The indirect organisation both of a firm and of a state is generally more firmly entrenched in its position than the direct labour which it controls, and more capable of finding impressive but superficial reasons for the perpetuation of the existing arrangements.

6. He seems to have changed his mind by the general meeting on 30 January 1920, for his speech included the following paragraph: 'We want no discontent amongst our workpeople – Rolls-Royce goods cannot be made in such an atmosphere – such a suggestion must never arise. We want our workpeople to recognise that their and our interests are identical, and that we appreciate their having built up the business of Rolls-Royce Ltd., by their loyalty and devotion, and their determination that its name shall head the list. We want it to be a distinction to be a member of the Rolls-Royce community, by reason of our pride in our workpeople and their pride in us.'

7. The ten chosen for consideration were: free dentistry, baths and dressing rooms, recreation ground, sports apparatus, gymnasium, flower gardens, swimming bath, recreation hall, bandstand and educational welfare.

CHAPTER 3

1. The Power of Attorney which was prepared for Johnson gave him specific authority to make financial arrangements with Aldred & Co., so it would appear from this that it was the English company's intention that they should do the financing, and not any of the other houses mentioned.

2. The board cabled Mackenzie for his opinion on the best procedure to be followed and he replied by cable on 23 June as follows: 'Strongly advise the best way for you to obtain full value American rights is by incorporating separate company here, getting it going successfully for time then if you wish sell your interest. Price should be very good. Patterson's opinion is that common stock will be worth $250 per share in very few years. Selling now would make price very problematical and taking up now might injure chances proper financing new company.'

3. The four schemes were:
   (a) Patterson's (Duke's backing)
   (b) Aldred's
   (c) A. B. Leach & Co.
   (d) Ensuth, McLeod and Euhne.
   Details of the last two schemes have not survived.

4. L. J. Belnap, who later became President of the new company, was well known to Rolls-Royce because of his work with the British Purchasing Commission under Sir Henry Jupp.

5. Some exceptionally interesting details and photographs of the Springfield plant are given in *The American Rolls-Royce* by A. W. Soutter (published by Mowbray Co., 1976) in Chapter II, 'Setting up Shop'.

6. Calculated as follows:

	$
Labour, 2880 hours @ 60 cents per hour	1728
Overheads 175% on labour cost	3024
Material	2041
Accessories	1012
Sales expenses	500
Profit	1500
	$9805

7. H. J. Fuller was a director of the Bosch Company at this time and was probably responsible for the very full co-operation given by this company to Hives when he visited their works.

8. George Bagnell, an old friend and associate of Royce, was one of a substantial number of senior supervisors sent out from Derby to Springfield to help establish the new enterprise.

9. This car had right-hand drive, petrol tank fillers on the wrong side of the body with a nozzle which was too small for the standard American pumps; it also lacked a petrol tank gauge. Since all modifications had to be sanctioned in England at this stage the process of adapting the car to local conditions was slow and cumbersome.

10. The horn button was a particularly good example of the cost of the rigid application of this policy. The replica of the English button was produced locally at a cost of between $12 and $14, when a standard button could have been purchased for seventy-five cents. Special Dunlop wire wheels were at first imported from England, but these were eventually manufactured in the United States, at very great cost.

11. American costs and equivalent English costs:

	$	£
Crankcase: lower	19.49	
upper	69.88	
Crankshaft	91.00	
Cylinders, front	46.77	
rear	46.78	
Valves (12)	31.20	
Radiator matrix tubes	82.44	
Gearbox	35.71	
Flywheel	7.50	2 16 9
Torque tube	25.00	
Rear axle gearbox	26.77	
Rear axle tube	26.70	
Outer brake drum	11.35	5 10 0
Inner brake drum	5.00	2 11 0

	$	£
Wheels (Dunlop)	246.00	
Frames	57.25	28 0 0
Front axle	21.00	
Steering wheel	16.79	
Dashboard	14.25	
Battery	25.40	
Tyres	192.24 ⎫	78 0 0
Tubes	22.26 ⎭	
Speedometer drive	32.50	
Lamps	58.00	

	$	*Cost of U.S. Substitute*	Price $
R.R. starter	216.68	Bijur	40.00
Watford magneto	92.74	Bosch	40.00
Lucas dynamo	116.31	Bijur or Wesths	40.00
Cambridge thermometer	21.33	Foxbore	12.00
Oil/pressure gauge	5.20	U.S. equiv.	3.40
Fuel gauge	5.20	U.S. equiv.	3.40
Front springs	69.51	Sheldon	23.50
Rear springs	103.70	Sheldon	22.00

$1841.95

12. On his many visits to Derby H. J. Fuller was never able to obtain information on comparable English costs. Both companies probably suffered from the lack of mutual confidence which this behaviour implied.

CHAPTER 4

1. English-made chassis were being retailed by the American company until their own production could absorb the whole of the demand.
2. I am indebted to Arthur W. Soutter (op. cit.) for the following figures on production:
      1922   230 R.H. drive Silver Ghosts
      1923   365 R.H. drive Silver Ghosts
      1924   320 R.H. drive Silver Ghosts
      1925   50 R.H. drive Silver Ghosts
             309 L.H. drive Silver Ghosts
      1926   291 L.H. drive Silver Ghosts
              35 'New Phantoms'

1927   340 'New Phantoms'
1928   275 'New Phantoms'
1929   50 'New Phantoms' (cast-iron blocks)
       201 'New Phantoms' (aluminium blocks)
1930   100 'New Phantoms' (aluminium blocks)
1931   100 'New Phantoms' (aluminium blocks)
       (73 imported Phantom IIs fitted with bodies)
1932   100 'New Phantoms'
       (16 imported Phantom IIs)
1933   50 'New Phantoms'
       (30 imported Phantom IIs)
1934   Production ceased

It is an astonishing comment on the policy of both parent and subsidiary that no less than 1000 right-hand Silver Ghosts were produced and sold from Springfield before effect was given to the decision to switch to left-hand drive, six hundred of which were made.

3. In fact, a calculation made on 10 August at a Springfield executives' meeting shows the narrow margin on which the company was working:

Estimate of production based on 8 cars per week

	$
Overhead per month	50,000
Productive labour, $1100 per car	38,500
Administrative and general expense	7,500
Selling and advertising	50,000
	146,000
÷ 35 per month	4,170
Material cost	2,000
	6,170
Assumed sales price	7,200
Profit per chassis	$1,030 \times 420 = 432,600$ chassis
Body profits ($450 × 420)	189,000 profit

4. The attitude towards this problem is clearly revealed in the subject for discussion at a conference which Henry Fuller had with Claude and Basil Johnson when he visited England in the autumn of 1922. This was entitled 'Quality *versus* Production' (from an entry in Mr Fuller's personal journal, 8.9.22). The writer was granted the privilege of reading Mr Fuller's journal for the period covering his association with the company (1919–35), and is indebted to this source for a considerable amount of information.

5. See Chapter 5, note 8.

6. The Knox Company was one of the earliest U.S. automobile manufacturers. It produced a tiller-steered three-wheeler at its Springfield plant in 1901 and developed a considerable reputation for its six-cylinder vehicles, one of which competed successfully in the 1911 Indianapolis race. The company finally ceased manufacture in 1922. See Soutter, op. cit., p. 54.

CHAPTER 5

1. See Soutter, op. cit., p. 123, for further information on the 20 h.p. Goshawk, of which only 81 were finally imported new into the U.S.A.
2. For an interesting discussion of the origins and development of this company see Soutter, op. cit., pp. 58 and 59.
3. This holding no longer gave the English management full control over the American board. Through the failure of the American company to pay any dividends the preference shares had acquired full voting rights. But the English company was still a most important shareholder and could still exercise considerable control by virtue of the original agreement between the two companies.
4. A. W. Soutter (op. cit., p. 126) has since published some interesting details of a Springfield proposal, based on the Rolls-Royce Phantom I engine, gearbox, rear axle and braking system, but having several U.S.-built components such as the Stromberg SU carburettor. No full prototype was built, but a Phantom I was extensively modified for test purposes. This is almost certainly the car which Fuller had in mind and which Maurice Olley and he discussed with Derby.
5. See Appendix III.
6. See Appendix IV.
7. For cars sold to a dealer, 12½ per cent of the retail price within 6 months; 5 per cent of the retail price within 6–12 months.
   For cars sold to a customer, 20 per cent of the retail price within 6 months.
8. The board of Rolls-Royce of America in 1928 consisted of the following:

President and Chairman	H. J. Fuller (later Chairman, Shawnigan Falls & Power Co., Canada)
Vice-President	H. C. Beaver (later managing director of Worthington Pump Co.)
Vice-President	W. E. Hosac (later head of Metropolitan News Advertising Company)
Directors	
J. E. Aldred	Senior partner of Aldreds & Co. (a multimillionaire)
A. P. Spence	Senior partner, Barrow, Wade & Guthrie
R. M. Smith	Partner in Aldred & Co.
W. L. Wright	Managing director of the Savage Arms Co.
R. E. Fulton	Chairman of the Mack Truck Co.
William Brewster	Head of Brewsters
J. C. Wells	Chairman of the American Optical Co.

Royce, B. Johnson, Lord Herbert Scott and Mackenzie were also on the Board but not of it, with the exception of Mackenzie. Mackenzie's partner, J. J. McManus, was secretary of the American company throughout its existence, and later became the English company's legal representative in the United States.

9. A. W. Soutter (op. cit., pp. 118 and 119) has given a particularly interesting example of the way in which the Rolls-Royce chassis involved substantial additional expenditure for the achievement of a comparatively limited objective. The hand controls on many cars of this period in the U.S. used simple Bowden cables attached to push–pull knobs. The entire mechanism could be purchased for under $1, whereas the Rolls-Royce, seeking to avoid this inferior design concept, used straight control rods, operated by levers on a quadrant, to adjust the governor, ignition, carburettor and magneto. This assembly involved 227 components assembled with 205 special fasteners. The special tools required for this process – 23 patterns, 22 drop-forging dies, two punch-press dies, a hard rubber moulding die, and numerous drill jigs, milling fixtures, chuck jaws, turret tools, engraving fixtures and brazing fixtures – cost over $69,000.

10. It is interesting to note that not even Fuller was entirely free from the wishful thinking of this attractive theory that rich people *must* buy Rolls-Royce cars, for in an interview to the *New York Times* on 28 January 1926, shortly after Johnson's last visit to the U.S., he made the following statement: 'When it is realised that in England, a country perplexed by unfavourable conditions and mounting taxes, sales of Rolls-Royce cars are three times those in America, it may be seen that we have but tapped the field in this country. *It is now only a question of time before the U.S. will correctly reflect the buying power of the two countries*' (italics mine).

11. This impression was not lost on Sidgreaves, for it was under his managing directorship that Rolls-Royce eventually built up one of the finest research organisations in British industry.

12. This sum was made up as follows:

Duty 33⅓%	£544	
Packing and freight	88	
	£632 =	$3,160
Bumpers, mascot, body, delivery charges, selling expenses and profit		9,283
		$12,443

CHAPTER 6

1. Hs. – the Derby initials for Hives.
2. Italics mine.
3. Italics mine.
4. Italics Royce's.
5. A. W. Soutter (op. cit., p. 132) has pointed out that all Rolls-Royce steel specifications were based on British experience and took no account of American S.A.E. standards.

CHAPTER 7

1. The *Automobile Engineer*, October 1929.
2. The first Goshawk, though it was commended in the trade press for the 'meticulous attention to detail' which characterised the design of the 40/50 h.p., did not have four-wheel brakes or a four-speed gearbox. In questions of this kind Royce displayed a growing conservatism, as the following memorandum to Johnson on the four-speed gearbox clearly demonstrates:

> For a central-change speed and brake position the four-way (three speed) change-over lever is particularly well suited, and it is no use handicapping ourselves and driving ourselves to another scheme of chassis because the crowd consider four-speeds are necessary. I give my time to consider these matters, and I know all the 'ins' and 'outs' and difficulties of design, and advantages of use, and the continually changing conditions, and consider that I am duty bound to follow my own judgment until it is proven unsound. This is a question of the best compromise and the best way of spending money, and I would certainly rather spend extra money on putting more work to produce a more perfect engine. By putting all the time and money possible into this we should always end with a less satisfactory job with a four speed box than a three speed, and I would not handicap our designers and works for ever for some slight advantage in sales.

3. See Appendix VII.
4. The trade discount paid by the Bentley Company, then an independent concern and an important competitor of Rolls-Royce in the high-class field, also averaged 17 per cent on turnover during the years 1926–31, when this company was in full production. This figure remained more or less constant, but as there was a steady fall in the number of chassis produced, which was offset by a rise in prices, the actual figure of discount per chassis shows a continual increase throughout the life of this company, from £132 per chassis in 1924 to £243 in 1931. For a full discussion of the Bentley Company, see pp. 104–113.
5. Calculation based on a production of 400 chassis p.a., 8 per week.

Average discount	*Net price*	*Profit per chassis*	*Total profit*	*Extra discount allowed*
	£	£	£	£
12½% (max 15)	1619	448	179,500	—
15 % (max 17¼)	1572	402	161,000	18,500
17½% (max 20)	1426	356	142,500	37,000
If 300 per annum				
12½%	1619	448	134,625	—
15 %	1572	402	120,750	13,875
17½%	1426	356	106,875	17,500

6. See Appendix VIII.
7. This remark might seem to imply that conventional cost accounting practice is not based on a careful theoretical calculation in the economic sense. This is to some extent true, not because the cost accountant is necessarily unaware of the economic nature of the problem, but because the system which he designs must be practical and inexpensive. It thus tends to become conventional, and conventions frequently conform to the criterion of convenience rather than to that of accuracy.
8. The figures given in Captain Turner's memorandum are as follows:

Year	Published	Actual	Difference
1923	156,000	159,000	+ 3,000
1924	163,000	78,000	−85,000
1925	165,000	80,000	−85,000
1926	100,000	39,000	−61,000

9. The development of the Kestrel revealed several weaknesses which led to one most significant change in the organisation of Rolls-Royce. The supercharger gave such poor results that it was decided to bring out an unsupercharged engine as an interim measure. As a long-term remedy J. E. Ellor, who had previously been responsible for supercharger work at the R.A.E., was brought in, at the government's suggestion, to direct all supercharger development at Derby. It was the excellence of this work which in subsequent years, and especially during the Second World War, did more than anything else to maintain the superiority of the Merlin. Subsequent supercharger work at Derby was directly supported by government development contracts quite separate from the engine development contracts. No technical limitations whatever were included in these contracts, which gave Rolls-Royce *carte blanche* to pursue supercharger development as the company thought fit.
10. The main differences between the 'H' and the 'R' were the following:
    (a) Double-sided centrifugal supercharger;
    (b) Air intake inside the 'V' to avoid spray;
    (c) A modified reduction gear;
    (d) Sodium-cooled valves – the first occasion on which these were used in a Rolls-Royce engine.
11. For detailed account of the technical history of these engines see Schlaifer and Heron, op. cit., p. 206–14.
12. See Appendix VIII.

CHAPTER 8

1. *The Economist*, 28 July 1928.
2. See p. 74.

3. There is a very strong similarity between the situation of Bentley Motors and that of the Springfield Company which proved equally incapable of solving almost identical problems. In both cases the manufacturing profit on a small turnover was too small to support overhead expenditure.

CHAPTER 9

1. In conversation with the sculptor Eric Gill, at West Wittering, Royce once made the statement: 'I have always believed that whatever I do, however humble the job is, if I do it as well as I can, it is noble.' Gill was so impressed by this that he had it translated into Latin and Royce in turn had the Latin inscription worked into the stone of his fire-place at West Wittering. It seems as relevant in 1977 as it was in 1927.
2. It is at least probable that Charles Lindbergh's flight across the Atlantic in 1927, in an aircraft powered by a small radial air-cooled engine, had some influence on Royce's thinking and design activity. The influence of this flight on American aviation thinking was profound.
3. He indulged his susceptibility with considerable discretion however and his aversion to certain features was occasionally expressed in a most picturesque fashion. 'Bumpers I hate, but I suppose they are needed to justify fashion, etc. In the case of accidents or even small collisions the usual bumpers are almost valueless, and suggest horrible manners.'
4. Italics Royce's.
5. The very successful General Motors type of independent suspension was designed by Maurice Olley, who had joined General Motors after leaving the Rolls-Royce Springfield design team.
6. Royce, more than most perhaps, had appreciated the increasing strain on the resources of the Experimental Department and in December 1930 he remarked, on the subject of the amount of experimental work undertaken by American firms, that he was 'sure we cannot stand the present tax upon our best workers'.

   He was thus justifiably resentful of the increasing volume of criticism directed at this department, and though rarely given to complaint – at least in his written memoranda – he twice rebuked the critics somewhat severely. In September 1930 he replied as follows to criticism of delay in the work he was doing on compression ignition.

   Believe me we are doing our best to get our work equal to our competitors, and you will realise that it is not easy to produce designs sufficiently good to be worth making; one firm fully engaged against many. Very few indeed care to strive for hours, days, weeks, months, on the drawing board, to produce something worthy of the name of a design. Like our 'dear to memory C. S. Rolls,' after a very short time they think it is good, when it is still only worthy of the name of a sketch.

The final quotation from Royce's memoranda from West Wittering and Le Canadel was on the subject of 'Experimental Car Work and Design Generally'. It is the last which he wrote on the subject.

It should be clear that I am not an obstructionist, but wish anything hopeful to be tried that can be bought both for test and special customers.

I have preached for many years the practice of – 'when in trouble find out what others are doing, and that we have enough well educated and inexpensive young men to take a personal interest in any special subject, and give them a chance of showing their ability and ingenuity.' We older engineers will use our experience to pick out that which we think is worth working on, and it must be remembered that time and money will not allow us to try or make everything and someone knowing most of our history is best able to make the choice.

We want to avoid the resources of the Experimental Dept. being crowded by ill-considered, half thought out, schemes, so that things which have had much time and thought are never made, or are pushed aside before they are tested to a finish.

I have no desire to spend the small hours of the morning seeking solutions of our difficulties, and features of design, etc., because this practice (forced upon me) has done much to make my life – through ill-health – nearly unbearable.

R.

At Le Canadel   5.3.32.

CHAPTER 10

1. See p. 122.
2. One of the most striking examples of this attitude occurs in a comment which Wormald, the works manager, made on the subject of Merlin production which was at this stage still carried out in the same factory under the control of the same executives. At a production conference he argued that 'the question of ease of manufacture should not be considered as whichever design is found to be desirable the manufacturing problem can be dealt with satisfactorily. The question [of cylinder block manufacture] should be discussed purely on its technical merits and there is no necessity for methods of manufacture to influence the decision.
3. During the years immediately before the war a fairly close technical liaison was established between the design and development divisions of Rolls-Royce and of the Rover Co., a long-established concern with a considerable reputation in its own field. The proposal to establish an independent plant to manufacture crankshaft forgings for both companies came originally

from the managing director of Rovers, S. B. Wilks, but the general uncertainly of the international situation at this time postponed any further developments in this direction.

4. Robotham considered that a production of 10,000 cars per annum was necessary to justify the expense of dies for all steel bodies and specialised machine tool equipment.

5. The following comparison between the Bentley and Rover gearboxes illustrates this argument:

	Bentley	*Rover*
Number of pieces	819	327
Number of machining and assembly operations	1431	412
Cost	£49 19s 2d	£26 3s 0d

A comparison of the Phantom III and Cadillac independent front suspension (which Robotham had recommended should be adopted on the Phantom III) revealed a similar disparity.

6. Material cost of:

Model in Current Production	£	*Replacement in Rationalised Range*	£	*% Saving*
Phantom III	425	8-cyl. Silver Wraith	225	47
Wraith	276	6-cyl. Silver Wraith	200	27
Bentley M	252	Bentley V	216	14

7. *Analysis of the Bentley V Production Costs*

Material	209	0	0
Labour	107	15	0
Factory	242	5	0
Development	55	0	0

(225% overheads)   Total direct manufacturing cost = £614

Guarantee	23	0	0
Sales	165	0	0
Discount	212	10	0
Pensions	7	15	0

Total indirect cost excluding profit = £408

	1022	5	0
Net Profit	127	15	0
	1150	0	0

8. In investigations of this nature the questions which are not asked are often more revealing than those which are, and it is significant that throughout this period the influence of restrictive practices was mentioned only once. In a discussion of suspension costs Robotham remarked that his estimates were 'based upon what one might call normal working conditions, i.e. conditions which would obtain in another factory. It was obviously taken for granted that however deleterious these conditions might be, there was no question of their being altered in the foreseeable future.

9. Sidgreaves was very sceptical as to whether or not this output could be sold, since the cheapest of the five cars was still £1100.
10. In a letter to the author written in June 1949, W. A. Robotham has stated that 'The instigators of the rationalised programme had never agreed that the Phantom was an economic model to produce. It was only included in the range because of the policy requirement that we should produce a chassis upon which the biggest and most luxurious body which the customer could demand, should be able to be fitted.
11. The existing models (Phantom III, Wraith and Bentley 4½-litre) were to be replaced by the following models in the rationalised range:
Silver Phantom 8-cylinder (successor to the Phantom III)
Silver Wraith 6-cylinder (successor to the Wraith)
Bentley V (successor to the Bentley 50)
Silver Dawn (existing production Bentley with RR radiator)
Silver Ripple (Bentley V with a Rolls-Royce radiator)
Cresta (8-cylinder engine in a Bentley 50 chassis)
(The Bentley V, of which ten experimental models were actually produced before the outbreak of war, was the first complete rationalised car to be built, and must be distinguished from the Bentley 50 which was the standard 4¼-litre which had been in production from 1935 to 1939.)

CHAPTER 11

1. The figures for aero-engines were:

	Total output (U.K.)	R.R. output
1928	539	67
1929	721	35
1930	726	122
1931	637	315
1932	738	315
1933	730	545

2. 'Aircraft Production: Quality' memorandum by Professor M. M. Postan, made available in typescript form to the present author in 1948.
3. Calculated as follows:

£ 777,200	Extension to factory and Drawing Office
2,105,200	New Plant and Machine Tools
420,000	Jigs, tools and gauges

£3,302,400

4. Programme dated 20 September 1935:

Month	1	2	3	4	5	6	Total
A.M. requirements	157	491	491	496	495	566	2696
Derby production	180	180	180	180	180	180	1080
New plant	100	180	260	340	360	376	1616
	280	360	440	520	540	556	2696

5. See Appendix XII.
6. Parry: Memorandum on Aero Engine Production, made available in typescript form to the present author in 1948.
7. The Air Ministry contemplated an expenditure of £1½ million for this purpose and suggested paying a bonus per engine in addition to the management fee on the following scale:

    2s per rated h.p. for the first half-million horsepower
    1s 6d per rated h.p. for the second half-million horsepower
    1s per rated h.p. for the third half-million horsepower

8. Winston Churchill, *The Gathering Storm*, p. 179.
9. The company divided its sub-contractors into two classes:
    (a) Those firms which Rolls-Royce had built into efficient and prosperous units almost completely dependent on this work;
    (b) Those firms which took on Rolls-Royce work as a stop-gap and could not be depended upon always to renew these contracts.
10. Winston Churchill, *The Gathering Storm*, p. 180.
11. Air Ministry December 1936 Programme:

Year	J	F	M	A	M	J	J	A	S	O	N	D	Total
1936	—	—	—	—	—	—	—	—	—	1	9	19	29
			(cumulative total)							1	10	29	
1937	17	22	25	44	47	48	75	130	134	151	157	164	1014
	36	58	83	127	174	222	297	427	561	712	869	1033	
1938	175	190	191	211	212	212	211	212	212	196	175	108	2305
	1208	1398	1589	1800	2012	2224	2435	2647	2859	3055	3230	3338	
1939	65	53	25	11	5	—	—	—	—	—	—	—	159
	3403	3499	3525	3535	3540								

12. Chester Barnard, 'Organisation and Management', in *Selected Papers* (Harvard University Press, 1948).
13. A simultaneous strike at the Fairey aircraft factory gave some cause for suspicion that the strike had an ulterior motive.
14. W. Lloyd and L. O. Low, *The Social System of the Modern Factory: The Strike – a Social Analysis* (Yale University Press, 1947).
15. Swift's report on this visit contained the following observations: 'We soon realised that Germany was thinking, planning and acting on a very much larger scale than we were . . . They are well on their way to possessing the finest air force in the world both as regards performance, numbers and rapid production.' Four engine firms were each producing 20–25 engines a week, and in contrast to Britain this was entirely absorbed by the airframe production. Far more resources and energy were expended on design and

development work than in comparable British firms, and the whole impression was one of an industry with a 'clear objective'.

16. On 28 March Colonel Disney had written informing Hives: 'I do not anticipate production will start until May 1940.'

17. On 19 March 1937 Colonel Disney had informed Colonel Darby, the Aero Sales Manager, that the Avro Manchester (AP 13/36) for which the Vulture was intended was expected to fly in March 1938, and that a production of 20 per month was expected by June. On this basis Rolls-Royce was required to produce 480 Vultures between April 1938 and March 1939. This was only a rough estimate, but it is significant that only seven Vultures were produced in 1938, nine in 1939 and 88 in 1940. The engine was never produced in any quantity. Its fate was ample confirmation of Hives' contention that no reliance should be placed on the attainment of rapid volume production of an undeveloped engine.

18. This report was favourably received by the Air Ministry, and particularly by Colonel Disney, then head of the Directorate of Aeronautical Production, who commented: 'I have studied your memorandum on the engine position with great interest. While it is a great disappointment to me that the Vulture will not be available until 1940 I am glad to know the exact position. The extravagant and ridiculous promises of contractors in the past have caused me so much work in trying to get them sorted out and put in the proper perspective that it is a great comfort to get a forecast of this sort which one feels is genuine and can be relied upon.'

19. In this connection the conclusion of the Harvard Report on the problems of accelerating aircraft production during the Second World War is interesting: 'In a very real sense management problems constituted the ultimate limiting factors on the peacetime aircraft industry's ability to expand during the war. These limitations were not so tangible and easy to understand as, say, a shortage of plant space or of aluminium forgings, nor could they be statistically measured. Nevertheless when the Companies were forced overnight into the vast wartime expansion they could progress only as fast as the upgraded and outside management personnel could learn their new duties. *The physical difficulties* encountered were in large part simply evidence of the bottleneck of human abilities and experience' (T. Lilley *et al.*, *Problems of Accelerating Aircraft Production During World War II* (Bailey Bros, 1952) p. 67).

CHAPTER 12

1. The number of Merlins actually produced in this period was 1815, of which 47 were produced at Crewe, without the suspension of chassis production.

2. Of a total of 4700 on aero work, 3716 were skilled, 900 unskilled. Only 84 were women. The total employee force in December 1937 was 7517.

3. The sub-contract man-hours increased as follows:

1933	Negligible
1934	70,000
1935	670,000
1936	1,470,000
1937	1,760,000
1938	3,140,000
1939	3,790,000

4. Parry, op. cit.
5. Directorate of Aircraft Production, Air Ministry.
6. This factory cost £792,000 to erect and equip. Of this figure, £149,000 represented building costs, and on the basis of building costs of £451,000 (estimated) it was calculated that the Rolls-Royce shadow would cost £2,400,000.
7. The Crewe factory was in consequence planned to achieve the maximum productive flexibility rather than as a mass-production factory. It was nevertheless decided that wherever possible the latest techniques should be employed with the object of reducing machining times. The following general principles were applied:
   (1) Forgings or pressings were to be used instead of machining straight from bar;
   (2) Die-castings were substituted for sand-castings;
   (3) Bar work was transferred from capstans to automatics;
   (4) Multiple setting was employed on milling and drilling machines;
   (5) Continuous rotary milling machines, borematics and multi-spindle drilling and reaming machines were employed;
   (6) Surface broaching was substituted for milling;
   (7) Improved fixtures employing cam-acting devices for rapid loading and pneumatic work-holding devices were installed;
   (8) Gauges were provided for semi-skilled operators.
8. A similar instruction was received in connection with one of the earlier expansion schemes. When Rolls-Royce enquired how many engines they should produce the Air Ministry replied, 'As many as possible bearing in mind the sum of money available.'
9. On the agenda for a conference with Air Ministry officials on 7 December, there appears the following item: 'Who is the responsible authority at the Ministry for Rolls-Royce expansion? Present system unsatisfactory because of delays and evasions.'
10. Winston Churchill, op. cit., p. 258.
11. In this connection the following observation from a company report on the Crewe expansion scheme gives an unusual insight into the problem of rearmament in the Britain of 1938. 'An interesting fact about sub-contracting is that it is much easier to get this done in towns which are busy, such as Birmingham or Coventry, than in the depressed areas. The engineering firms in the depressed areas have been trying for so many years to spin out jobs as long as possible that they have lost the art of rapid production. We started in 1936 with 12 firms in Lancashire but eventually we had to give them up.'

CHAPTER 13

1. In a letter to Air Chief Marshal Sir Wilfrid Freeman written on 10 March Hives commented that 'we are nothing like going to meet your suggested requirements.'
2. The Peregrine engine was a developed Kestrel produced for the Westland Whirlwind fighter. In all 290 were produced, production continuing to the early part of 1942.
3. Italics mine.
4. This is further supported by the details of the two original estimates of the cost of erecting and equipping this factory which were made in a letter to Sir Wilfrid Freeman on 10 March. It was estimated that a production of 60/70 Merlins per week would require a factory three times the size of Crewe, and that the production of 90/100 engines per week would require a factory five times the size of Crewe (including a foundry, pattern shop and tool room). The former was estimated to cost £4,100,000, the latter £6,300,000. On the basis of this estimate the lower rate of output gives a lower cost of production (£58,000 per engine per week) than the higher rate of output (£63,000 per engine per week). These estimates were based on a 10 per cent allowance for contingencies, indicating a possible margin of error of £400,000–£600,000.
5. The only parts of the engine not completely manufactured in the Glasgow factory were carburettors, split pins and joint washers.
6. It is important to bear these facts in mind in connection with the comparisons of output which are made at a later stage in this study. An output of 100 engines at Glasgow under the above conditions is equivalent to an output of 192 at Derby and 172 at Crewe. In consequence of the fact that Glasgow production was independent, while that of Derby and Crewe was intimately dependent on hundreds of sub-contractors of varying types and efficiency, any attempt at an *overall* comparison of the productive efficiency of these three factories, the Ford Factory at Manchester, and the Packard Factory in the United States, is so subject to qualification in every direction as to be almost meaningless.

CHAPTER 14

1. *The Economist*, 1 Dec. 1923.
2. Almost the entire history of the American company in the twenties (see Chapters 3–6) illustrates the danger of an overwhelming preoccupation with short-term problems.

3. The reports of the Anglo-American Council on Productivity bear testimony to the profound influence on the productivity of American industry of comprehensive industrial statistics and the relative freedom with which information is exchanged between firms.

4. This conclusion received striking confirmation in the reports of the Anglo-American Council on Productivity.

5. It may fairly be argued that when aberrations become permanently established it is legitimate to question the system itself. Ortega y Gasset has made this useful distinction in his discussion of an entirely different subject – the reform of higher education – which applies equally to an industry or an institution.

> Reform is always the creation of new usages. Abuses are always of minor importance. For either they are abuses in the most natural sense of the word, namely, isolated, infrequent cases of departure from usage; or else they are so frequent and customary, so persistent and so generally tolerated, that they are no longer to be called abuses. In the first case they will presumably be corrected automatically; in the second case it would be futile to correct them, for their frequency and acceptance indicate that they are not exceptions to a rule, but manifestations of usages which are bad. It is something in the usage, the policy . . . and not the breach of it, which needs our attention.

But whether the attack is on abuse or on usage, it will be much more successful if the purpose of the organisation, which usually serves remarkably stable and compatible ends, is clearly defined.

6. Bentley Motors, Rolls-Royce (Springfield, U.S.A.) and Rolls-Royce (G.B.).

7. See Schlaifer and Heron, op. cit., p. 550: 'A company solely engaged in any branch of the aviation business goes out sooner or later if technical prestige is lacking.'

8. *The Economist*, 30 April 1949: 'Unless the mills re-deploy, cotton and rayon manufacturing "will have had its day" as an exporting industry . . . The skill, craftsmanship and accumulated knowledge at the disposal of the Lancashire trade can offset only for a limited period the almost incredible waste of manpower and technical conservatism which, as the Commission's report shows, persist.'

Index

Abyssinian crisis, 157, 159

A.C. cars, 108

Acceptance tests, standard of in U.S.A., 121

Admiralty, and the British United Shoe Machinery Co., 178

Advertising and sales techniques, limitations of, 79

Aero-engine industry (British), production pattern of, 206; nature of competition in, 214, 215; proposals to change, 217

Aero-engine industry (French), efficiency of, 205

Air Council, Committee of Supply of the, approves shadow scheme, 180; intimates further order, 181; letter from Sidgreaves to, 192

Aircraft industry (British), assessment of potential, 169; influence of motor industry methods on, 170

Aircraft industry (German), assessment of potential, 169; Fedden's views on, 170

Air Ministry, patronage of, 83; and cost allocation, 91; abandons Condor engine, 96, 97; and aero-engine profits, 137; attitude towards Rolls-Royce, 148; and national production policy, 149; considers Kestrel production, 150; and Treasury constraints, 153; responsibilities, 154, 155, 156; relationship with Rolls-Royce in wartime, 157; and stock acquisition, 158; inactivity in 1936, 159; kept informed of Merlin plans, 161; conference at, 162; supports formation of Rotol Ltd, 164; reduces Merlin orders, 169; receives Fedden's report on Germany, 171; advised of Rolls-Royce acceptance of shadow scheme, 172; confidence in 1937, 173; enquiry from, 174, 176; and utilisation of chassis plant, 175; indecision at, 177; suggests conversion of Derby, 179; provides information on Daimler factory, 180; inability to define requirements, 181; attitude towards

Crewe, 183; and long runs, 185; authorises second Crewe extension, 186; and January '39 programme, 187; contemplates third factory, 188; and 1940 programme, 189; rents shadow factory, 192; and control of production orders, 194; value of Rolls-Royce orders from, 195; questions consultants' fees, 198; support for aero-engines, 205

Air Staff, resists pressure to expand R.A.F., 153

Alcock and Brown, first transatlantic flight, 22

Aldred, J. E., enters American negotiations, 25; offers to finance issue, 26, 27; joins board of Rolls-Royce, Inc., 28; discusses U.S. prices, 35; visits England, 40; and confidence in future of Rolls-Royce Inc., 41; influences U.S. bankers, 42; and charge for raising capital, 43; continues negotiations, 44, 45, 46; maintains confidence, 48; suggests ten year notes, 49; supports stock convertibility, 50, 51; proceeds with conversion, 52; describes conditions for maintaining confidence, 53; warns Johnson against takeover, 58; manipulates quotations, 59; growing dissatisfaction of, 60; loses interest, 61, 62; attempts takeover of U.K. company, 64; considers further advance, 66, 67; continues financial support, 70; approves settlement agreement, 75; and effect of guarantee, 76

Allis-Chalmers, Co. Inc., and Rolls Royce managers, 58

Alloys, the 'RR' Series, 99

Amalgamated Engineering Union (A.E.U.) and grinder's strike, 167

America, competition from, 1; and early consideration of market in, 23

American manufacturers, workmanship of, 37

Apprentice schemes, Hives' view of, 166

Armstrong-Siddeley Ltd, and work on

19; Eagles power Vickers Vimy, 22; market prospects of, 73; and production cross-subsidisation, 91, 92, 93; redesign of Eagle and Condor, 96, 97; emergence of Kestrel engine, 98, 114, 117; 'R' engine performance, 99; V-16 considered, 100; supremacy of liquid-cooled designs of 102; radial engine merits canvassed by Royce, 114; economic dependence of company on, 119; Sidgreaves' view on U.S. lead in, 122; and cost of forgings, 131; profit on, 137; and effect of rearmament work, 140; market for liquid-cooled, 143; Merlin, development of, 148, 153, 161; effect of 'R' engine on reputation of, 148; and quantity production of the Kestrel, 148, 150, 153, 157; and liquid cooling, 151; radiator drag of, 152; Buzzard, development of, 160; Goshawk, development of, 160, 161; 'R' unsuitable for fighter aircraft, 160, Peregrine, development of, 162; Vulture, development of, 162, 169, 175, 190; production of untried, 173; and absorption into aircraft, 177; proposal to switch from Merlins to Vultures, 183; development of 'Exe' 188, 190; production standardised, 196; and company's reputation, 200; importance of technical merit in, 204; contribution of, 205; nature of competition for, 208, 214; production tables of, 232, 233; and work on superchargers, 243

Board, decides to continue merger negotiations, 4; asks Royce to design 20 h.p. car, 12; authorises manufacture of 'Goshawk', 13; considers reducing wages, 15; reduces output, 16; rejects request for development funds, 19; considers workers shares, 20, 21, 22; congratulates Royce on first transatlantic flight, 22; discusses Mackenzie cable, 26; advises Johnson on U.S. terms, 27; and relationship to U.S. Board, 28; attitude towards duplication policy, 29; receives Johnson's report on U.S., 33; meets Aldred, 40; agrees guarantee, 41, 46; considers U.S. proposals, 42; refuses cash, 43; declines to underwrite U.S. issue, 45; enquires about Aldred, 46; specula-

tion as to motives of, 50; controversy with U.S. Board, 54; considers selling out, 59; maintains product policy, 63; knowledge of takeover proposal, 64; reaction to U.S. selling costs, 64; refuses to cut losses, 65; Fuller's opinion of, 69; suggests schemes to Fuller, 75, 76; considers buying Barkers, 108; discusses Bentley proposals, 110; rejects Bentley scheme, 111; receives Royce memorandum, 114; acquires Park Ward, 135; receives chassis policy report, 144; leases Hucknall aerodrome, 151; decides to co-operate on Spitfire development, 153; and discussions on shadow factory scheme, 159; and acquisition of Phillips & Powis, 159, 160; authorises expenditure on foundry, 174; declines to finance rearmament, 192; implied criticism by, 198

Cars, Silver Ghost, manufacturing procedures, xvii; electric starters in, 1; chassis programme restored, 1; 40/50 remains principal product, 1; and post-war situation, 5, 10; Goshawk design undertaken, 11; post-war prices of, 12, 15; and post-war market estimates, 14; post-war design of, 17; and decision to produce Phantom I, 19; Goshawk introduced, 19, 46, 84, 86, 88; price of 40/50 h.p., 84; Silver Ghost design continuity, 87; Goshawk output reduced, 90; excessive production costs of, 94; gearing design of, 115; Phantom II replacement, 115, 116; Phantom II orders, 117, 120; Bentley 3½ litre sales, 119; Phantom III design begins, 120, 121; Wraith carburettor, 127; Phantom II, 128, 130, 136; Wraith, 128, 129, 136; Bentley, 3½ litre, 129, 130, 138; Bentley 4½ litre, 129; rationalised range of, 129, 138, 146, 147; Spectre, 130; Phantom III, 130, 136, 137; components of, 131; Bentley standard bodies for, 132, 133; and chassis costs, 137; Bentley V, 138; Bentley 50, 139; Phantom III jig and tool costs, 140; Myth, 142; production of suspended, 143; 5½ litre straight eight, 144; Phantom type, 144, 145; Silver Ghost, 145; decline in demand for, 175; chassis costs of, 200;